Ireland

20TH-CENTURY ARCHITECTURE

Ireland

Edited by

ANNETTE BECKER, JOHN OLLEY,
AND WILFRIED WANG

With contributions by

HUGH CAMPBELL, SARAH CASSIDY,
EDDIE CONROY, LOUGHLIN KEALY,
PAUL LARMOUR, FRANK McDONALD,
ORLA MURPHY, JOHN OLLEY,
SEÁN O'REILLY, SEÁN ROTHERY,
JOHN TUOMEY, AND SIMON WALKER

Building descriptions and
biographies by

PAUL LARMOUR, ORLA MURPHY,
JOHN OLLEY, SHANE O'TOOLE,
TOM RUSSELL, AND SIMON WALKER

Prestel
Munich · New York

First published on the occasion of the exhibition '20 th-Century Architecture, Ireland', Deutsches Architektur-Museum, Frankfurt am Main, 4 July-24 August 1997

Edited by Annette Becker, John Olley, and Wilfried Wang
for the Dezernat für Kultur und Freizeit,
Amt für Wissenschaft und Kunst der Stadt Frankfurt am Main,
Deutsches Architektur-Museum

Front cover: Blackwood Golf Centre, by Sheila O'Donnell and John Tuomey, and The Ark, by Shane O'Toole and Michael Kelly Architects

Spine: 'River of Life' floor mosaic in the Honan Hostel Chapel, by James McMullen

Back cover: 'The four Winds', Dalkey, by Michael Scott (Photo: John Olley), and Beckett Theatre, Trinity College, by de Blacam and Meagher Architects (Photo: Peter Cook)

Frontispiece: Lambay Island (Photo: Aerofilms)

Photo credits see page 200

Library of Congress Cataloging-in-Publication Data is available.

Prestel books are available worldwide. Please contact your nearest bookseller or write to either of the following addresses for information concerning your local distributor:

Prestel Verlag, Mandlstrasse 26, D-80802 Munich, Germany
Phone (89) 38 17 09-0, Fax (89) 38 17 09-35

and 16 West 22nd Street, New York, N.Y. 10010, USA
Phone (212) 627 81 99, Fax (212) 627 98 66

Designed by
Gino Lee and Matthew Monk, Cambridge/ Mass.

Produced by
Tom Harwerth, Frankfurt am Main

Edited by
Mike Foster

Offset lithography by
Fischer Repro Frankfurt am Main

Printed and bound by
Gorenjski Tisk, Slovenia

Printed in Slovenia

ISBN 3-7913-1719-9

Contents

Foreword

I welcome a timely exhibition on Ireland's contribution to architecture this century. While it would be impossible – or at least rash – to write a history of English literature of the twentieth century without mentioning Irish writers, we may readily admit that familiar accounts of European architecture in the twentieth century have, reasonably, few conspicuous Irish heroes or heroines. Notwithstanding this, it is genuinely exciting to watch how, in the recent past, this century's activity in building throughout this island of Ireland has received fresh attention from historians and critics (among whom the Ulster Architectural Heritage Society was a pioneer).

It should not surprise us that the study of Irish building in this period, which was one of radical political transformation in Ireland, as well as one of radical architectural transformation in Western architecture, is rewarding. The hospitals, the schools, the power stations, the local authority housing are an index of how energetic and evolving communities chose to represent themselves to the world. That they did this in the clear knowledge of contemporary architectural development abroad is now documented in Seán Rothery's pioneering book *Ireland and the New Architecture*. Sometimes, as in the case of Henman and Cooper's Royal Victoria Hospital in Belfast, Ireland was not merely reacting to outside influence but taking the lead, and the sheer quality of some of the other work presented here will probably come as a happy discovery to many. This volume breaks new ground. In proudly introducing it, I hope others will be inspired to follow its lead.

Mary Robinson
Uachtarán na hÉireann
President of Ireland

8

1 Sir William Chambers
Casino at Marino, Dublin,
begun 1758

2 Passage grave, Newgrange, 4th millennium BC

3 Round tower, Glendalough,
c. 10th–12th century

Architecture in Ireland prior to 1900

SEÁN O'REILLY

The history of Ireland's architecture has been shaped by its relationship to Europe. As an island situated on the western reaches of the continent, Ireland has found itself shielded from the influence of Europe by sheer distance. European developments reach this outland only later in their life, often distilled through the perspectives of neighbouring Britain or after the continental melting pot has proven them to be more than passing fancies.

Ireland, observing from afar the turmoil associated with progress in Europe, appreciates the value of tradition. Retaining a fundamentally conservative attitude, its response to new ideas is reserved and it absorbs them only slowly. In this, Ireland takes on a self-imposed role as protector of traditional values, the guarded outpost of Europe's most respected mores.

At first sight, Ireland's architectural evolution appears to have been determined by a succession of cultural incursions punctuating its history: Celtic, Christian, classical and modern. Yet such monumental foreign invasions, whether of armies or of ideas, are invariably confronted by a wall of tradition and find themselves more often moulded than moulding.

Invasions may exist as grand gestures or convenient tools in the sketching of Ireland's history, but their real impact on the country's native culture has often been restricted. Ireland's size gives it a peculiar advantage here, for its relatively small scale is perfectly suited to the creation and maintenance of a unified culture – too big to stagnate and too small to splinter easily. Too vibrant to be overwhelmed by invasion, yet sufficiently small to be moulded by a single person, the nation's cultural evolution has found itself most susceptible to enthusiastic promotion by individuals, whether patrons, scholars, artists or priests.

In common lore Ireland's conversion to Christianity is linked with the success of St Patrick in securing the support of the native kings. Similarly, Ireland's introduction to the mature pan-European Enlightenment of the later eighteenth century may be associated with a patron of unique importance, James Caulfield, Lord Charlemont, and with an event of special significance, the building of the Casino at Marino (fig. 1). The Casino was designed by the British architect Sir William Chambers from about 1758 as a museum for part of Charlemont's extensive collections. Charlemont was one of the most sophisticated Irish patrons of his day and aspired to the ideals of the Age of Reason, promoting learning, taste and progress as self-justifying principles. The Casino, as both architecture and gallery, provided perfect testimony to his ideals and confirmed a whole new era in Irish architecture.

4   Gallarus Oratory, possibly as early as the 8th century or as late as the 12th century

While unified through its scale, Ireland has always encountered different levels of simple subdivision, a kind of national bifurcation. Such divisions, though often superficial, have been no less important in determining history. Within Ireland's cultural geography one may contrast the open seaboard districts with the more reserved inland regions. Sea-borne communication has granted Ireland's coastal reaches easier access to the passing fancies and tastes of international culture. Inland, in contrast, one frequently finds a solid and justified scepticism towards such frivolous variety.

Important in the shaping of Ireland's architectural culture, and bifurcating otherwise comparable traditions, has been the impact of historical circumstances. From medieval to modern times, Dublin, as the seat of a succession of foreign cultures, has displayed a particularly strong tradition of respect for established orders. More recently, the northern counties of the island gained a social and cultural character of their own, a phenomenon evident in the architecture of the industrial revolution. Belfast, in particular, triumphed in the Victorian era in a manner unmatched by the former capital, Dublin. Indeed, no other Irish town or city can boast Belfast's authoritative array of the architecture of capitalism.

The history of Ireland's architecture reflects the evolution of its cultural heritage and its intense, if intermittent, dialogue with Europe. The earliest surviving remnants of an Irish architectural tradition, though primarily archaeological, already evince the genesis of the Irish mind within a European framework. The most impressive of these remnants originated in a Celtic tradition. This marks a significant cultural continuity between Ireland and Europe. Newgrange, in County Meath, has been described as 'one of the finest passage graves in the whole of northern Europe' (fig. 2). Here stone ramparts help support a mound or cairn spreading over more than an acre and containing an estimated 200,000 tonnes of material. Inside, a passage built of huge monoliths cuts into the mound. Many of the stones are incised with abstract patterns of Celtic origin, giving to the structure a symbolic import that reverberates through Ireland's history.

The relationship between European development and Irish assimilation appears most strongly in the country's response to Christianity. The new religion came to Ireland only some four hundred years after Christ's birth, yet it was to remain one of the strongest forces in the nation's history. In the turmoil following the fall of the Roman world, aided by its distance from the Continent, Ireland preserved the combined cultural traditions of the classical and Christian civilisations. Not surprisingly, Ireland created its own unique amalgam, which reached its height in the production of illuminated manuscripts such as the Book of Kells. Here Christian text and classical ethos are overlaid on a pure Celtic language to create a new spirit.

In contrast to the usual assumption that the early medieval period distrusted the beauties of the natural world, the Christian Celtic spirit is distinguished by its special sympathy with nature. Like so many early Irish monasteries, that at Glendalough in County Wicklow has a setting of true natural majesty. The complex consists of a series of Christian monuments that weave their way along an isolated and otherwise secluded valley. The monastery originated in St Kevin's selection of this place as his hermitic home; his followers expanded the settlement, elaborating the simple stone structures.

Towards the end of the first millennium, monastic complexes such as Glendalough found themselves dominated by a new and distinctive form, the round tower (fig. 3). This takes the form of a tall, tapering stone cylinder, often rising more than thirty metres and topped by a conical cap. Probably developed as a defensive refuge from the marauding Vikings, it could also serve as bell-tower and surveillance post. The efficient form and multiple usage, features that reverberate through Irish architecture, may well have encouraged its development, and the round tower may be credited as the first Irish contribution to architectural typologies. Its profile dominated the landscape but, less happily, it must also have acted as a signpost to the very Vikings from whom it was intended to provide protection.

Ireland's architectural development over the centuries prior to the appearance of the Gothic style is well illustrated by the contrast between the Gallarus Oratory in County Kerry and Cormac's Chapel on the Rock of Cashel in County Tipperary. The date of Gallarus is uncertain, but its primitive form suggests an origin early in the Christian era (fig. 4). The characteristic outline of this impressive building has inspired the popular name 'boat-shaped oratory'. Entered through a single doorway and with only a single window to give further architectural expression inside, its restraint embodies the ascetic philosophy of its Christian builders.

As Gallarus encapsulates the almost natural aesthetic of a largely anonymous early Christian tradition, Cormac's Chapel represents Ireland's most sophisticated expression of a nascent classical spirit, of European derivation, and reveals the impact that an inspired patron could have on native traditions (fig. 5). The chapel was erected from 1127 under the patronage of Cormac MacCarthy, King of Desmond. Its comparatively complex spatial organisation, sophisticated vaulted construction and adoption of classical formulas all impress. Asserting the importance of Cormac's Chapel in Irish architectural history, vestiges of its distinctive classicism reverberate through later Irish Romanesque architecture and reappear in the revivals of the later nineteenth century.

By the end of the same century the developed Romanesque of Cormac's Chapel had been superseded. The incoming new technology and formulas of Gothic architecture permitted a whole new scale of construction and an increasing complexity of internal arrangement. St Patrick's Cathedral in Dublin, dedicated in 1192, represents the imported style in relatively pure form. It is also one of a long series of Irish buildings to have originated in English traditions rather than in immediate Celtic or in Continental sources. Continuing the pattern for native responses to such innovations, Irish Gothic reduced the style to fundamentals, notably the pointed arch. Hence, a more distinctively Irish form of early Gothic is to be found in the smaller, simpler, more severe church at Boyle in County

Roscommon. Similarly, the trans-continental inspiration for Norman castles, seen at Carrickfergus in County Antrim, was modified to become more typically indigenous in the tall, stark tower houses of later centuries.

A good rule of thumb for assessing the changing relationship between Ireland and the Continent is that the greater the vibrancy of Europe, the closer Ireland's ties to it. With the rise of post-medieval Europe, benefiting from the revival of the classical tradition in the Renaissance, the ties between the island outland and its mainland mentor grow closer. In Ireland the seventeenth century sees a most vibrant conjunction of the Renaissance world and the native medieval order. In the social flux of this period influences appear from an uncommon breadth of sources, including Italy, Spain, France and Holland, in addition to Britain, each of these countries sharing a progressive interest in the developments of the Renaissance.

Kanturk Castle in County Cork, built by Dermod MacOwen MacDonagh from about 1601, captures Ireland's early response to these innovations (fig. 6). Its sturdy walls and corner towers indicate the retention of a defensive posture. The classically composed symmetry, the large, regular windows, and the occasional Renaissance touch all represent the burgeoning of a new mood. When news was received of the building's sophisticated nature, work was ordered to cease, and it remains incomplete to this day.

As Kanturk intimates a brave new world in architecture, so Leamanagh in County Clare (1643) embodies a more pragmatic, representative and suitably economical Irish response – the extension (fig. 7). The modern formal composition is simply tacked on to a monolithic tower house dating from 1480. Displaying a foresight of particular relevance in a century of turmoil, the O'Briens, responsible for its construction, might still find refuge in their castle if the need arose, while in quieter times they could enjoy the pleasures of a home. The incorporation of earlier fabric follows a practice repeated throughout the country's history and gives to the building a self-consciously historical air. While the process might detract

5   Cormac's Chapel, Cashel, 1127–34

6   Kanturk Castle, c. 1601

from the purity of the design, it does have the advantage of both practicality and economy.

The fabric of the Royal Hospital at Kilmainham, dating from the end of the seventeenth century, is entirely new, and its background European (fig. 8). However, as one might expect, it possesses a distinctive native colour. The architect, Surveyor–General Sir William Robinson, found inspiration in a classical expression of international authority of England, France and, ultimately, Italy, but he retains in the design a memory of an older world. Thus a stone tracery window in the chapel destroys the classical symmetry of the eastern front, and the arched windows of the main front decline the use of imposts. Despite its conscientious bowing to tradition, Kilmainham represents the earliest expression in Ireland of a pan-European Renaissance aesthetic.

It is not until the eighteenth century, and the development of Ireland's Georgian architecture, that a pure manifestation of the Renaissance ideal is attained. Purity, of course, remains the exception rather than the norm. The architecture of the Georgian era holds a special position within the country's heritage yet, contrary to popular opinion, its distinction lies not in the strength of the foreign implant, but rather in the manner in which it retains a curiously local character. Again the country stamps its own cultural tradition onto new forms.

The Georgian country house represents well the imposition of native idiosyncrasy on international norms. The Palladian paradigm remains the starting-point. Here a tripartite composition, with a central residential block and flanking service pavilions, is subordinated to the rules of classical symmetry and order. With flanking buildings so often omitted or left incomplete, the proportions of the central block gain a vertical emphasis out of sympathy with the original classical conception. Instead, as at Mount Ievers in County Clare or Ledwithstown in County Longford, the tallness is more in keeping with the more vertical massing of medieval houses (fig. 9). On the original front the former Irish Houses of Parliament of 1728–9, now part of the Bank of Ireland on College Green (p. 80),

7 Leamanagh Castle; tower house *c.* 1480, extension 1643

8 Sir William Robinson
Royal Hospital, Kilmainham, *c.* 1684

9 Richard Castle (?)
Ledwithstown, early 18th century

10 James Gandon
Emo Court; begun c. 1790,
completed c. 1860

11 James Gandon
Custom House, Dublin, 1781-91

possess almost vertiginous erectness. Designed by Ireland's finest architect of the early eighteenth century, Sir Edward Lovett Pearce, the effect cannot be considered accidental. Perhaps it was in response to this taste that, as late as the 1760s, one finds diminutive flanking pavilions in the Provost's House in Trinity College Dublin.

The assimilation of classical horizontality into the native building tradition does not begin until the mid-eighteenth century. William Chambers's pupil, James Gandon, learned the lessons of his mentor's French-inspired classicism at first hand. As Ireland's foremost architect in the later Georgian period, Gandon promoted a more horizontal disposition in Irish architecture. His only major country house, Emo Court in County Laois, indicates the potential of broad and low proportions in free-standing domestic buildings (fig. 10). Following this pattern, a lower massing seeped into the Irish vernacular, giving to later Georgian farmhouses in the Irish countryside a more classical orientation. The new horizontality also returns the domestic building to its own vernacular roots, as the farmhouse regains the elongated proportions of the Irish country cottage. Usually of one storey, perhaps with attic accommodation, and enlarged by lateral extensions, the long and low orientation of the traditional cottage offers an interesting and surprising precedent for Georgian farmhouses.

Though born and trained in England, Gandon succeeded in representing traditional Irish interests in his architecture. He recognised that in Ireland tradition moulds the broad aesthetics of the culture and that craftsmanship has ever been more highly valued than innovation. It can have come as no surprise to him that there would be more appreciation of the magnificently sculpted riverine heads on his first Irish master-work, the Custom House in Dublin, than respect for his daring in dropping the pilaster-responds to the *in antis* columns (fig. 11). Yet the artistic reserve in his architecture reflects perfectly an austerity that might also be considered an attribute of the country's national style.

If Irish Georgian architecture remains, with certain notable exceptions, resolutely regional despite its Europhile fancies, Irish Victorian architecture takes a proud place on the stage of the internationally progressive. The architect who brought to Ireland the applause of leaders in taste was Benjamin Woodward. A civil engineer by trade and largely self-taught as an architect, in the mid-nineteenth century he was the main inspiration in the Cork firm of Deane and Woodward. Together with his partner, Thomas New-enham Deane, he replaced an often pedestrian later Georgian Irish manner with a self-

confident and hugely influential Victorian architectural aesthetic.

The Museum Building in Trinity College Dublin, built to the designs of Deane and Woodward, marks a new level of achievement in Ireland's architecture

(fig. 12). The freshness of the museum's design lifted Ireland's status at a crucial moment in its history and, on the basis of this building, the firm gained real success in Britain. Ireland at last could show the world a possible future for a modern architectural aesthetic, one that incorporated personal ingenuity, artistic variety and traditional architectural values centred on sound construction.

Ireland's international success in architecture in the reign of Queen Victoria was matched by the industry and inventiveness of its engineers. As leading figures in the world's foremost industrial economy, people as yet little-known outside the circles of enthusiasts brought Ireland respect and prestige. Richard Turner was among the most successful of Irish engineers and his talent is well represented by the curvilinear glasshouse at the Botanic Garden, Glasnevin, Dublin (fig. 13). The success of people such as Woodward and Turner indicates the increasing significance of the country's nascent internationalism.

New architecture in Ireland has always been promoted by a few genuine enthusiasts. With exemplary new buildings indicating possibilities, from Cormac's Chapel and the Royal Hospital, Kilmainham, to the Casino at Marino, the Trinity College Museum Building and Dublin's Busárus bus station (pp. 118-9), the response of a more reflective populace is reserved, and the architectural principles modified.

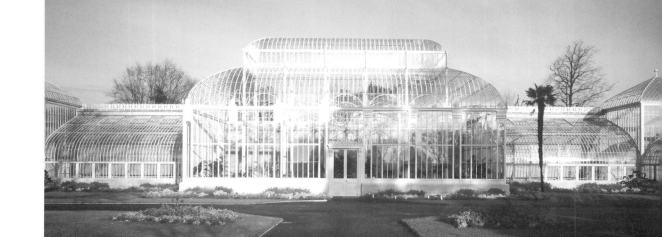

13   Richard Turner et al.
Curvilinear glasshouse,
Botanic Garden, Glasnevin,
Dublin; 1843, enlarged 1869

Ireland and the New Architecture
1900–1940

SEÁN ROTHERY

The period 1900–1940 is of particular significance because it saw the culmination of many avant-garde design movements. In Ireland, as elsewhere, an examination of architecture charts the impact of these international influences.

Ireland has been portrayed as a backwater, unaffected by, and unaware of, the great and revolutionary architectural events of other countries. *Contemporary Architects*, an encyclopaedic survey of the profession, has only one entry on an Irish architect, Michael Scott, and refers to Ireland's 'relative isolation': 'Little effective dialogue with European mainland influences was possible. It is doubtful that Corbusier's *Towards a New Architecture* of 1927 would have reached Ireland, or Pevsner's *Pioneers of Modern Design* of 1936, not to mention the *Architectural Review* and its famous essays of Morton Shand or Wells Coates.'[1]

On the contrary, Irish architects were very much aware of the new movements in design. All the principal architectural journals and most pioneer works on modern architecture were available and discussed. Le Corbusier's book was reviewed in 1928 in the long-established Irish architectural journal, *The Irish Builder*, just after the first English translation had appeared. The essays of Morton Shand in the 1930s were widely commented upon and *Architectural Review* had been in Irish architects' libraries since it

was first published in 1896. More importantly, the visible products of the new architecture – the revolutionary buildings and those now recognised as milestones of the modern movement – were enthusiastically sought out and visited by Irish architects.

On a wider front, Ireland was in touch with cultural developments on the Continent. For instance, there were important artistic and scholarly links with France and Germany from the end of the nineteenth century, particularly in the study of languages. Other connections with European countries were established through Irish literary figures on the Continent. John Synge travelled and studied in France, Germany and Italy. George Moore and James Stephens lived in Paris, and James Joyce worked in France, Switzerland and Trieste. Paris and Antwerp were hosts to Irish painters, who included Walter Osborne, Paul Henry, Roderick O'Connor, Nathaniel Hone, Maine Jellet, William Leech and Dermod O'Brien.

With the development of political nationalism in the late nineteenth century, Irish figures returned to the problem of breaking ties with Britain. This was well illustrated by Arthur Griffith's publication of *The Resurrection of Hungary: A Parallel for Ireland*. After the establishment of the Irish Free State in 1922, there seemed an even stronger desire to move away from the influence of the British Empire. In 1925 the fledgling state looked beyond Britain when examining models for a new national electricity supply system. The result was the commissioning of the German firm of Siemens Schuckert to harness the waters of the Shannon in a hydro-electric scheme, probably the greatest engineering project the country had ever seen (pp. 104-5).

By the beginning of the twentieth century, a *new* and *modern* architecture had emerged in America in the work of the Chicago School and H. H. Richardson. The bold new structures with multi-storey steel frames caught the imagination of European architects. During the early years of the century the influence of America, especially Chicago, became apparent in Ireland, even in relatively modest buildings.

If a single building could be said to epitomise this Richardsonian influence, it must be the great Market Street Store House (fig. 1 and pp. 94-5). Completed in 1904, it housed the fermentation process as part of Guinness Brewery in Dublin. The building is large by Irish standards. Almost forty metres high, with nine storeys, a deep plan and central light-wells, it is close in form to Richardson's Marshall Field Store in Chicago. Brick outer walls conceal its real structure of steel framing, which is then fully exposed and celebrated in the interior (fig. 2). The Guinness Store House appears as the first steel-framed, multi-storied building not only in Ireland, but in Britain too, just pre-dating London's Ritz Hotel of 1904.

A sample of the pioneering work in reinforcing concrete with iron and steel in Ireland appears in the fire-proof floors of the National Gallery, Dublin, constructed in 1850. In 1870 Bindon Stoney, the 'father of Irish concrete', used giant blocks of pre-cast concrete in the Dublin Liffey Quays, which attracted international interest.[2] The Hennebique system of reinforced concrete structure, patented in France in 1892, first appears in Ireland in 1904, at the Somerset linen factory, Belfast, with its thin panel walls and con-crete framing. However, the nine-storey Granary in Waterford of 1905, with its simple cubic form, reinforced concrete

columns and horizontal steel windows, gives a premonition of the rational modern architecture of the 1920s (fig. 3).

William A. Scott returned to Ireland from early professional experience working for London County Council in the Fire Brigade Section. This adventurous and innovative group proved a strong influ-ence on his later career. Scott's highly original design for the Diocesan College in Galway of 1912 seems to anticipate the Art Deco pavilions for the 1925 Paris Exhibition. With abstract cubic forms framing the entrance, this building might claim to be the first *modern* building in Ireland.

Despite its revolutionary birth in 1922, the new Irish Free State did not espouse a national style of architecture but, from the very beginning, quietly yet positively supported an international image for Ireland. Addressing the Architectural Association of Ireland in 1922, a Govern-ment minister, Darrell Figgis, condemned the idea of an 'Irish style' as an architec-tural falsehood. With its pleas for 'simpli-city and truth', for the abandonment of 'antique manners' and the 'cleansing' of minds of imitations, the Figgis address could have been an extract from an Inter-nationalist manifesto.[3]

As with the commissioning of the Electricity Supply system, the 1930s pro-gramme of new hospital building sought inspiration in Continental European models. The architect Vincent Kelly was employed to make a study tour of con-temporary hospitals in Switzerland, Sweden, Germany, France, Austria, Holland, Italy and Czechoslovakia. In just over three months he visited sixty-five hospitals. Following these studies, a number of new hospital buildings were begun (fig. 4). An image of clean and modern efficiency was clearly achieved with these large, horizontal, white struc-tures, most with flat roofs and many sporting sun balconies and projecting concrete canopies. The language of modern architecture was spread throughout the country with this contem-porary reformulation of an essential building type.

There was one other important build-ing programme carried out under the patronage of a state agency in the early

1 A. H. Hignett
Guinness Store House, Dublin,
1903-4

2 A. H. Hignett
Interior of the Guinness Store
House, Dublin

3 W. Reil, engineer
Granary, Waterford, 1905

4 J. V. Downes
Kilkenny Hospital, 1935

6 R. S. Wilshere
McQuiston Memorial School
(now School of Music),

5 Herbert Simms
Flats at Poplar Row, Dublin, 1938
Drawing by C. Stevenson

years of independence – the provision of large-scale urban housing in the form of apartment blocks. Early in 1923 the clearances of slum tenements in Dublin prompted a huge municipal rehousing effort. Again, the inspiration and appropriate model came from the Continent. From 1925, when Herbert Simms was appointed Dublin Housing Architect, until 1941 a total of 16,000 dwelling units were built in the capital. Influence of the Amsterdam School is evident, even though the more idiosyncratic details of Piet Kramer's and Michel de Klerk's work are missing. Some significant features of the Amsterdam model – the brick buildings aligned along and forming the street facades, the Expressionist definitions of the corners, entrances and balcony features – were followed in the Dublin schemes (fig. 5). To this might be added the influence of the architecture of J.J.P. Oud, bringing two streams of Dutch modern architecture to mix happily in Dublin and resulting in strong horizontality, rounded corners and reinforced concrete cantilevers.

Dutch influence was also felt in Ulster, where the plain brick architecture of Willem Dudok provided inspiration for the large programme of school building in Belfast. This was demonstrated in the work of R.S. Wilshere, architect to the Belfast Corporation Education Committee, whose Avoniel, Finiston and McQuiston schools of the mid-1930s have a strong Dudok feel (fig. 6). Also in the 1930s, a further Dutch connection arose with the appointment of J.D. Postma to design a series of factories for the production of industrial alcohol. Plants were built at Carrickmacross, Ballina, the Cooley Peninsula, Labbodish, Carndonagh and Convoy. The Irish practice of Buckley and O'Gorman built houses for the excise officers serving at these factories. Their designs were all in an early International Style – flat roofs, white walls and horizontal steel windows. Another industrial project that furthered the cause of modernism in Ireland was the vertical Retort Houses for the Dublin Gas Company, built in the period from 1925 to the 1950s (fig. 7). Constructed with H-shaped steel framing and an infill of panels of Accrington engineering and

8 J. V. Downes,
'Dunboys', Foxrock, County
Dublin, 1939

7 Unknown engineer
Retort Houses, Dublin, 1925-50s

glass brick, with some panels of open brickwork for ventilation, they have resonances with Hans Poelzig's industrial architecture and can even be said to recall the early work of Mies van der Rohe.

Whereas the role of the Irish State was positive in its widespread patronage of modern architecture, the attitude of the Catholic Church, the next single most important patron, was in total contrast. For more than the first half of the twentieth century, new churches commissioned were traditional in plan and followed historical styles. However, one very important exception was the Church of Christ the King at Turner's Cross in Cork (1927-31) by Barry Byrne from Chicago (pp. 106-7). At the time it was the most advanced of the architect's churches and a pioneering work, not only for Ireland, but also for European modern architecture as a whole. Byrne began his career in the Oak Park office of Frank Lloyd Wright, where he trained and worked from 1902 to 1908. Then, in the early 1920s, he built three Roman Catholic churches in the American Midwest that were original in their functional planning and notable for their economy of cost and their modern appearance.

In 1926 Byrne made a trip to Europe, where he saw many of the new modern buildings in Germany, Holland and France. He met Dominikus Böhm, whose modern churches had excited great interest. The influence of this contact with contemporary European architecture is clearly evident in the design for the Cork church. Oval in plan and with serrated walls that admit light through long slit windows, the interior is free of columns, giving it a feeling of spaciousness. The church is built of concrete with cranked steel trusses spanning the wide nave. The front facade is a striking expression of the plan and was boldly sculpted by John Storrs to show an interesting integration of ornament and structure. This elevation can be compared with the Expressionist Grundtvig Church in Copenhagen (1921-6) by Jensen Klint.

The first *modern* house in Britain is reckoned to be New Ways in Northampton, completed in 1925 by Peter Behrens; but the first by a British architect was that designed by Thomas Tait of Burnet, Tait and Lorne at Silver End in Essex, a garden village established by the Crittal Casement Company. The company's factory was later to supply windows for Walter Gropius's Bauhaus building at Dessau. However, it was Tait's assistant, the Irishman Frederick MacManus, who designed most of the other houses on the estate. MacManus designed two houses in Ireland in the mid-1930s, both in the suburbs of Dublin and both using white walls, flat roofs and horizontal steel windows to articulate the language of the new architecture. Although most Irish modern houses of the 1930s were small, their designers managed to enliven the simple forms with a limited vocabulary of international modernism (fig. 8). Projecting porches, balconies and cantilevers were all used to produce shadow effects. The most innovative house of this period was Michael Scott's own, 'Geragh', in Sandycove, County Dublin (pp. 114-5). Scott was one of the small group of young architects who enthusiastically embraced modernism in the early 1930s. He went on to lead one of the largest architectural firms in the country, and the one most associated with the development of modern design.

Often built for the use of architects themselves or for members of their families, Irish houses in the International Style are modest in scale and small in number. However, these white cubist designs with their flat roofs, large windows, sun balconies and steel railings were very much part of the 1930s dream of an exciting and promising future.

While domestic architecture in Ireland had limited the creative exploration of the new architecture, the Dublin Airport Terminal (1937-41) allowed a full-blooded and innovative engagement with the International Style (pp. 110-13). Desmond Fitzgerald was appointed Airport Architect for the project, which was carried out in the Office of Public Works. Fitzgerald was only twenty-six and had just graduated from the School of Architecture at University College Dublin. The team of young architects who worked under his direction included the talented Dermot O'Toole, who played a major role in the design of the terminal. The contract for the new airport was placed in November 1938, implying that the preliminary drawings must have been executed in 1937: the design therefore represents a mature and elegant exercise, in the same league as the best of contemporary European architecture. The building was completed before the end of 1940 but, since the Second World War was in progress, for state security reasons it was forbidden to publish any details. The delay in giving this building appropriate publicity denied it proper recognition as a pioneer design.

The Irish Pavilion at the New York World's Fair of 1939 was commissioned by the Irish Government in 1937; the architect was the committed modernist, Michael Scott. The Irish authorities were determined to create a separate and modern image for Ireland at the Fair, and went to some lengths to secure a site far removed from the British compound. The final design for the Pavilion, with an all-glass curved wall, was a frank expression of the International Style (fig. 9). However, the major contribution of the firm of Michael Scott was yet to come, with Busárus, the Dublin bus station, of 1946-53 (pp. 118-9).

At the end of the 1930s one other notable and enthusiastic Irish exponent of modernism emerged. Noel Moffett, who had worked for Serge Chermayeff in the mid-1930s in Britain, was one of the most brilliantly inventive young modern architects of the immediate post-war years. It was the presence of Chermayeff, along with Erich Mendelsohn, in England in the 1930s that acted as a catalyst to an energetic group of young architects whose work established modernism in Britian. Among them was Raymond McGrath. Born in Australia, he went to England in the 1920s. His particular contribution can be seen in designs for the British Broadcasting Corporation and in his exceptional house, on St Ann's Hill at Chertsey (fig. 10). The outbreak of war in 1939 put most architects in Britain out of work and, in the same year, McGrath came to live in Ireland, where he was to have a major influence on art and architecture until his death aged seventy-four.

Another kind of Irish connection to European modernism is represented by Eileen Gray. Paradoxically, this Irishwoman was to be one of the pioneers of modern French design and architecture. In 1902 she left Ireland for France, where she was to become a friend and neighbour of Le Corbusier. In 1926 she designed an International Style house at Roquebrune in collaboration with Jean Badovici.

The small corpus of early International Style work in Ireland, generally dating from the 1930s, remains almost intact. The best building of the period, the first Dublin Airport Terminal, is perfectly preserved and, although dwarfed by later development, remains the most significant and original piece of architecture on the site. The geometric, white-painted, flat-roofed buildings of the 1930s may have promised far more than they delivered, but they are integral to our national architectural history and may yet be invested with nostalgia.

9 Michael Scott
Irish Pavilion,
New York World's Fair,
1939

10 Raymond McGrath
House St Ann's Hill, Chertsey,
1936-7

Notes

1   Muriel Emmanuel (ed.), *Contemporary Architects* (London, 1980).
2   See John de Courcey, 'A History of Engineering in Ireland', *The Engineers Journal* (Sept./Oct. 1985), pp. 23-35.
3   The address was printed as a booklet entitled *Planning for the Future* (Dublin, 1922).

1, 2   Michael Scott with Patrick Scott
Bus Garage, Donnybrook, 1946-51

Architecture in Ireland
1940 – 1975

SIMON WALKER

The past fifty-five years in Irish architecture have been concerned with the rise and demise of modernism, which has been coloured by Ireland's unusual industrial history. The effect of a small, isolated economy, and of the intimacy of the country's architectural profession, is that key buildings have become symbols of significant industrial and social developments. These buildings are inevitably entwined with a heated polemic about the direction of social change and the cultural identity of our built environment.

In the 1920s architecture became the business of the Free State and, from this point onwards, the evolution of architecture mirrors almost exactly the political forces at work in the emerging Republic. Patronage shifted into the hands of Government, the semi-state companies were established and a programme of building was begun. The promise of industrialisation seemed to presage a new era with a very different character. The spirit of the new nation was embodied in the building of the hydro-electric power station at Ardnacrusha (pp. 104-5). This huge complex on the River Shannon brought home the fact that Ireland could be a cement-rich country and therefore self-sufficient in a basic building material: concrete. And this material, even in its poorest form – blocks and render – lent itself easily to the production of a stripped-down, elementarist aesthetic.

During the 1930s a number of individuals began to introduce Ireland to the language of modernism, so that debate on, and the practice of, modern architecture were already well advanced in architectural circles by the outbreak of the Second World War. However, the Dublin Airport Terminal by Desmond Fitzgerald, begun in 1937, signalled the start of a very different conception of modern building in Ireland (pp. 110-13). It was no longer good enough to imitate the Dutch style with plain sand and cement-rendered block walls, the treatment of windows and nervous experiment in flat roofs – the whole project of building was now infused with the heroics of innovation and invention.

The spirit of rebirth and renewal was palpable, Raymond McGrath's editorial for the 1946 Royal Institute of Architects of Ireland (RIAI) Yearbook describing the 'delicious smell of Portland cement, wet timber and midnight oil in this new world!' This publication contained messages of support from Le Corbusier, J.J.P. Oud, Walter Gropius and Frank Lloyd Wright, as well as an article from the Danish engineer Ove Arup on concrete shell construction that contained an extensive range of detailed drawings and designs. For the Irish concrete industry, Arup was the person who finally suggested the link between production and *design*.

3   Raymond McGrath
Pink Nuns, undated
Private collection

5 Andy Devane
'Journey's End', Howth,
1962

4 Raymond McGrath
Proposal for a
JFK Memorial Concert Hall,
1964

The application of this technology is nowhere better illustrated than in the programme of building undertaken by Michael Scott for Coras Iompair Eireann, the state transport company. Scott's office was attracting many of the best young talents, which enabled him to keep abreast of the quickening pace of architectural innovation in late 1940s Ireland. Designed with Brendan O'Connor, the chassis works factory in Inchicore used a combination of concrete vaults and structural steelwork. But Arup's advice was first employed in a radical way at Donnybrook Bus Garage, designed with Patrick Scott (figs. 1, 2).

The garage was to be the first of eight planned for the country, using the same formwork throughout. This plan never material-ised. The economy was still rather fragile and large developments were often tortuously slow, as proven by the next and most ambitious work in the programme, the Central Bus Station, or Busáras, in Dublin (pp. 118-9). Begun in 1944, abandoned in 1949 when the Government decided to convert the building to an employment exchange, then restarted, Busáras was shrouded in controversy from an early stage owing to the initial siting and to a misleading newspaper article about its intended height. But the scale and location of the building undoubtedly heralded the arrival of modernism in central Dublin; in Scott's characteristically self-assured claim, it was 'the first major building in Europe after the War'. Throughout the nine-year saga of its construction, there was, perhaps for the first time within the country's architectural profession, a sense that Ireland was on a par with European development, allied with a certain giddiness in the face of potentially unlimited modernisation.

There was also a degree of social revolution in the making in the post-war situation. An arts community consisting of what were loosely called 'modernists' existed in Ireland during the 1940s. Many architects enjoyed close proximity to this community, among them Patrick Scott and the White Stag Group, Noel Moffett and Raymond McGrath. The young architects provided a conduit for the commissioning of artists to decorate new buildings, and the first 'Exhibition of Living Art' in 1943 further established the new artwork.

The White Stag Group was founded in Bloomsbury, London, in the 1930s by artists Basil Rakoczi and Kenneth Hall. In 1940 they, and several other artists or 'conscientious objectors', including McGrath, an Australian architect working in Britain, moved to Dublin to avoid the war. They promoted 'modern' art, as opposed to academic convention, and attracted important artists, such as Maine Jellet and Evie Hone, to their exhibitions of paintings. Other emerging Irish and expatriot British artists found support within the group, notably Nano Reid, Ralph Cusack, Robert Dawson, Doreen Vanston, Louis le Brocquy and Patrick Scott, the architect, who was now dividing his time between art and architecture.

McGrath began to draw and paint on coming to Dublin, exhibiting his work in Waddington's Gallery. His wife, Mary, became involved in textile and graphic design, and ran an agency with the help of Michael Scott. McGrath became Architect to the Office of Public Works, where he remained until 1968. In this capacity he designed a little-known, but beautifully conceived, pumping-station in Dublin's Phoenix Park, the first of numerous such small buildings that were erected throughout the 1940s by a number of architects – examples are Vincent Kelly's Lucan bus shelter and Daithi Hanly's 1947 Rathfarnham kiosk – and that combined local traditional materials, such as

6 Alan Hope
Aspro Factory,
Dublin, 1947

7 James Brennan
Dolphin Bar, Dublin, 1939

8 James Brennan
Dolphin Bar, Dublin, 1939

stone, with flat-rendered planes, oversailing concrete slab roofs, interesting modern detailing in the doors and rooflights. McGrath, however, had little luck with architectural commissions – his major schemes for Civic Offices (1948) and a JFK Memorial Concert Hall (1964; fig. 4) were never realised – so it is as an artist and interior designer that he is best remembered in Ireland (fig. 3). His final work was a design for the Royal Hibernian Academy Gallery, Dublin, completed after his death by Arthur Gibney.

Unlike their predecessors in the heady days of hospital building and large projects in the 1930s, most of these young architects and artists relied on smaller works – for instance, J. Arthur Douglas's 1946 Carrickmines House in Dublin. Here, in addition to the by now familiar look of 'international white', there was a genuine attempt to develop a synthesis between, on the one hand, modern planning and construction and, on the other, a native, 'organic' language, no doubt influenced in part by a building such as Le Corbusier's 1935 Weekend House, which combined concrete and glass block with natural stone walls. This tendency can only have been reinforced by the work of Frank Lloyd Wright in America, whose Taliesin complex was visited by the young Andy Devane. Devane wrote a letter, published in the 1946 RIAI Yearbook, in which he talks, prophetically, of 'the real root of art - the root of natural and sincere life that grows from God, not the Industrial Revolution'. On his return from America, Devane built 'Journey's End' in 1962 in Howth, County Dublin, which paid homage to Wright's 'organic' use of natural stone and to his cantilevering decks and roofs (fig. 5). In 1949 Hubert Banahan built the Astor Ballroom in Roscommon, which exploits a madcap juxtaposition of rough stone cladding with

an undulating concrete shell roof, and has floors of coloured asphalt with aluminium strips. The integration of rustic masonry and local vernacular with modern construction has been a recurring theme in Irish architecture.

Noel Moffett, whose wife, Margo, was secretary of the White Stag Group, was one of the most active of architects in Ireland before the war. He had graduated from Liverpool University, where his fellow students included Reggie Malcolmson, who later worked with Ludwig Mies van der Rohe in Chicago, and Liam McCormick, who became a significant church architect in later years. All three worked for a brief time as Town Architects in Northern Ireland and must have contributed to the excellent standard of housing in the North, which continued to win many awards and commendations from the RIAI in Dublin. Returning to Dublin after working in London with Serge Chermayeff, and following short periods of work with Michael Scott and as a planner with Dublin Corporation, Moffett set up his own studio and design school. As a planner, he was involved in several major exhibitions in Dublin during the war, including one on national planning. He proposed a visionary scheme, sadly never implemented, for a riverside park for the Dodder, stretching ten miles from the mountains to the sea. Committed to the ideas of modular design, Moffett produced the first Irish designs for prefabricated houses, under the auspices of the Irish Times' Tomorrow Club and presented with accompanying lectures. Only three of these houses were built, in County Cork, one of them lived in by his friend and patron, Major Freres. Moffett published his designs for low-cost housing in Ireland in the November 1946 issue of *Architectural Design*.

9   Ronald Tallon
Knockanure Chapel, 1960-4

Moffett was continually involved with theatre. He produced set designs for the Gate Theatre in winter 1940-41 and, when he and Margo went to Freres' residence on Achill Island, they designed and built an open-air amphitheatre cut in turf, at which the Abbey Players performed. It was here also that they had met Monica Pidgeon, editor of *Architectural Design*, an acquaintance that continued when Moffett was the only Irish representative at the C.I.A.M. in 1947. From this association he guest-edited a special edition of *Architectural Design* on new Irish architecture in 1947. It illustrated many new materials appearing in the aftermath of war and gave expression to renewed confidence in modern design. Michael Scott's bakery on Dublin's Parnell Street, for example, used teak, terrazzo and glass block for its front, with murals embossed on glass by Louis le Brocquy; James Brennan's Dolphin Bar also used glass block, and polished black marble (figs. 7, 8). Innovative houses completed just before the war by Brennan, J.V. Downes and John O'Gorman were illustrated, but more interesting are the unbuilt house projects by Brendan O'Connor and, again, Noel Moffett, which used all-glass fronts and expansive open planning. O'Connor finally did get to build a house, in Carrickmines in 1949, an excitingly modern work with an unusual, long monopitch and polychromatic rendered wall planes.

One of the unique aspects of actual construction at the time was the re-use of waste products, necessitated by material shortages, which prompted some innovative responses. Perhaps the best-known example of this post-war aesthetic was Jammet's Restaurant and Grill Room in Dublin, by Moffett, which made startling use of plywood, glass bricks, tubular steel, armour-plated glass, concrete and mosaic tile – all materials that recently had been decommissioned.

Architectural Design also contained some references to the new wave of factory buildings that was sweeping the country. Most impressive of these was Alan Hope's Aspro Factory, which won the RIAI Triennial Gold Medal in 1950 but sadly has been demolished (fig. 6). Hope, who had been one of the students of Professor Reilly at Liverpool University, came to Ireland in the 1930s at the time of the hospitals programme. He set up in partnership with Freddie Hicks and became an enthusiastic and influential member of the profession.

Although deemed appropriate for factory buildings, modern architecture encountered resistance when it started to overlap with social functions, as at Busáras. The 'modern' artists and architects had emerged in opposition to the 'social realism' prevailing in the work of the artists of the Royal Hibernian Academy and also supported by the de Valera regime during the 1930s. Eamon de Valera was a former revolutionary turned conservative nationalist who formed a Franco-like alliance with the Catholic Church. While de Valera was promoting his vision of a Catholic Ireland, enacting the 1937 Constitution and ultimately creating a Republic in 1949, he relied heavily on the Catholic Church to share the mantle of patron of architecture, helping extensively the programme of schools and hospitals.

The flavour of this collusion between Church and State is epitomised by the building of Galway Cathedral in 1957-65, under the diocesan control of Bishop Browne and designed by the favourite architect of the hierarchy, John Robinson of Robinson Keefe. This huge Hiberno-Romanesque pile represents the apogee of the inward-looking, fiercely traditionalist Catholic society and sent a clear warning to those entertaining thoughts of 'corrupting' Ireland with modern values.

Despite the conservatism of the bishops, especially McQuaid of Dublin, the emerging modern movement was to have a major effect on ecclesiastic art over the next two decades. When de Valera and his party, Fianna Fail, fell from power in 1948, the new centre-left coalition established the Cultural Relations Committee under Minister Seán McBride (later to become Secretary-General of the United Nations), leading to the setting up of the Arts Council in 1951.

The importance of the Church should not be underestimated: beginning with the 1949 RIAI Yearbook, and continuing until well into the 1960s, architectural publications are filled with little but articles on church art and design and reviews of exhibitions of religious art – from Gerald McNicholl's complaints of 'ugly grottoes' and 'mean and shoddy buildings' to the young Arthur Gibney's enthusiasm that church architecture might be grounds for a national synthesis of art and architecture to exercise 'our national genius for decoration'. McNicholl, together with the writer Seán O'Faolain, Director of the Arts Council, put on an exhibition of French ecclesiastic art, entitled 'Eglises de France Reconstruites', in Maynooth College, which introduced a very modern look to the design of sacred buildings. Parish priests were now encouraged to start commissioning sculptors such as Michael Biggs and Oisin Kelly to furnish the new churches. During this time there began a kind of introspection, a search for national identity in the realm of art and visual expression that might result in the emergence of a 'Celtic Modern' aesthetic.

In 1960 Michael Scott joined the board of the Arts Council, of which Fr. Donal O'Sullivan, a Jesuit priest, had been appointed Director. They renewed the effort to establish a national profile for modern art and design. In 1962, following a commissioned report on Scandinavian design, a private company, Kilkenny Design Workshops, was established and soon achieved a high standard of quality and innovation. Scott's work in this field reached its peak in 1967, with the opening of the first of a series of major international art exhibitions, called *Rosc*. These gave a new level of public exposure to modern art. Throughout the 1960s, there was a conscious attempt to synthesise modern and native, best exemplified by

two contrasting but complementary schemes: Liam McCormick's church of 1964-5 at Burt, County Donegal (p. 131), and Ronald Tallon's Knockanure Chapel, County Kerry, of 1960-4 (fig. 9). Burt is a circular building with a stone perimeter wall and an asymmetric conical roof, while Tallon's is a simple rectangle with brick sides and glazed ends, a steel roof, and a terracotta screen by Oisin Kelly depicting the Last Supper.

The 1950s had been a time of great hardship and economic recession in Ireland. The 1954 RIAI Yearbook presented a bleak picture: no competitions, no lectures by outside visitors, no site visits, no buildings illustrated. Among the many young architects who emigrated was Robin Walker, who left Scott's office to join Mies van der Rohe's post-graduate programme at the Illinois Institute of Technology in Chicago. Cathal O'Neill and Peter Doyle followed. All were to return to make a major impression on the Irish architectural scene.

Robin Walker returned to Michael Scott's office in 1958, inspired by Mies's teaching, and soon made the presence of a new discipline felt. He signalled his intentions as early as 1959, with the Cork Opera House, and then with the Bord Failte Building in Dublin, completed in 1966 (fig. 10). Walker's concern was that, by displaying total honesty of structure and fabric, and by using inexpensive local materials, the building could relate in spirit to the eighteenth-century Georgian vernacular. Ronald Tallon, too, entered Scott's office in 1958, coming from the Office of Public Works. He took over the commission to build the Abbey, Dublin's new National Theatre, which won the RIAI Gold Medal on its completion in 1966. This group of buildings – Cork Opera House, Bord Failte, the Abbey Theatre – represent a new twist in the story of modern architecture in Ireland. The formal assemblages, cultivation of new materials and surfaces, and abstract patterning of 1940s design were replaced by a new structural discipline that, at its best, entailed a refinement of approach to produce simple, unadorned buildings of striking integrity.

1960s Ireland is popularly known as the time of Lemass, the Prime Minister

10   Robin Walker
Bord Failte Building, Dublin, completed 1966

11   Ronald Tallon
Bank of Ireland Headquarters, Dublin, 1975

12 Niall Scott
Port and Docks Board Headquarters,
Dublin, 1978

who brought an economic boom and hence a revival of commissions for big buildings. There was a new confidence and a determined attitude to technological progression. In 1962 a Building Centre was set up in Dublin to provide an up-to-date source of reference material and an exhibition centre for new methods and materials, as well as to publish a regular review, *Forgnan*. At the forefront of this architectural activity was Michael Scott and Partners, later to be renamed Scott Tallon Walker. Walker employed concrete and other local basic building materials, but pushed beyond prescribed Miesian formulas to make truly original works. It was Tallon who, in classical Miesian mode, made a more overt use of steel on the exterior of his buildings. The obvious chemistry between these two architects produced a remarkable spate of work between 1960 and 1975.

All Walker's work - his own house at St Mary's Lane, Wesley College, the O'Flaherty House (pp. 134-5), the Maynooth Arts Faculty, the University College Dublin's Restaurant (pp. 136-7), St Columba's Science Laboratory – shows a deep concern for the expression of structure and material and for the possibilities of horizontal spatial planning. Tallon's work forms the greater volume in the partnership's output and includes perhaps the better known and more recognisable buildings. From the auspicious beginnings of the Abbey Theatre, he went on to design the 1959 GEC Factory and the 1960 RTE Television Studios, both of which were awarded an RIAI Gold Medal. Under Tallon, along with major public buildings, the practice produced a staggering number of industrial buildings over the following decades, with the Carroll's Factory, Dundalk, of 1973 also winning a Gold Medal (pp. 132-3). Tallon's early works use exposed concrete at the ground-floor columns, but the upper floors are enclosed in an elegant metal and glass skin. Later, his best work is where the language combines with an original conception of form, as at University College Galway, the RTE Radio Building (p. 123), the Goulding House (p. 146), or Carroll's.

However, the pure and successful structural resolution of these works was perhaps pushing Tallon closer to a confrontation with the relationship of the structural form to the outward appearance of the building. The Lisney Building, 1974, in white-painted steel on an infill site on Dublin's St Stephen's Green, addressed the same issue of 'scaffold and exhibit' as Bord Failte, but proposed instead to solve the problem of modern architecture's intervention in the urban fabric by attractive cladding. The transplantation of Miesian forms to Irish soil might have seemed complete with the Bank of Ireland Headquarters, Dublin, of 1975 (fig. 11). Yet, when placed in the context of eighteenth-century Baggot Street, with dark-coloured bronze and glass simply cladding a massive, hidden concrete bulk, the expression of the building was at once forceful and strangely mute. The problem of skin had finally caught up with architects and remains the prevailing question for Irish architecture.

In his late buildings Walker refused to accept the dominance of skin over structure: St Columba's Science Laboratory, 1972 (p. 141), and PMPA Building, 1973, both investigate the possibilities of steel and glass skins, but the structural expression of the buildings behind remains clear and dominant. Scott Tallon Walker was boosted by the inclusion of Michael Scott's son, Niall, who developed his own, very clear formal approach, as in the 1978 Port and Docks Board Headquarters, in which an externally expressed concrete armature is emphatically separated from the gridded glass envelope of the internal volume (fig. 12).

One of Walker's last projects is his own house at Bothár Buí, County Cork, an example of how to build sensitively in a remote and beautiful landscape (p. 78). It is an infinitely humble, yet uncompromisingly modern work, which demonstrates a perfect symbiosis between the simple whitewashed stone, pitch-roofed cabins restored on the site, and the simple three-sided whitewashed block, mono-pitched enclosures set into the steep slope. This house provides a salutary example of modern architecture's integration with context and, if better known, would surely have influenced the debate that was to come.

From Concrete to Contexturalism

Irish Architecture 1970–1995

SIMON WALKER

Concurrently with Scott Tallon Walker, several practices in Ireland were operating on almost the same scale, while others were making smaller, considered contributions to the advancement of the architectural dialogue. Cathal O'Neill built the Egan Warehouse in Phibsboro, an elegant work using concrete panels and double-height glazing under a projecting concrete roof. Peppard and Duffy's churches at Greenhills and Donnycarney were extraordinary exercises in formal engineering, while Pearse MacKenna and Seán Rothery's St Michael's Church in Dun Laoghaire of 1973 evinced a more relaxed, structuralist approach. There were smaller gems, too, such as Downes and Meehan's Munster and Leinster Bank at Leeson Park in Dublin, which used fine materials to produce a simple, unpretentious building with pleasing proportions. One aspect of modern construction at this time that should not be forgotten is the often extraordinary level of craftsmanship that still existed in the trades; it was exploited to the limit in the deceptively difficult task of realising 'minimalist' buildings.

Projects of all sizes in virtually every townland in the country were realised in the 1960s and early 1970s, including schools, social buildings and housing. In 1970 the Royal Institute of Architects of Ireland (RIAI) awarded its Medal for Housing to Neil Hegarty's Dundannion

Court in Cork, which was reminiscent of Mies van der Rohe's Lafayette Park Housing and at the top of its class internationally at the time. Hegarty went on to become an influential spokesperson for housing and urban planning in the post of Cork City Architect.

Robinson Keefe Devane was an enigmatic practice that ranged from an inheritance of the hospital building programme of the 1930s and the churches of the 1950s to the seeming promise of the Carroll's Building in Dublin and the holistic thinking of Andy Devane (fig. 1 and p. 130). But 1977 brought the Irish Life Centre complex of buildings, behind the Custom House, which had an enormous, if understated, influence on Dublin's city planning. This was Dublin's first 'groundscraper', the result of planning policy to limit the height of all future development in the city to six or seven storeys. As such, the Irish Life Centre represents the failure of planning to respond to the problem of redevelopment of the centre. With a pedestrian 'mall' at ground level, it set the example for such disastrous future schemes as the Irish Life Mall in Henry Street.

Building in concrete, which had held the key to architectural progress in twentieth-century Ireland, and whose subsequent demise reflects the wider problem of the decline of modern architecture in general, received some significant influ-

1 Robinson Keefe Devane
Carroll's Building, Dublin,
1962-4

ence from abroad in the 1960s. In 1961-7 Trinity College built the Berkeley Library by Ahrends Burton Koralek (ABK; pp. 124-5). Its powerful use of raw concrete to model three-dimensional forms had a profound effect on Irish architects. Later, ABK were to build St Andrew's College, also in Dublin, which again uses innovative concrete forms and detailing, as well as unusual blockwork; and in 1968 David Cronin built the Tayto Factory in the city, with an excellent use of exposed concrete, ramped and cut away in places to reveal an inner glass skin. In the north, concrete was turned to explore the Brutalist aesthetic in the extension to the Ulster Museum of 1963-71 by Francis Pym of London and in Portadown Technical College of 1972-6 by J. B. Kennedy (fig. 2 and pp. 144-5).

3 Sam Stephenson
Central Bank, Dublin,
1975

2 Francis Pym
Extension to the Ulster Museum,
Belfast,
1963-71

Andrej Wjechert, while still a student in Poland in 1964, won an international competition to design the layout of the new University College Dublin campus at Belfield, along with the commission to design the Arts Building, Administration Building and Bank, all of which were built between 1970 and 1973. The buildings feature exaggerated horizontal bands of white aggregate concrete following the stepped line of the 'landscaped' plan and standing out against slots of deep shade, in pointed contrast to the slender, floating quality of Walker's Restaurant Building nearby (pp. 136-7).

Wjechert was part of a wider European response to modernism, involving the use of expressionistic sculptural forms whose effect had not gone unnoticed by Arthur Gibney. In 1969 Gibney and his partner, Sam Stephenson, won a competition to build the new offices for the Electricity Supply Board, in Dublin's Lower Fitzwilliam Street. From the start, this building, clad in brown, pre-cast concrete panels, was immersed in controversy as it involved the demolition of a terrace of prized eighteenth-century Georgian houses, breaking the unique and heretofore intact 'Georgian Mile' of Fitzwilliam Street. It was a controversy that would dog modern architecture in Ireland. Along with the Ballymun Tower Housing of 1969, this building seemed to suggest that modern architects were bent on destroying the entire architectural heritage of the city.

Further controversy was to ensue with the building of the Central Bank in Dame Street in 1975 (fig. 3). An astonishing and ambitious work, it used pre-cast concrete floor slabs hung by bronze-clad cables from a huge, nine-storey umbrella structure on a central concrete core. It was easily the most notorious project since Scott's Busáras over twenty years earlier (pp. 118-9). Stephenson became Ireland's most public architectural figure, helped by his voluble and gregarious Dublin nature. Again an interesting dialogue took place between two architectural partners. Stephenson employed dramatic, if sometimes crude, gestures, such as the external steel bracing on his Coolock Shopping Centre, the strange brick-clad volumes of the 1973 Molyneaux House and the Fitzwilliam Tennis Club, or the mirror-glass curtain wall of the 1975 EBS Building. Gibney's approach was more sober, concentrating on the strong modelling of forms within an expression of structure, as in the 1972 International Airport Hotel. He was to win the RIAI Gold Medal for his Irish Management Institute at Sandyford (pp. 142-3). In Gibney's most famous drawing of this building, from the year 1973, dark and ominous clouds loom over it, a sign that the end was near for modernism in Ireland (fig. 5). Events finally came to a head with Stephenson's illfated scheme for the Civic Offices at Christ Church, which was halted halfway through, ostensibly owing to the ongoing archaeological excavation at Wood Quay.

The real cause, however, was the public outcry at the appearance of these two stone-clad monoliths, which was intensified by their being identified with the much-criticised City Corporation and the destruction of the Wood Quay dig.

In retrospect, the modern dream always carried within it a self-destruct mechanism. This activated in the late 1970s, as modernism was forced to confront the issue of its relationship to context. Also, increasing 'Internationalism' only begged the question of 'national' identity. In a very brief period, from 1960 to 1975, there had been an intensive burst of activity; different aspects of modern architecture – concrete formalism, steel structuralism, even a native organic style – were pursued to their limits and beyond. Inevitably, it seems now, modernism was followed by fifteen years of murky mediocrity, a grinding period of economic depression, confusion and loss of innocence, when modern architecture adopted extraordinary and ever more degrading measures to disguise itself, among them red bricks and pitched roofs.

As with any period of inactivity, debate and introspection resulted in a spate of 'paper projects'. Young architects graduating in the mid- to late 1970s began to re-examine the notion of context, in an attempt to uncover the significance of the legacy of urban fabric. A very few firms maintained a thread of continuity with the early 1970s, most notably de Blacam and Meagher, and Peter and Mary Doyle, who won an RIAI Gold Medal for their school at Birr (pp. 150-51). Shane de Blacam had studied under Louis Kahn in Philadelphia and this, along with John Meagher's experience of Alvar Aalto's architecture, had given them a committed, yet sensitive, appreciation of what might be called the more 'human' side of modernism, and of the lessons that it held for making a place-specific architecture. Their church at Firhouse (1976-8) remained true to a simple modern language, yet its plan, with an external courtyard space before the church, reflected a more specifically Irish pattern of use (pp. 148-9). This approach was continued in new buildings and in sensitive intervention in, and renovations of, old buildings, particularly at Trinity College (pp. 154-5). Another

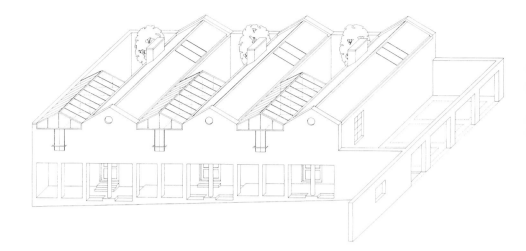

4   Shay Cleary
Design for houses at Swan Place, Dublin, 1980

architect who studied with Kahn is Noel Dowley, who has also fought to maintain an individual sense of continuity, from his Kilfrush houses in the early 1970s to his Dublin Airport Carpark buildings of 1991 and the school at Ashbourne, County Meath, of 1995.

Other architects were also able to marry an acceptance of pre-existing conditions of context to the modernity of their own ideas without loss of integrity. Shay Cleary, in his Swan Place houses project of 1980 (realised in 1983), successfully manipulates familiar urban elements and combines them to maximise the spatial planning of the houses within the rigid framework of the existing mews plots (fig. 4). That year, his collaboration with Frank Hall, Tony Murphy, Yvonne Farrell and Shelley McNamara (who later became Grafton Architects) produced an apartment complex at Chapelizod, Dublin, that uses brick cladding, but maintains distinctly modern, yet relaxed, proportions.

The emergence of this new sensibility at the end of the 1970s, called 'new regionalism' or 'new rationalism', depending on whether one's preoccupation was predominantly English (Kenneth Frampton) or Italian (Aldo Rossi), coincided with the development of a large body of 'paper projects', many of which were included in an exhibition of architecture, 'A Sense of Ireland: Traditions and Directions', that was shown at the Royal College of Art in London in 1980. As the English architect Ed Jones remarked in the catalogue, 'architecture cannot be the product of osmosis or the

5   Arthur Gibney
Perspective drawing of the Irish Management Institute, Dublin, 1973
Collection of the RIAI

6   Michael McGarry and
Siobhan ní Éanaigh
Riverside house,
County Meath, 1993

7   Shane de Blacam and John Meagher
Beckett Theatre, Trinity College Dublin,
1993

spontaneous free will of the people recalling distant Celtic origins, but is rather the product of conscious cultural exchange'. The show combined the new paper projects with the best work of the 1960s and 1970s by established architects in an attempt to establish a thread of continuity in Irish architecture, while freely admitting foreign influences. Among the contributors to the catalogue was Derek Tynan, then studying urban design at Cornell University with Colin Rowe. Urban design projects by Gerry Cahill, Shane O'Toole and Grafton Architects were also included, as well as work by many young graduates, including Sheila O'Donnell and Paul Keogh, M.A. students at the Royal College at the time, John Tuomey, Michael McGarry, Siobhan ni Éanaigh, Michael Kelly and Liz Morgan.

The polemics contained in this new 'contextual' (urban) or 'regional' (rural) architecture provided a firm base for the continued propagation of ideas and, when all these young architects came together in Dublin, the work continued apace. The lack of real building activity served only to reinforce the campaign for a new architecture, particularly where it involved urban design. The City Architecture Studio of 1984 and the 1986 Quays Project, co-ordinated by Gerry Cahill, involved students and graduates of the School of Architecture at University College Dublin in a scheme to complete the renewal of the Quays and the adjoining districts. As head of the school, Cathal O'Neill was probably the figure most instrumental in bringing these architects together and fostering a climate of creativity and aspiration.

In tandem with the urban work, there was the development of what Cahill called a 'non-provincial regionalism' – a notion, influenced to a large extent by Aldo Rossi's work in Lombardy, that revolved around the idea of 'appropriate' buildings, ones that can appear blunt in form and expression, but that have subtle, underlying roots in a place-specific architectural tradition. An exhibition of Rossi's drawings, organised by Paul Keogh in Dublin in 1983, helped to introduce the look of this new European classicism to an Irish setting. Much of this new Irisch Work

was shown in 1986 in an exhibition at the Architectural Association in London called 'Figurative Architecture, which included projects by Paul Keogh, John Tuomey, Rachel Chidlow, Valerie Mulvin and Niall McCullough.

Meanwhile the economic recession continued, and the Government gradually shifted the onus for development onto the private sector. Over the course of the 1980s figures for private estate housing, for example, showed a drop in Government-financed projects, expressed as a percentage of the total, from 70 to 7 per cent. In deprived inner-city areas in Dublin, the young architects' exploratory project work may have helped the urban environment to become a more pressing public concern. Here the mechanism of tax incentives was introduced to stimulate renewal. Unfortunately, these incentives were mostly abused by developers, who speculated on the tax relief itself, having concluded there was more profit in reselling sites than in actually developing them. The corollary to this increasing reliance on the private sector to take on the mantle of urban renewal was that certain design-build corporations were able to conceal their approach to planning under mock-contextual garments. They developed a pastiche formula of brick cladding and old-world decoration that worked to the detriment of serious architectural initiative in urban design.

The RIAI and its medals became less relevant to the direction of new architecture, as the agenda for change was by now being set mostly by the Architectural Association of Ireland, which sponsored a yearly awards scheme. The quickening pace of a new, rooted yet modern, architecture, spurred on by such established architects as de Blacam and Meagher, can be measured by the awards given. To date, the awards have consistently featured certain architectural practices, including O'Donnell and Tuomey, McGarry and ni Éanaigh, Ross Cahill O'Brien, Paul Keogh and Rachel Chidlow, and Shay Cleary.

A significant amount of the work now being taken on by Irish architects is in the area of intervention in existing buildings, structures or settings. Perhaps the given conditions of site and shell offer an improved climate for innovation, sheltered, as it were, from naked newness by the received imprimatur of the historical building. Sheila O'Donnell's stitching of the Irish Film Centre into the urban fabric of Temple Bar (pp. 156-7), the placing of the Beckett Theatre in the grand architectural setting of Trinity College Dublin by de Blacam and Meagher (fig. 7), Shay Cleary's interiors for the new Museum of Modern Art in the Royal Hospital at Kilmainham (pp.158-9), Phelim Dunne's Tropical Fruits Building, and the sheltered housing by Gerry Cahill that has created a minature urban complex around a nineteenth-century convent building – all are happy results of an improved, realistic approach to urban renewal that places value on rescuing old structures that, in another age, might well have been demolished. This kind of work has been able to demonstrate that there is no *a priori* relationship between progress and loss of heritage, and in itself has applied the kind of necessary pressure to public and private sector alike to forge ahead with renewal initiatives.

In 1991 Group '91, a consortium of eight small architectural practices, was established to design the project 'Making a Modern Street'. For a Corporation-owned site in Dublin, the group designed a terrace of houses, each with an individual, yet complementary, expression (fig. 10). This finally dislodged the inertia affecting the task of rehabilitating the centre of Dublin. When the Government designated

8   Murray O'Laoire
Visitor Centre, King John's Castle, Limerick, 1992

the city's Temple Bar district a cultural quarter in 1991, a competition held to design an overall 'Architectural Framework Plan' was won by Group '91 (p. 161). Phase one of the development of the area, which has recently been completed, involved the creation of a dozen cultural institutions and extensive residential building, and represents a significant and exciting approach to urban renewal in Europe.

In the 1990s architecture has not just been limited to urban renewal, however; a new sensibility to landscape and context in regional buildings, much of it centred around tourism, is now everywhere in evidence. In their restoration work at King John's Castle in Limerick, Murray O'Laoire have juxtaposed ancient stone masses with a refined modern enamelled white steel and glass structure. This introduced a confident new approach to modern materials and aesthetics in an historic setting (fig. 8). The same can be said of some of the new 'interpretive centres', buildings for tourist information that occupy scenic locations. Mary McKenna's Ceide Fields Visitor Centre of 1993 for the OPW (p. 41) is a half-submerged pyramid with glass lantern at the apex, reminiscent of the approach of de Blacam and Meagher, in their Knock Chapel of 1990 (p. 65), to cutting into the site. De Paor and O'Neill's Ballincollig Visitors' Centre in Cork, 1992, adopts a

9　Grafton Architects
Department of Production
Engineering, Trinity College Dublin,
1996

more fluid attitude to the received conditions of site, incorporating them into a looping circulation pattern punctuated by small buildings or rooms (p. 173).

The now improved economic conditions have brought what seems to be almost an *embarras de richesse* of projects allowing experimentation and invention in architecture, among them many significant urban buildings. With its cantilevered roof and multi-tiered stands, phase one of Gilroy McMahon's Croke Park Stadium in Dublin, completed in 1995, makes an architectural statement in a field once reserved for engineers (fig. 11). The emphasis in urban residential development is gradually moving away from maximum-density speculative schemes to embrace designs that offer more variety of spaces and provisions for urban living, with commercial and infrastructure development as yet lagging behind. Towns and cities have been transformed in the past five years: Cork, Limerick, Athlone, the villages of West Cork, all now enjoy a revitalised outlook in answer to the 'cultural imperative' demanded by tourism and sustainable environmental policies. Dublin's day will not be long in coming.

The year 1996 has seen the completion of two projects, Grafton Architects' building for the Department of Production Engineering at Trinity College (fig. 9) and de Blacam and Meagher's Cork RTC Library (pp. 178-9), both of which display a new and easy confidence. Many more

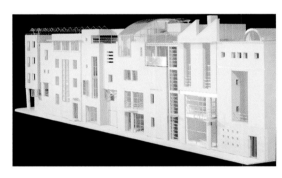

10　Group '91
'Making a Modern Street', 1991

11　Gilroy McMahon
Croke Park Stadium, Dublin, 1995

projects in towns and in the landscape, by all generations of architects, seem to have found a new freedom of expression. This is the result of a growing maturity that, having eschewed the crudest simplistic dogmatism of the 1960s, has emerged from the nightmarish confusion of the fall of modernism and the beginnings of contextualism, and that allows architects to practise their art with a broader and deeper understanding both of the nature of modern building and of its relationship to our natural environment.

1 Deserted *clachan* on Achill Island

2 Rundale Relics

3 Lenankeel *clachan*, County Donegal

Building in the Irish Landscape

ORLA MURPHY

When Heinrich Böll wrote *Irisches Tage-buch* he took back to Germany the image of a desolate paradise, clinging on to the edge of an increasingly wealthy Europe. Its troubles – poverty, a dispersed and ever-decreasing rural population – were also to become the pathetic charms of 'Der grüne Insel' (fig. 3). The sense of connection between man and the land-scape that so seduced Böll was one rooted in social and political tradition, reinforced in text, ceremony and nomenclature.

The earliest example of this codifica-tion can be found in the Brehon Laws, which structured the Celtic land-use sys-tem through definition of field boundaries and ownership. Nomenclature and devel-opment of names are extremely powerful weapons in the preservation of a culture. As the character Manus tells us in Brian Friel's play *The Gentle Island*: 'There's a name for every stone about here sir, and a story too.' The Irish language not only represented a code through which every mark on the land could be signified, defined and elaborated; it also provided for the people a way of weaving them-selves into the land, through their own names and stories. Ceremonies such as treading and perambulation were used to reaffirm field boundaries in relation to distinctive marks on the landscape, such as ringforts, high crosses and cairns, all of which bear their own culturally evolved name and associated history (fig. 2).[1]

Through the English Plantation of Ireland the social relationship between man and the landscape was changed to one of peasant tenure, existing outside the walled demesnes of the great estates. The Celtic land-use patterns ceased to function under the pressure of the popu-lation explosion of the nineteenth century, and famine and emigration were left to redress the demographic balance. With the dawn of the Free State, the Irish Government attempted to symbolise national cultural identity as that contained in the vernacular thatched cottage on the mountain. Eamon de Valera went as far as to say: 'We are prepared to get out of the mansion, to live our lives in our own way, and to live in that frugal manner'.[2] To a public weary of colonial oppression this was a simple and eloquent way of appeas-ing anti-British bitterness and equating a natural life-style with independence and liberty. Through the conscious turn away from all things colonial, the notion of building in the landscape became loaded with political overtones and implications. The Big House was bad and the thatched cottage was good. This tenet was also proposed by the Dublin cultural élite of the turn of the century, as Fintan O'Toole has argued: 'The notion of the peasant, and of the country which the peasant embodied, was not a reflection of the Irish reality but an artificial literary creation, largely made in Dublin for Dubliners.'[3]

4　Simon J. Kelly and Partners
Houses, Mincloon,
1986

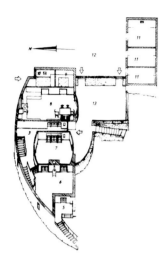

5　Ross Cahill O'Brien
House in Bofara, 1995

The rural dwellers themselves had more pressing cares than their elevation to the level of national symbols. Their day-to-day worries were not those of W. B. Yeats's character Kathleen Ni Houlihan, but rather of where the next meal would come from and of the increasing tide of emigration that was burgling the nation's bank of youth. Through a centralised Government programme, the rural poor were relocated to the more fertile land and the great estates portioned out. However, in many places these resettlements broke irredeemably the cultural connection between man and the landscape. It is a tragedy of Ireland's recent past that landscape has been shaped through the minds and political intervention of urban dwellers, which allowed a blight of bungalows to stretch itself endlessly along the national routes, with none of that consideration for site, topography, scale and materials that their forerunners seem to exhibit effortlessly (fig. 1).

Against this political background, buildings that connect with the landscape in a contemporary context become all the more remarkable. In a conservative planning environment such qualities can be difficult to achieve, but may often be found in the most unlikely places. For example, the last thing you would expect to find, walking along the heavily overgrown and very steep-sided Dargle Valley in County Wicklow, is a pristine glass box, cantilevering over the river. This summerhouse of 1975 (p. 146), designed by the rigorously modern firm Scott Tallon Walker, is a poetic realisation of the theoretical transparency of the modern movement in architecture.

The qualities that make buildings in the landscape work are not scale-dependent. They are present in the strength of conviction of the Mourne wall, a structure that stretches around the ridge of an entire mountain range in County Down with the sole purpose of delineating the territory belonging to the Silent Valley reservoir. They are equally present in some of the smallest dwellings.

The approach to a cluster of three houses in Galway built by Simon J. Kelly and Partners in 1986 offers a glimpse of angled gables that call to mind the paintings of Paul Henry (fig. 4). On closer inspection the gables reveal themselves as belonging to an intimate group of modern houses, each with its own public forecourt and strong formal presence on a site that extends out to a private connection overlooking Galway Bay to the Clare coast beyond. Greene House (1992) by the same architects appears from the distance as a tower, barricaded against the elements, in a field of wild flowers (fig. 6). The living area of the house is entered across a walkway, stepping down in section to allow the private rooms of the house to enjoy direct access to the site.

A change that the twentieth century has seen in rural Ireland is the increase in large one-family houses standing on their own, distinctly separate sites, which may or may not be connected with a farm. This has given rise to the problem of scale and proportion, as the new houses can fall between two precedents, achieving neither the presence of the Big House, nor the organic sympathy of a smaller dwelling. A solution to this problem has been proposed by several architects in recent years. Ross Cahill O'Brien's house in Bofara, County Mayo (1995; fig. 5), Derek Tynan's house in the Barrow Valley, County Wexford (1987; fig. 7), and Grafton Architects' house in Doolin, County Clare (1995), all make use of the one-room-deep, middle-sized farmhouse proportions to achieve a modern

6 Simon J. Kelly and Partners
Greene House, Galway,
1992

7 Derek Tynan
House in the Barrow Valley,
1987

alternative to the unfortunate 'bungalow blitz'.

The last of these buildings attempts to adapt a simple form to the needs of modern living, while framing views of the extended landscape through holes punched in its protective boundary walls (figs. 10, 11). The distinguishing factor of all three houses is the architects' confidence in the positive contribution of the building to the landscape. No attempt is made to hide the houses. They are proud of their proportions. In a sense they allow the site into the building.

Related to the farmhouse and quite often a more successful inhabitant of its site are the omnipresent red corrugated barns, which are to be found across the country in a multitude of forms, colours and sizes. These barns are a modern interpretation of many of the principles latent in Irish vernacular building that worked with the landscape. They may stand tall and proud, open to their leeward side, exposing their innards of hay and their spindly steel construction while closed to the wind, a sheet of red oxidised metal barring the elements. At other times they are small integrated parts of a complex of farm buildings that now seems the natural inheritor of the *clachan* (hamlet). Today, however, one family inhabits the settlement, made up of a house, barn and cowshed that are usually brought together loosely around connected courtyards of varying degrees of privacy (figs. 8, 9).

A new typology that has arisen from the political attempt to make landscape a marketable product is the interpretative centre. Being without precedent, these buildings often disguise themselves as traditional forms, without any regard for the latter's original logic. The most notable examples are the Ceide Fields Visitor Centre in County Mayo (fig. 12), the Glenveagh Visitor Centre in the Donegal National Park and the Blasket Island Centre in Kerry. These buildings were designed and built amid increasing controversy. Public outcry at the decision to build interpretative centres in areas of acute environmental sensitivity, in particular the Burren and Lugalla, called into question Government immunity from the planning process.

The majority of realised interpretative centres exhibit their dubious right to inhabit the landscape by their buried forms: the centre at Ceide Fields, the Valentia Island centre in Kerry and the Glendalough centre in Wicklow are just three examples of 'embarrassed' buildings, which seek invisibility by concealing themselves beneath grass and peat. A notable exception to this trend is the Ballincollig Gunpowder Mills Visitors' Centre in County Cork (fig. 13 and p. 173). This is a small building designed by Tomás de Paor and Emma O'Neill. The visitor moves along routes through the landscape on the tour – routes that form a focus of entry and exit at the point where the visitors' building is located. Through considered planting and use of materials, another layer is added to the sensuous experience of the site within its own immediate context and thus to the wider context of the landscape.

Perhaps the one building form that has thrived under the political evolution of twentieth-century Ireland is the church. Churches have been allowed to become physical and social beacons, positively encouraged to respond to their context. The churches of Liam McCormick are

8 Typical Irish barn

worthy of particular note. St Aengus in Burt, County Donegal, is the full stop in a flow of primitive circular forms, beginning with the ringfort of Grianan na n-Aileach on the peak above, spiralling down the mountain, and winding to the circular church in the valley below. Within the building this language is continued, as the symbolic landscape is brought into the space through a high ring of clerestory light and through a funnel in the conical spire (p. 131).

At Creeslough, also in County Donegal, McCormick's St Michael's Church appears as a sculpture of clear curved protecting walls, at once graceful in form and powerful in its pride of place on the land, a pride that it seems to arouse in the landscape beyond. The walls, at once massive and protective, resonate with the rolling hills, resulting in a poetic symbiosis of building and site (pp. 138-9). The exterior walls of the same architect's church of 1977-9 at Fossa, County Kerry, undulate in two directions, forming a reverent foreground below the towering Kerry mountains.

In Ireland there exists a deep-rooted tradition of the architectural palimpsest – that is, the adaptation over hundreds of years of forms and buildings to new uses. This tradition continues in the twentieth century, from social housing projects built within the walls of King John's Castle in Limerick to the conversion of desanctified churches into apartments. In Ireland buildings in the landscape do not just live and die. They are reclaimed by the land out of which they came, transmuted into adapted forms to serve new functions, added to, built on and built around, all the time reinforcing their relationship with the earth.

If Heinrich Böll could return to Ireland today, he would no doubt find a

9 Typical Irish barn

10 Grafton Architects
House in Doolin, 1995
Interior

11 Grafton Architects
House in Doolin,
1995

12 Mary McKenna
Ceide Fields, Visitor Centre,
1993

country different from that portrayed in
his diary. It is still a nation 'catching up
on two centuries and jumping over another
five',[4] but it is jumping quicker all the
time. I hope that it is an Ireland in which
the people are slowly learning that to be
part of the rest of the world does not
mean to imitate it. Equally, it is of no
benefit to dress up the country for the
sole interest of tourists. Amid the rush to
modernise an agricultural economy and to
halt rural depopulation it is essential to
consider the likely repercussions of
political decision on the formation of the
terrain.

The Irish landscape is a paradox of
colours, smells and textures under ever
changing light that both repel and attract,
that can arouse a sense of shame, but also
great pride. It was the inherent unpre-
dictability of the paradoxical Irish landscape and people that Böll most admired.
The one constant about this unpre-
dictability is that it will always be with us.

13   Tomás de Paor and Emma O'Neill
Gunpowder Mills Visitors' Centre, Ballincollig, 1992

Notes

1 A discussion of treading and perambulation ceremonies can
   be found in J. H. Andrews, *Plantation Acres* (Omagh, 1985).
2 Quoted in Brian P. Kelly, 'The Traditional Irish Thatched
   Cottage', in Adele M. Dalsimer (ed.), *Visualising Ireland*
   (London, 1993), p. 176.
3 Fintan O'Toole, 'Going West: The Country versus the City in
   Irish Writing', *The Crane Bag* 9:2 (1985), pp. 111-16.
4 Heinrich Böll, *Irish Journal* (London, 1995), p. 122.

1 Georgian townscape,
North Merrion Square,
Dublin, begun 1760s

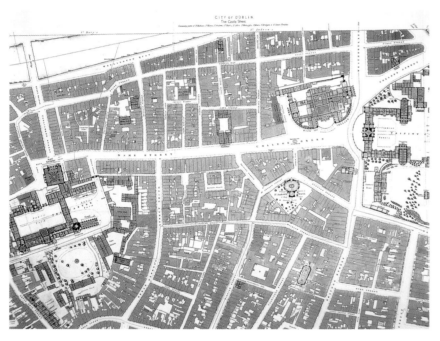

2 The area centred on College Green,
Dublin, in 1847

Weaving the Fabric of the City

Urban Design and Dublin

JOHN OLLEY

In the history of urban design, the reputation of Dublin is usually tied to that of Bath, Bristol, Edinburgh and London. Each city contains fine pieces of Georgian townscape (fig. 1). However, Dublin has its own particular character, specific to the conditions of a capital of a colonial country harbouring an irrepressible desire for the assertion of independence and the creation of a national identity.

In Dublin the eighteenth century saw the eastward expansion of the city in the speculative development of landed estates by laying out streets and squares. A more organic spread of the city came down the hill from its medieval core and moved along the River Liffey to meet the Georgian estates in the vicinity of Dublin's first university, Trinity College (fig. 2). This junction between the expanded old town and the Georgian new seemed likely to become the monumental focus of the city. The university had a new eighteenth-century facade that, along with the adjacent Parliament building, framed an emerging public urban space. From this bridgehead, axes were aimed across the Liffey and back to the medieval core to engage the Cathedral of Christ Church and the Castle, the administrative stronghold of the British. The landed estates of the north and south side of the Liffey were joined and the older parts of the city penetrated to establish coherent streets and vistas. Streets were widened and new, more uniform facades imposed.

This was part of the work of the Wide Streets Commissioners, a body set up in 1758. These neo-classical planners sought to heal the ideological suture between organic growth and the formal order of the new estates, etching the new forms onto the old (fig. 3). In addition they completed the construction of the Liffey Quays. Begun in the late seventeenth century, the Quays reversed the previous practice of turning away from the water's edge and, with the addition of a pair of Dublin's grandest eighteenth-century public buildings, the Four Courts and the Custom House, the river became a grand watery boulevard, lined with quays and terraced with architecture (fig. 4). All this was neatly packaged by the dual cordon of the circular road, begun in 1763, and the Royal and Grand canals, built in the 1790s. The diagram of all these urban design gestures has retained to the present day a nostalgic afterglow in the minds of planners and architects (fig. 5).

For Dublin, this eighteenth-century neo-classical moment did not form a sudden blooming to be followed by precipitous decay brought on by the Act of Union in 1800. Although usually remembered for its more diagrammatic lines of vistas, streets and squares, it was absorbed into the continuing complex evolution of the city, which has woven a subtler and richer tapestry. A new public building might, for example, take the opportunity

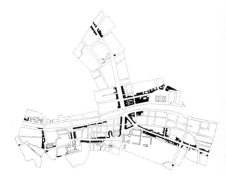

3   Map of Dublin showing the projects promoted by the Wide Streets Commissioners

to enter into a dialogue with the city, asserting its presence and becoming a figure in the urban landscape. It could embroider itself onto, and weave itself into, the fabric of the city, discovering and creating new patterns and relationships (fig. 6). In addition, a building of distinction would encourage the readjustment of its surroundings to make an architectural and urban virtue of its specialness, or it might be picked up by some distant part of the city and incorporated into the composition of another locality. Alternatively, unpretentious insertions would be involved in the subtle fusing of one small development with another, transforming the ordinary into the extraordinary as each fragment worked to reveal and contrive echoes across the city and reflections across the street. Modest buildings played their part in two ways: either they acknowledged their immediate surroundings, submitting themselves to a setting from which a public building could emerge with importance, or they adjusted their posture to combine with humble neighbours to transform the commonplace into something exceptional, as the whole became much more than the sum of the parts.

As the Protestant Anglo-Irish Ascendancy lost its instrumental power to fashion both politics and city fabric, Dublin in the nineteenth century became the battlefield for the complex political climate. The two Churches, the emancipated Catholic and the Disestablished Church of Ireland, now marked the urban skyline with a dialectic, not a consensus. Furthermore, commerce and the merchant princes sought to add their individual identity to the streets, with associations and sympathies seasoning the political and religious stew. And, with a weak and lethargic Dublin Corporation, the nostalgia for the grand urban design of the Wide Streets Commissioners could not move beyond paper projects. All the uniformity that had been imposed on the older parts of the city centre fragmented as a multiplicity of secular and sacred concerns sought individual expression (fig. 8).

Isolated interventions, however, were achieved. In 1886 Lord Edward Street was cut to open up Christ Church Cathedral to Dame Street, but now more as a transportation route than for reasons of either

4   Thomas Cooley and James Gandon
The Four Courts, Dublin,
1776-1802

5   Taylor's map of Dublin, 1816, showing the city's overall form

6   William Lynn
St Andrew's Church,
Dublin, 1860.
View from College Green

7   View towards Christ Church Cathedral up Lord Edward Street,
cut in 1886

aesthetic delight or sound real estate logic (fig. 7). Otherwise, civic gestures were generally limited to individual buildings, receiving generous patronage from powerful citizens. Christ Church was 'restored' by Henry Roe, and the Guinnesses replied with a refurbishment of St Patrick's Cathedral, although Sir Benjamin Lee Guinness then failed to cut a street to join his adopted monument to his residence in St Stephen Green. The aspirations of the Wide Street Commissioners lived on, but the executive will and means were lacking. Yet, with the power of their purse and strong localised influence, the Guinness dynasty set out, under the guise of philanthropy, to improve the presentation of St Patrick's to the city. A labyrinthine tangle of streets hung over by tottering tenements crowded in around the newly restored cathedral. *The Irish Times* wished that 'Round the Cathedral should extend a fine, clear space, a lung of health in the dampest portion of the city. Let the place be covered with earth and sown with grass, and planted with trees. Nothing mean or hideous should mar the precincts of the Cathedral.'[1] Space and air were given to the cathedral as St Patrick's Park was laid out and, at the turn of the century, a further swathe between the two Protestant cathedrals was razed to improve the social and physical fabric of the neighbourhood. The Iveagh Buildings resulted (pp. 92-3). A self-contained urban project, this disciplined layout of blocks and buildings sought to reflect order onto the community. Social improvement was implicit in the mix of apartments, a hostel for homeless men, public baths, shops and a community centre to promote educational and cultural activities. All this looked across the park to the authoritative bulk of the cathedral. The Iveagh Buildings were a response to a growing problem. Housing was a critical issue for the capital. The grand Georgian residences that lined the streets and squares had become tenements, some with a family to each room. Meanwhile the rhetoric of nationalism was inventing a rural image for Ireland, promoting further neglect of its fine urban heritage.

In 1914 the Marquis of Aberdeen sponsored a competition to 'elicit designs...for "Greater Dublin" calculated to suggest measures for the development of the City, and especially to outline proposals for meeting the housing needs of the population'. The winning scheme was that of Professor Patrick Abercrombie and his associates, Sydney and Arthur Kelly of Liverpool.[2] By citing the grand dimensions of O'Connell Street and Dublin's most conspicuous neo-classical public buildings, and by invoking the authority of Haussmann's Paris, but claiming a superior stance, the plan latched onto the geometric figure presented by the circular roads and canals, in order to reduce the city to a spoked wheel radial pattern of roads that fanned out to spawn peripheral and barren suburbs (fig. 9). The city was to be a transportation network, its centre 'in no sense a civic centre – it is a traffic heart, to which arterial roads and railways converge: it has therefore not been treated with a lavish use of formal gardening: the shapes of building sites are dictated by the necessary lines of streets, and complete symmetry is impossible owing to the complexity of axial lines'.[3]

With a glance over their shoulders at Haussmann's Paris, these planners also wanted to infect the city with a rash of gargantuan public buildings (fig. 10). Fortunately, none of the destruction or pomposity required for the radial routes or public buildings was within the realm of possibility for the faltering economy. However, the plan did bequeath a mentality that was later to wreak havoc, unravelling and negating the cumulative and syncretic achievements of the past. The 1970s and 1980s saw the rapid expansion of Dublin. Fiscal policies and incentives stimulated aimless suburban sprawl. The absence of a public transportation infrastructure forced the motor car onto the roads. In the dash to provide new road systems, by construction and blight swathes were torn through the fabric and communities of the inner city. A vicious circle was established whereby traffic converged on the inner city from the suburbs and roads were built to service the perceived need. The centrifugal forces of expansion were now disembowelling the inner city.

Back in 1922 the distinguished public buildings, the Four Courts, Custom House, Post Office, City Hall and Castle,

8 William Murray and Thomas Drew
National Irish Bank, Dublin,
1867-73

were in ruins, the symbolic targets of uprisings and civil strife. A plan to provide a seat of Government and a constellation of public buildings sought to repair, refurbish, reuse and reallocate existing edifices of significance, stretching the high points of the public domain from the western approaches of the city to the docks in the east.[4] Even though this might have been a worthy programme for using architecture as the seed of urban regeneration, again its conception was pompous in style and form, demonstrating a nostalgia for the neo-classical heyday of Georgian Dublin (fig. 11). Such imperious urban design statements were alien to the politics and economics of the new State.

Earlier in 1922, on 2 February, a contrasting vision for Dublin had appeared: *Ulysses*. Published in Paris, James Joyce's epic novel attempted to 'rewrite' the city of Dublin. As implied by the name of the author's fictional alter ego, Stephen Dedalus, Joyce was the architect of the labyrinthine journey of the ordinary man, Leopold Bloom. B(loom) threaded his way through the city, weaving his wanderings into a new urban fabric for the capital of an independent Ireland. For Joyce the architecture of the city is the weftage that is embroidered by the daily activities of the citizens.

Yet Joyce's narration of the city went unheard, as the contrary literary vision of W. B. Yeats's Celtic nostalgia triumphed to impose a rural identity on the new Irish nation-state. The wanton neglect of the urban heritage of Southern Ireland that followed independence may have sprung from this or may simply have been another manifestation of the universal malaise of the twentieth-century city. The political rhetoric of independent Ireland sought disjuncture from the country's colonial past. Modern movement urban design disengaged itself from surviving city fabric. Each was a denial of history.

Modernity in architecture and urban design terminated a tradition that had favoured the creation of urban spaces, streets and squares by carving them out of the built fabric and, in its stead, planted a landscape of autarchic objects. Although Dublin was spared the worst ravages of redevelopment experienced elsewhere in Europe, there were prominent incidents

of aggression against the city. Foremost among these was the building of the Central Bank in 1977. This edifice bullied its way into the heart of Dublin like King Kong, alien in scale and expression (fig. 13). However, there is an alternative to the invention of city monsters, a process of inclusion not exclusion, of repair and addition not clearance and isolation.

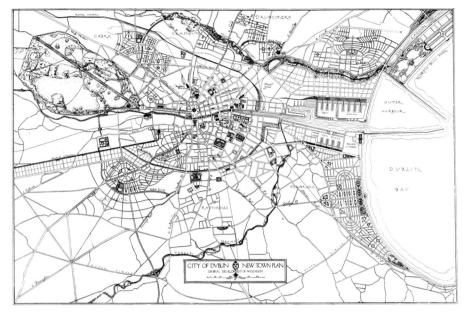

9 Patrick Abercrombie
New Town Plan for Dublin, 1914

This alternative has emerged from the shadow of the Central Bank, both literally and metaphorically. The lacuna of the 1960s and 1970s produced a reaction in a younger generation of architects. They sought to understand their urban heritage and to discover a more evolutionary tradition for renewing the city. Initially, they researched through mounting exhibitions, writing and producing paper projects, but are now doing so more concretely, in their contribution to the physical regeneration of Temple Bar (pp. 160-71). This central city area was blighted by the protracted threat of redevelopment as a transportation centre – the final realisation of Abercrombie's vision of a traffic city.[5] After winning the 'Architectural Framework' competition for the area, a consortium of young Dublin practices, Group '91, built a series of individual buildings, often incorporating existing fabric, that came together to create a number of urban 'rooms' – Meeting House Square, the Curved Street and Temple Bar Square (fig. 12). These new

10 Patrick Abercrombie
Scheme for improvements to central Dublin, 1914

11 Part of the proposal by the Greater Dublin Reconstruction Movement, 1922

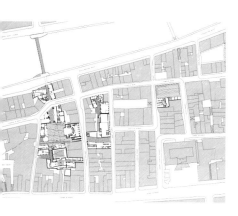

12 Plan of Temple Bar, Dublin, showing some of the new buildings by individual architects of the Group '91 consortium that have been stitched into the existing urban fabric

13 View east along Dame Street, Dublin, dominated by the Central Bank of 1975 by Sam Stephenson

public spaces have exploited circumstantial dereliction in the backlands of a city block or adjacent to existing roads in urban backwaters, making each a humane respite from the domination of motor traffic. Any other place within the public domain that might have been celebrated as an outside space in the past has now been invaded and dominated by the noise, pollution and dangers of motor traffic. Down the Quays it thunders; in O'Connell Street it asphyxiates the shoppers; and in front of Trinity College it speeds round and divides, scattering pedestrians.

In Temple Bar, the Irish Film Centre, by O'Donnell and Tuomey, and its neighbouring Meeting House Square, with which it is functionally and spatially interwoven, demonstrate an urban design strategy to counter the imperious and trivialising layout of formal boulevards and the establishment of axes or perspectivally contrived vistas (pp. 156-7). By pushing apparently invisible tentacles into surrounding contextual crevices, an individual building or an ensemble can replan its locale, a process that discovers and exploits contingencies.

The approach to urban design seen in the work of Group '91 in Temple Bar is not an isolated instance. The same sensibility governs the work of others. The interventions and repairs in Trinity College Dublin by de Blacam and Meagher,[6] and the minimal alterations by Shay Cleary to the Royal Hospital, Kilmainham, to create the Irish Museum of Modern Art (pp. 158-9),[7] resonate with their ancestral typologies to awaken dormant potential. Analogous results are achieved in the creation of communities in the

social and sheltered housing by Gerry Cahill.[8] Even in new-build, a similar strategy can be recognised. The library for the Regional Technical College in Cork by de Blacam and Meagher looks beyond the confines of the given site and building function to discover and imply a wealth of interaction in space and time (pp. 178-9). This then forms a template for evolution rather than remaining a mute element trapped in the rigid matrix of a master plan.[9]

In any planned city or quarter with grid-iron rigidity, the forces and activities of occupation soften the matrix to allow its plastic deformation as life moulds it into different forms and establishes a complexity of relationships. By the single act of writing, Joyce had hoped to refigure the city of Dublin for the ordinary citizen, whose daily tracing of the labyrinth remakes the city. At Temple Bar and elsewhere, the approach to urban design remembers something of *Ulysses*. The fabric of the city is being recycled. The interventions of Group '91 and others are stitching new uses and activities into the spaces and buildings of the existing fabric. The urban tapestry is enriched while its material worth is conserved and an ecological alternative is formulated to suburban expansion and the process of destruction and rebuilding. However, submissive sympathy to conservation is eschewed in favour of an active empathy with the natural processes of evolution and change inherent in the tradition of Irish architecture and urbanism.

Notes

1 *The Irish Times*, 15 Feb. 1865.
2 The proposals were later published as Patrick Abercrombie, Sydney Kelly and Arthur Kelly, *Dublin of the Future: The New Town Plan* (London, 1922).
3 Ibid., p. 38.
4 The Greater Dublin Reconstruction Movement produced a scheme that was announced in *The Irish Times* of 14 Dec. 1922.
5 In 1941 Abercrombie had suggested Temple Bar as the location for a Central Omnibus Station: Patrick Abercrombie, Sydney A. Kelly and Manning Robertson, *Town Planning Report: Sketch Development Plan* (Dublin, 1941), pp. 20-1.
6 See John Olley, 'Rebuilding in a Classical Tradition', *Architects' Journal* 185 (17 June 1987), pp. 37-51.
7 See John Olley, 'Sustaining the Narrative at Kilmainham', *Irish Arts Review* (1991/2), pp. 65-72.
8 See John Olley, 'The Theatre of the City: Dublin 1991', *Irish Arts Review* (1993), pp. 70-8.
9 See John Olley, 'The Art of Reading', *Architectural Research Quarterly* 1 (Winter 1995), pp. 30-41.

2   'Showy homes'

1   Bungalows littering the
Irish landscape

3   Bungalows along the
Connemara coast near Carraroe

4   Bungalows littering the Irish
landscape

Ireland's Suburbs

FRANK McDONALD

It has often been said that the Irish are not really an urban people. And this unusual trait, more than anything else, helps to explain why the suburbs of Ireland can now be found strung out along nearly every rural road. 'Bungalow Bliss' is not only the title of a best-selling book; it also encapsulates the aspirations of a great number of Irish people to carve out a niche for themselves in the landscape.

Many visitors to Ireland, particularly from continental Europe, are amazed by the seemingly endless ribbon of housing that lines the approach roads to cities and towns, even more so by the often ostentatious bungalows and houses littering the countryside – some inspired by Spanish haciendas, others by the *ante bellum* pastiche of Southfork, from the popular American TV series 'Dallas' (figs. 1-4).

To the more discerning, it must appear that Ireland has no planning laws at all, that anyone can build what they like where they like. Of course, such laws do exist. But in what is still a post-colonial society – the only one in Western Europe – there is no consensus on the need for rules and regulations of any kind. Everyone wants to make a mark on the landscape, whatever the planners might say.

Throughout the 1980s over half the total national output of new private housing consisted of bungalows in the countryside. In other words, for every house built in an urban or suburban location, at least one other was built in the middle of nowhere. As a result, the clear distinction that ought to exist between town and country has become increasingly blurred in the Irish Republic.

This is particularly true of the West of Ireland, an area renowned for its rugged scenery. Here, in places where the Irish language is still spoken, the spread of suburban-style bungalows has been unremitting, compromising the very landscape that had made it so attractive to foreign visitors. It is almost as if its people have consciously reverted to the dispersed pattern of Celtic settlement.

There is no better vantage point from which to get an overall impression of the chaos created by the 'bungalow blitz' than Black Head in County Clare. On a clear day, high above Galway Bay, you can look across to Connemara and see an almost continuous white strip along the coast, stretching from Salthill to Inveran (fig. 3). And that white strip is made up of bungalows that have been built over the past twenty-five years.

Seamus Heaney, the Irish poet and Nobel laureate, once reminded architects that every time they designed or built a new building they were 'in a profound metaphorical sense, recreating the world'. It is an awesome responsibility that few, if any, of the bungalow builders considered when they decided to make their indelible

5 Thatched cottage in County Donegal

marks on the relatively unspoiled rural environment.

The truth, however, is that most of these houses with their big picture windows were copied from pattern books, such as *Bungalow Bliss*, rather than designed by architects who might be expected to take climate and orientation into account (fig. 7). They are also characterised by a rejection of the Irish vernacular tradition – notably thatched cottages, which are associated with poverty, dispossession and the Famine (fig. 5).

The ostentatiousness of so many of the new houses is intended to show that their owners have arrived, that they have 'made it' and established their place high up on the social scale. They are in the countryside, but not of the countryside, and this incongruity is emphasised by their overwhelming preference for suburban lawns and showy shrubs, replacing the native species of the roadside ditch.

For the 'bungalow blitz' is largely an urban-generated phenomenon. The doctors, lawyers and shopkeepers who were once quite content to live in towns began moving out in the 1960s, as homes in the tranquil rural environment became more fashionable, even *de rigueur* (fig. 6). And farmers were more than happy to dispose of small patches of land on their road frontages to meet the demand for housing sites.

Jack Fitzsimons, the author of *Bungalow Bliss*, which has sold more copies than the most popular cookery books, says what he offered people was a real alternative to the bleak, homogenised suburban housing areas created by planners, road engineers and speculative developers. He was also, of course, tapping into the cult of rabid individualism that is very much part of Ireland's post-colonial psyche.

Greater affluence, including the availability of cars, has also made it possible for people to live in a rural setting and commute to work in nearby towns. So, too, has the massive EU-funded road-building programme. Newly built houses, with easy access to one of the new motorways, are often advertised as being 'in a sylvan setting only twenty minutes from the city centre' – by car, of course.

The fact that so many thousands of Irish people have chosen to live in the countryside, for their own selfish reasons, not only puts additional pressure on public services – such as roads, public lighting and garbage collection – but has also contributed in no small way to the physical degradation of Ireland's cities and towns. Indeed, it could be argued that urban decay is the flip-side of bungalow bliss.

As people evacuated the towns, they left behind the traditional idea of living over the shop. The upper floorspace of many historic buildings on the main streets, once alive with families, was

6 Houses near Clonmel,
County Tipperary

turned over to storage or simply not used at all. If this trend had continued, Irish country towns would have lost their most important feature – the informal streetscape formed by an accretion of buildings over time.

In the mid-1980s it came to be accepted at Government level that something would have to be done. A major urban renewal programme, based on tax incentives, was launched, initially for Dublin and the other (much smaller) cities. But it has since been extended to many other towns and even villages, and the aim is to make them more attractive places to live as well as to conduct commerce.

Dublin, as Ireland's capital and by far its largest city, exhibited the worst problems of inner-city decay and suburban sprawl (fig. 8). At one stage, in the early 1980s, the historic core of the city was so blighted by dereliction that it seemed as if large parts of it had simply been abandoned; the middle classes had fled to the suburbs and the working classes, with less choice in the matter, were rehoused on the outskirts.

During the 1970s Dublin was hailed as 'the fastest-growing capital in Europe', as if that were a particular badge of pride. Certainly, the city's expansion over the past thirty years has been spectacular; but the vast new suburban areas created to accommodate the increase in population to more than one million have been less than successful, in both social and environmental terms.

For the most part, Dublin's urban expansion consists of featureless housing estates, built at a density of twenty-five units per hectare, each house with its own front and back gardens, but with no historical reference points or sense of place (fig. 9). Once fine manor houses were often the first casualties of suburban sprawl; indeed, so few have survived that

7 A recent bungalow pattern book

they might almost be regarded as an endangered species.

Dublin is undoubtedly one of the most socially stratified cities in Europe, with each class living in its own 'ghetto'. To the north and west, it is ringed by Ireland's version of the South African townships – virtual Sowetos, where unemployment may be as high as 70 per cent – while the city's middle class congregates around the shoreline of Dublin Bay and the more salubrious southern suburbs (fig. 11).

Arguably, the only major achievement of 'planning' in the city was to decant the former working class to the periphery, out of sight and out of mind. The pattern of extended family relationships that sustained people during the worst period of slum-

8 Dereliction around the corner from Dublin's O'Connell Street

dwelling in the inner city was broken and, although the quality of housing was better, it is already clear that this dislocation represents a sociological timebomb.

Ironically, Dublin's low-density suburbs were designed on the assumption that every family would have at least one car; the fact that this has not happened has meant social isolation for certain groups, particularly women in the home. It has also meant that the suburbs are difficult to serve by public transport, with the result that the city is now choked to death by commuters converging on its centre by car.

The depopulation of the inner city and the consequent decay of its housing stock left it ripe for major road schemes, to cater for motorised suburbanites. Whole areas of its historic core were laid waste over decades to prepare for the installation of dual-carriageways, as the authorities remained blind to all the evidence from abroad that traffic in an urban area inevitably expands to fill the available road space (fig. 10).

However, since the decision-makers themselves all lived in the suburbs, it was hardly surprising that the city became a victim of their relentless suburban mentality. They could not conceive of the inner city as a residential location; for them, and for most Dubliners, it is a place for work, shopping and entertainment. After all, less than one in ten of the city's inhabitants actually lives in its historic core.

But Dublin, no less than other Irish cities and towns, could not remain forever immune to the European ideal of urban living. Over the past six years, since the first private apartment block in the inner city was built on the Liffey Quays, thousands of middle-class people – mainly young singles and couples – have flooded into the city centre, reclaiming it as a place to live in a phenomenal reversal of the historical trend.

Many of the new city dwellers had lived, worked in or even just visited other European cities – Amsterdam, Barcelona, Hamburg, Paris or wherever – and experienced the vitality of urban life there. On their return to Dublin, they saw no reason why it, too, should not offer something similar. Thus, even though it took the property developers some time to appreciate it, there was a huge suppressed demand for apartments in the city centre, close to theatres, cinemas, restaurants and workplaces.

The same trend was evident in Cork, Galway, Limerick, Waterford and some of the large towns. Soon, there were cranes on the skyline as developers rushed to build apartment blocks, grabbing almost every site they could to respond to what seemed to be an insatiable demand for residential accommodation in the very heart of Ireland's cities and towns. What had previously been unthinkable was now happening.

9 Suburban housing estate, Dublin

10 Devastation of the High Street, Dublin, by road-building schemes

11 Middle-class homes on Dublin Bay

In 1995, incredibly, some 40 per cent of the output of private housing in Dublin consisted of apartments in the inner city. Many would be regarded as sub-standard in European terms – one-bedroom units with just 30 square metres of living space – and critics had nagging doubts about their long-term sustainability. Indeed, it was even suggested that they could become 'the tenements [slums] of the twenty-first century'.

There is also evidence from detailed surveys that many of the apartment dwellers see themselves as temporary residents of the city centre; as soon as they got married and had children, they would be off to the suburbs or, perhaps, even a bungalow in the countryside. For it is still true that middle-class Irish people cannot conceive of raising a family in the rough-and-tumble environment of the city centre.

None the less, at least the first steps have now been taken. The mood and atmosphere of Dublin, and other cities and towns in Ireland, have changed markedly for the better as a direct result of the influx of new inhabitants. And that, perhaps more than anything else, will serve to counteract the 'bungalow blitz' on Ireland's precious rural landscapes – those magical areas that so appeal to our visitors.

1   Suburb at Loùghlinstown,
County Dublin, 1970s

3   Horace O'Rourke
Croydon Park, Marino, Dublin;
designed 1915, built 1925-8

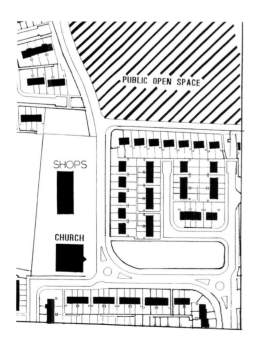

2   Plan of Loughlinstown,
County Dublin,
1970s

Centre and Periphery
Housing in Ireland

EDDIE CONROY

For a variety of cultural and historical reasons, the dominant trend in Irish housing in the twentieth century has been towards low-density, house-based suburban expansion to the edges of cities and towns. This has been underscored by an older tradition of high-density urban housing with more complex typologies and site responses. It is this minor tradition with its roots in a Victorian concern for coherent urban fabric that has become the foundation for a more complex, socially responsive and sustainable approach to housing in Ireland. Dublin has always been at the centre of the housing debate, reflecting and amplifying housing trends throughout the country, and is the focus of this essay.

Suburban Housing: The Dominant Trend

Migration to the suburbs began as early as 1834 with the opening of the first commuter rail line to Dun Laoghaire, just south along the coast from Dublin. The continuing drift of the middle class to the edge of the city was given intellectual and philosophical underpinning by the Garden City movement toward the end of the century. Two of its principal advocates, Patrick Geddes and Raymond Unwin, were invited to Dublin in 1911 and 1914 respectively.[1] Together they promoted Dublin's first working-class garden suburb at Croydon Park, Marino (fig. 3). The intense overcrowding of the city centre,

difficulties in slum clearance and urban renewal, and the need, calculated by Geddes, for 60,000 new dwellings to relieve the appalling congestion made the suburbs an obvious and economical housing location. The large-scale development of small outlying villages for both public and private housing and the consequent and consistent outward expansion of the city became the main housing process over the next sixty years. In 1940 Patrick Abercrombie, the English town planner, worried at the rate of the city's growth, proposed a Green Belt to limit its size.[2] However, the door was opened in 1966 for untrammelled urban expansion by the Myles Wright Planning Report on the growth of Dublin, with its call for four 'new towns' of 100,000 persons.[3] Around the same time, this process was echoed in the north of Ireland with the foundation of a suburban 'city' at Craigavan. Today's banal and formless nature of the city's edge owes much to this expansion coupled with the blanket implementation of simplistic building-density and plot-ratio standards under the new 1963 Planning Act, and the unyielding application of extravagant road design standards (fig. 2). Generous new-housing grants, income tax relief on mortgages and the tendency of financial institutions to favour new 'prime' sites all exacerbated this process. Finally, trade in older housing stock was slowed by a hefty Stamp Duty Tax.

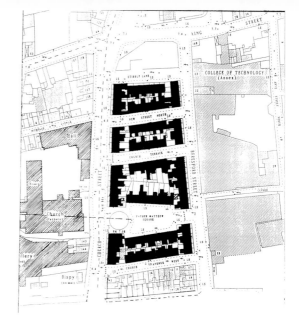

The cost of these trends is all too clear. There has been a prodigious waste of land and an endless extension of road and service networks (fig. 1). Large tracts of the city are built to densities too low to be readily susceptible to mass transit systems, forcing ever increasing reliance on motor transport with all that that entails in congestion, pollution and accidents. The low density and numbing uniformity of estate design has failed to produce urban legibility or sense of place, slowing the formation of community and increasing alienation. Low densities have restricted the intensity of economic and social activity, slowing the generation of civic, commercial and amenity facilities.

In working-class areas the monoblock nature of estates with up to 70 per cent unemployment and low spending base exaggerates these problems. Many residents were moved to these areas from familiar inner-city locations and existing community networks. Absence of public transport and low car ownership rates in these estates have resulted in geographical as well as social segregation and isolation. High levels of environmental decay, vandalism and social dysfunction are hardly surprising.

At the city-wide level, the increase in traffic and congestion led in the 1960s to a call for extensive inner-city road-improvement programmes. A protracted compulsory purchase system for obtaining the necessary land resulted in the creation of mass dereliction in the city centre over a long period. This dereliction caused continuing environmental decay and necessitated the removal of even more inner-city residents to the periphery.

4 Architects Department,
Dublin Corporation
Slab-blocks, Linenhall Terrace, Dublin,
late 1950s

6 Herbert Simms
Henrietta Place,
Dublin, 1937

Physical decay found a natural corollary in community decline and increasing social unrest.

The twelve houses per acre density established by the Garden City movement was based on the need to provide breathing space for the very large families typical of that period. This logic can no longer prevail. The average number of persons in a home in Ireland is currently 3.4 but falling towards the European average of 2.0. The family-based three-bedroom house with its front and rear garden can no longer be considered the standard building block of all housing in Ireland.

Urban Housing: A Continuing Tradition

From the turn of this century a minor, but important, trend of denser urban-based housing counterpoints the growth of the suburban model. The Dublin City Architect C. J. McCarthy argued powerfully against the first Croydon Park scheme on the grounds of land wastage and the hardship imposed on tenants through the cost and difficulty of travel to their workplace. He had realised a series of projects (for example, Church Street) that were high-density schemes built to a traditional urban pattern of streets and squares in a familiar and legible way (fig. 5).

The massive Reflationary Public Works Housing Programme began in 1932, under the direction of Herbert Simms, City Housing Architect. This quiet Englishman was responsible for building 17,000 units before his death at his own hand in 1948. His projects were flat-based and modelled on the work of the Amsterdam School of 1910-20 (fig. 6). Generally four-storey with deck access, they adhered to existing street patterns and evinced a concern for urban scale, context and event. Each was organised as a perimeter block around a communal access courtyard. They maintained existing communities in their locales, and remain in use and popular to this day.

In the 1950s the typology of these perimeter blocks was replaced by the free-standing modernist slab-block (fig. 4). The new type had a more complex composition of units: a ground-floor flat with two by two-storey maisonettes above with an access deck alternating between floors. With their cylindrical stair towers, butterfly roofs and maintenance-free detailing they retain a certain elegance. However, although some of these blocks stand happily among trees in an open and generous space, more typically they fail to define public and private territory and disrupt their urban context. The flat-building programme was brought to a close in 1974 following the social and aesthetic failure of Ireland's only high-rise housing scheme at Ballymun and the increasingly bad press for English deck-access schemes.

In the mid-1970s the City Quay Housing Competition changed the face of urban housing. The challenge was to find a new practical form for urban housing. Housing-led urban regeneration was growing throughout Europe. In Dublin, public anger over the fate of the city, derelict and unloved, and social concern for the imminent disappearance of long-standing urban communities forced a new politics of urban housing design. The winning schemes and those that followed in their wake were low-rise, medium density and house-based (fig. 7). The schemes, generally terraced, two or three storeys high and in a coherent street pattern, were reminiscent of a familiar nineteenth-century artisan housing language. Not only did they fill derelict sites, but successfully undertook other urban tasks as well: creating new corners and book-ends, hard edges to landscape features, settings for landmark buildings and even new small urban spaces. These schemes have been a powerful tool in the rebuilding of a shattered urban fabric.

However, over time the limitations of the schemes became more obvious. The principal building block was still the three-bedroom house. Changes in demographics meant that this type was no longer flexible enough on its own to meet differing needs. The three-storey houses, successful as they were in many areas, could not always match their older neighbours in height and scale. In the hands of less talented designers they began to tend toward the suburban, with curtilage parking and front and rear gardens. In many cases lower densities failed to make optimum use of increasingly scarce and valuable land. The houses were expensive to build and their tenants had to be maintained on social welfare payments owing to high unemployment. This consequent low-spending base meant that these communities could not on their own generate or maintain attendant service activities or employment in the city-centre areas.

It was clear by the 1980s that the urban regeneration begun by the programme of inner-city social housing could be extended into the private sector. There was a widespread shortage of good quality private and rented accommodation in the city. The dockland experience of Thatcherite London had shown that private housing development could extend urban renewal, generate and maintain service industries and ensure a good social mix. The Incentive Areas Tax Scheme in 1986 allowed generous offsets against new buildings in derelict urban areas. In Dublin alone this initiative has generated over 15,000 new apartments in recent years.

Problems of Form

The increasing development of city-centre housing has brought many benefits in its train. Large stretches of derelict land have been reclaimed and built upon. Gaping holes in the city fabric have been filled. The rise in the population of the inner city is already creating a new lively urban culture and a marked increase in social and service activities.

The growth in the number of apartments, both public and private sector, has raised the issue of the form of these developments. Typically, the private sector apartments are designed as shallow-plan

7 Burke Kennedy Doyle Associates
City Quay Housing,
Dublin, 1977

8 Developer-built apartment buildings,
Ellis Quay, Dublin, 1995

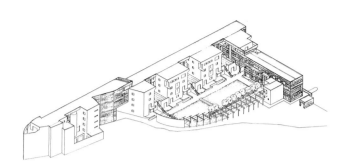

perimeter blocks built to the edge of the pavement and following existing street patterns (fig. 8). The space remaining between these buildings is often given over to car-parking, reducing its amenity potential. Even when landscaped, these internal spaces have not contributed to the quality of the adjoining streets. The visual richness of the European city is often the result of such inner spaces – courtyards, gardens glimpsed, if not always accessible, from the street.

This unwillingness to engage the street is predictably rooted in concerns about security. The tendency to open entrances from these secure inner spaces or to limit the number of entrances onto the street through the use of long and dark internal corridors has further reduced the capacity of these buildings to reinforce the public realm, and to keep streets busy and safe. The inclination to treat each project as an urban fortress must be replaced by the search for a useful semi-public realm in and around these buildings that, while respecting issues of privacy and security, can enliven street life and add to the visual texture of the city.

Urban Housing: New Models

There are already schemes that wrestle with these problems and find an encouraging way forward. Gerry Cahill Architects' proposal for the NABCO Housing Co-operative at New Street accepts its responsibility to the urban context (fig. 9). A four-storey block, it rises to five storeys at its corner with Patrick Street, a wide,

heavily trafficked road. Although a perimeter block form, it generates a generous semi-private garden at its centre overlooked by large-scale shared balconies. The vertical access systems through the building are linked to these balconies, giving them a clear architectural character. The scheme has a richness of scales in relation to site and city. The project is indirectly funded by Government through a co-operative, overcoming the limitations of direct-funded social housing with its restriction of social mix, tenure arrangements and meaningful consultation. At Patrick Street, consultation took place at design stage with the co-operative, who will be responsible for the management and maintenance after completion. A variety of apartment units and houses are included. Care has been taken over issues of energy saving and the reduction of the risk of fuel poverty. This scheme engages both social and architectural issues.

The new Dublin Corporation housing at Golden Lane by Eugene Gribbin is another interesting example (fig. 10). The scheme matches in scale and detail the Iveagh Buildings opposite (one of the city's earliest social housing projects; pp. 92-3). The four-storey elevation is composed of two by two-storey maisonettes stacked over each other. All entrances to these blocks are off the street and generate considerable activity around the building. The ample public stairways act as threshold spaces in the manner of a New York Brownstone, encouraging social interaction. Living-rooms are orientated south

11 Fitzgerald Reddy Associates
Apartment block, Patrick Street, Dublin, 1994

12 Fitzgerald Reddy Associates
Apartment block, Patrick Street,
Dublin, 1994

and west with generous glazing and out-door balconies addressing St Patrick's Park opposite. The internal courtyard glimpsed through a large arch contains two-storey units in a 'stable-yard' arrangement. The arch allows a view to the courtyard while retaining its privacy. The corner of the block is articulated and contains a greater variety of flat types. Once again, extensive consultation took place with the residents.

The apartment block beside St Patrick's Cathedral, by Fitzgerald Reddy Associates, is an interesting private-sector example (figs. 11, 12). This building matches its neighbours in scale and materials, and creates a surface against which the Cathedral and its park can be read. It adapts itself to corners and adjoining streets and lanes. The apartments open from the large number of stairways, banishing the dark internal access corridor. The numerous entrances and mixed commercial uses at ground-floor level enliven the adjoining streets. The apartments themselves have generous glazing and useful balconies. This pre-scription of four- and five-storey apart-ment-based buildings with commercial use on the ground floor is familiar from other European cities, but has hitherto been absent from twentieth-century Dublin, only now making a welcome reappearance.

Irish Housing: The Future

The twentieth-century demographic shift from rural to urban is reflected and explored in Irish drama. It is also part of the continuing story of Irish housing. Suburban expansion in towns and cities is slowing. Increasing education and con-cern about the environment has pointed up the overall advantages of denser, more compact settlement patterns. In cities, Dublin in particular, traffic congestion has already made public transport an attractive and achievable option. A new-found, but growing, interest in the advan-tages and opportunities of urban life is finding expression in the refurbishment of older buildings for residential purposes and the exploitation of derelict city centre sites for infill housing. And this housing is now as likely to be apartment-based as house-based.

Housing in Ireland now has the same priorities and challenges as in other Euro-pean countries – it must minimise its impact on the environment, be flexible and useful over its lifetime, and, in gener-ating a meaningful sense of place, hope to sow the seeds of sustainable community.

Notes

1 For the involvement of Geddes and Unwin in Dublin, see Mervyn Miller's 'Raymond Unwin and the Planning of Dublin', in Michael Bannon (ed.), *The Emergence of Irish Planning 1880-1920* (Dublin, 1985).
2 Patrick Abercrombie, Sydney Kelly and Manning Robertson, *Town Planning Report: Sketch Development Plan* (Dublin, 1941).
3 Myles Wright et al., *The Dublin Region: Advisory Plan and Final Report*, 2 vols. (Dublin, 1967).

1 Vincent Craig
Presbyterian Church, Hillhall, 1901

2 William A. Scott
St Patrick's Basilica, Lough Derg, 1919
(built 1926-31)

3 William A. Scott
St Enda's, Spiddal, 1903-7

Twentieth-Century Church Architecture in Ireland

PAUL LARMOUR

Gothic Revival, the predominant style of church architecture in Ireland for much of the nineteenth century, continued to make its presence felt for a while in the new century, although forms of Romanesque were to gain in popularity. The Roman Catholic cathedrals at Letterkenny, County Donegal (1890-1901), by Hague & MacNamara, and Loughrea, County Galway (1897-1903), by W. H. Byrne, both in Gothic style, and the Church of Ireland cathedral of St Anne at Belfast, County Antrim (1899-1904), by Sir Thomas Drew, in a French style of Romanesque, illustrate the prevailing approach for large works in the hands of the leading architects in their respective denominations at the turn of the century.

The influence of Art Nouveau, that most vital new style that swept much of Europe at the time, was slight in Irish church architecture and was largely confined to Non-Conformist work in Ulster. Its effect can be seen in the quirky forms and decorative details of the Presbyterian churches at Hillhall, County Down (1901), by Vincent Craig (fig. 1), and Letterkenny (1907), by Blackwood & Jury, two of the main exponents of a style that was never very widespread elsewhere in Ireland.

The inevitable reaction against the forms of highly ornate English- or French-inspired Gothic, which had prevailed for so long in the previous century, found its main expression in Ireland in a fashion for Hiberno-Romanesque. The revival of distinctly native forms of architecture of the Early Christian and Romanesque periods was of course just one facet of the Irish Revival, which had been developing for many decades and which, in the visual arts, sought to recreate the glories of the Celtic past.[1]

One of the most successful examples of a church designed in this 'national romantic' spirit was St Enda's Roman Catholic Church at Spiddal, County Galway (1903-7), by William A. Scott of Dublin (fig. 3). Characterised by rugged simplicity and boldness of form, it evoked the quality of early Irish work even if it was not archaeologically accurate.[2] Contemporary nationalist opinion referred to it as 'the first in-coming wave of what we may hope to be a fresh vigorous tide of architecture in Ireland…. It is a development of the ancient Irish Romanesque for modern architectural purposes. In this way it may be said to begin a modern native architecture in Ireland.'[3] Scott was generally regarded as the foremost of the new school of young Irish architects that was emerging in the first decade of the new century.

Scott's career was unfortunately too short for him to fulfil his architectural potential entirely. However, he did design one other significant church. That was the large pilgrimage church of St Patrick,

4   Rudolf Butler
Catholic Church, Newport, 1915-18

5   Henry Seaver
St Patrick's Memorial Church, Saul, 1932-3

6   Ralph Byrne
Kilmore Cathedral, 1937-46

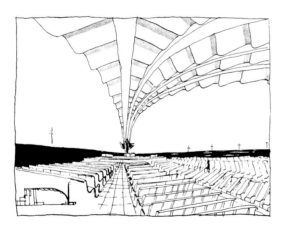

7   James M. Brennan
'Church Experiment', 1935

8   Patrick Haughey
St Theresa's, Sion Mills, 1960-2

sited on an island in Lough Derg, County Donegal, designed in 1919 but not built until 1926-31, by which time Scott had died (fig. 2). Laid out on an octagonal plan derived from San Vitale at Ravenna, and given an Irish flavour by the circular turrets and Celtic interlaced details, St Patrick's Basilica has been admired by some as the most important church of its period in Ireland.

Other architects took up the Hiberno-Romanesque mode, usually with more explicitly derivative features than at Spiddal or Lough Derg. The Roman Catholic church at Timoleague, County Cork (1906-11), by Maurice Hennessy is typical of many at the time in which an unprepossessing Romanesquoid design was given a distinctively Irish appearance by the prominent use of a conically capped round tower belfry, while the Honan Hostel Chapel at Cork of 1915-16 by James McMullen alluded to a number of revered Irish Romanesque precedents (pp. 100-1). Its arcaded west front was based on that of St Cronan's church at Roscrea; the placing of a miniature round tower at the junction of nave and chancel recalls the arrangement of St Finghin's church at Clonmacnoise; and the interior is barrel vaulted in emulation of Cormac's Chapel at Cashel. Over-dependent on such specific references, and rather mechanically handled, the architecture of the Honan Chapel is somewhat disappointing, but its chief merit lies in its furnishings, which represent much of the best Irish arts and crafts work of the time.[4] It includes fine metalwork in Celtic style designed by William A. Scott as well as brilliant stained glass by both the Tower of Glass studio and Harry Clarke of Dublin, the most exceptional native talent in that field at the time. The incorporation of Irish arts and crafts in modern Irish churches was not initiated at the Honan Chapel – the practice had already started at Loughrea Cathedral under the direction of Scott in 1903 – but the full range was demonstrated here more effectively than anywhere else.

One of the most imposing examples of the Hiberno-Romanesque style is the large Catholic church at Newport, County Mayo (1915-18), by Rudolf Butler (fig. 4). It displays such distinctive early Irish fea-

9 Joseph Downes
Our Lady of Lourdes, Drogheda, 1935

tures as battered walls, a tangent gable and sloping jambs to the west doorway, and also incorporates the Irish round tower motif. Butler pursued the Hiberno-Romanesque style through the 1920s in such churches as Belclere, County Galway (1920-5); Scottshouse, County Monaghan (1924); and Killanny, County Monaghan (1925-31).

Two other names who emerged as specialists in Catholic church work in this period were John J. Robinson, and Ralph Byrne. Robinson's early interest in the Hiberno-Romanesque, as seen in the freely treated example at Lusk, County Dublin (designed 1918; built 1922-5), soon gave way to Lombardic Romanesque as at Killester (1925), Cabra (1931-3) and Foxrock (1935), and the more modernistically treated Corpus Christi, Drumcondra (1938-41), all in the Dublin area. Byrne employed the Irish round tower type of belfry at Blackrock, County Louth (1919), and at the Church of the Four Masters in Donegal town (1930-5), but is best remembered for his full-blooded return to classicism in three of the most monumental churches of the 1930s. These are Mullingar Cathedral, County Westmeath (1932-6); the church of St Peter and St Paul, Athlone, County Westmeath (1935-6); and Kilmore Cathedral, County Cavan (1937-46) (fig. 6). Mullingar in particular is a fine piece of traditional cathedral architecture in a Roman classical style handled rather in the manner of Sir Edwin Lutyens. However, Cavan engagingly pays tribute to an earlier champion of Renaissance Revival in Ireland, Francis Johnston, in its front portico and spire modelled on that of St George's Church in Dublin of 1803.

While the majority of churches in the inter-war years were built for the Roman Catholic denomination, there were also some Protestant churches erected. Two notable examples for the Church of Ireland in this period are St Thomas's, Dublin (1930-2), a charming and elegant church in a Lombardic style for which its architect, F. G. Hicks, was awarded the first Triennial Gold Medal of the Royal Institute of Architects of Ireland (RIAI) in 1932-4, and St Patrick's Memorial Church at Saul, County Down (1932-3) (fig. 5), which was designed by Henry

Seaver to commemorate the 1500th anniversary of St Patrick, Ireland's patron saint, establishing his first church in Ireland in AD 432 on the site there of a barn (*sabhall* in Irish, pronounced Saul). The distinctive round tower belfry at Saul therefore provides a very appropriate symbol of the early days of the church in Ireland.

Whether Hiberno-Romanesque, Lombardic Romanesque, Classical or Gothic in style, historicist revivalism held sway among Irish church architects right through the inter-war years, much to the dismay of a younger generation enthused by the new architecture of the modern movement elsewhere in Europe and impatient to see its influence extended to all building types in Ireland.

The first overtly modern church to be built in Ireland was the Roman Catholic Church of Christ the King at Turner's Cross, Cork, designed in 1927 by Barry Byrne of Chicago and built in 1929-31 (pp. 106-7). Hailed at the time as 'the greatest break from conventional church architecture which has yet been made in this country',[5] Turner's Cross was, in an Irish context, revolutionary in its plan, its constructional technique and its modernist idiom. It did not, however, have any immediate or definite influence on Irish church architecture – the traditional styles were to prevail almost without exception for the next two decades or more.

Church design of an overtly modern type by Irish architects before the Second World War was confined to one unbuilt project by James M. Brennan, exhibited in 1935, and two small chapels built by Joseph Downes around the same time. Brennan's project, termed a 'Church Experiment', was for a reinforced concrete church that would provide an unobstructed view of the altar from all angles, to be laid out on a segmental plan (fig. 7). The scheme was not built as it was a theoretical proposition only, but it is of interest in the light of later developments.[6] The two

10 Frank Corr and Liam McCormick
Catholic Church, Ennistymon, 1948-54

11   Liam McCormick
St Aengus, Burt, 1964-5

chapels by Downes, Our Lady of Lourdes, Drogheda, County Louth (1935, but now demolished) (fig. 9), and Kilkenny Hospital Chapel (1936), were indicative of their author's affinity to the modern movement. Designed in a plain flat-roofed idiom, they were reminiscent of the more sober churches of the German heyday of modern church building some years earlier.

It was not until well after the Second World War that modern church architecture really got under way in Ireland, although progress was slow at first. The Catholic Church at Ennistymon, County Clare, can claim to be the first post-war church in Ireland designed in a contemporary idiom. The result of a competition held in 1947-8 and won by Frank Corr and Liam McCormick, it was not, however, built until 1952-4 (fig. 10). It was a design of some originality and, although it did not break radically with convention, its success must have given some encouragement to those who wanted to see a fresh approach to ecclesiastical design. Corr and McCormick themselves built a modern-looking church with weatherboard cladding on a steel frame at Ennis Road, Limerick, in 1951, and Brendan O'Connor built a small chapel of almost domestic simplicity at Rossguil, County Donegal, in 1954.[7] Even in the immediate post-war era, however, resistance was encountered in the attempt to make modern design entirely acceptable in ecclesiastical work; designs of a traditional style and plan were usually preferred, as typified by the Byzantine style with which the firm of Jones & Kelly found favour in the 1950s with such churches as St Francis in Cork (1951) and Clonskeagh, Dublin (1958),[8] and by the Romanesque-based design of Galway Cathedral (1957-65) by John J. Robinson. The elegant Garrison Church of St Brigid at the Curragh Camp, County Kildare (1958-9), by the Office of Public Works under the direction of Gerald McNicholl is a good example of the restrained type of modern design that found the widest acceptance in the 1950s.

In terms of architectural approach the most radical church of its time in Ireland was that at Knockanure, County Kerry (1960-4), designed by Ronald Tallon of Michael Scott & Associates (p. 26). Laid out on a simple rectangular plan with solid side walls and a completely glazed front, all standing on a podium, it heralded a new era of architectural boldness in Irish church design. St Theresa's, Sion Mills, County Tyrone (1960-2), adopted a somewhat similar plan and overall idiom, but its exterior was further distinguished by the majestic, full-width, incised slate frieze over the entrance, depicting the Last Supper, by the sculptor Oisin Kelly (fig. 8).

At the Convent Chapel in Cookstown, County Tyrone (1963-5), Lawrence McConville boldly connected a textured concrete cubic block to the front of the old Victorian convent and furnished it with work by some of the best Irish artists of the period, notably Patrick McElroy, whose metalwork also decorates the exterior. Equally novel was the Dominican church at Athy, County Kildare (1965), by John Thompson & Partners, where a dramatically conceived hyperbolic paraboloid concrete shell roof covers a fan-shaped plan.

By the mid-1960s the tide had clearly turned in Irish church architecture: not only had contemporary styling become established, but new plan forms were also being explored in response to a changing liturgical emphasis.[9] In a period when the rigidity of traditional rectangular plans was being abandoned, Liam McCormick (working initially in partnership with Frank Corr) emerged as the most important Irish church architect of his generation. At St Aengus, Burt, County Donegal (1964-5), he produced what is generally regarded as the first masterpiece of the post-Vatican II era in Ireland (fig. 11 and p. 131). It is circular in plan, echoing the ancient stone fort on the hill above it, with seating arranged around three sides of the altar.[10] Its intriguing form, with rubble stone walls and a tent-like copper roof, as well as its close relationship to the site, make it one of the most beautiful churches in Ireland. It won for McCormick the Triennial Gold Medal of the RIAI for 1971.

McCormick's partner, Frank Corr, also explored curvilinear plan forms at that time, being responsible for the elliptically planned St Clement's Retreat Chapel, Belfast (1966-7), and the similarly formed but much more imposing Church of the

Redeemer, Dundalk (1966-9). In 1968 McCormick and Corr parted company, and McCormick went on to produce a series of outstanding churches that demonstrated both a wide variety of architectural approach and an exceptional sensitivity to site and landscape. They include the churches at Creeslough, County Donegal (1970-1), the most successful of Irish churches inspired by Le Corbusier's chapel at Ronchamp (pp. 138-9); Glenties, County Donegal (1974-5); Maghera, County Londonderry (1975); and Fossa near Killarney, County Kerry (1977-9). They stand as testimony to their architect's innovative design ability as well as to his committed patronage of Irish artists in stained glass, metalwork and sculpture.

Apart from McCormick's work, other interesting Catholic churches of the post-Vatican II period in Ireland include Our Lady of the Wayside, near Leenaun, County Galway (1968), by Leo Mansfield, notable for its angular tent-like form; St Patrick's, Dunnamanagh, County Tyrone (1969), by Patrick Haughey, built of stone on a polygonal plan in a hilly setting; and St Fintan's, Sutton, County Dublin (1973), by Robinson Keefe Devane, an accomplished handling of textured concrete on a fan-shaped plan. Also of interest are two churches with more irregular and complex plans, the Church of the Holy Spirit, St Leonard's, Ballycullane, County Wexford (1971), and Our Lady of the Nativity, Newtown, County Kildare (1975), which involved, respectively, Wilfred Cantwell and Richard Turley, two of the most tireless workers for the promotion of a meaningful modern church architecture in Ireland.

Of the various architects working for the Protestant denominations in the post-war period the two most notable were, firstly, Dennis O'D. Hanna, whose Church of the Pentecost, Cregagh (1961-3), and St Molua's, Stormont (1961-2), for the Church of Ireland in Belfast showed his particular interest in cultivating the work of local artists in the service of religion, and secondly, Gordon McKnight, who produced an interesting series of mainly Presbyterian churches in which he explored varied plans and forms. Among his most notable examples are the church at Knockbreda, Belfast (1970-1), the High Kirk, Ballymena, County Antrim (1976), and the Corrymeela Worship Centre (1978), whose curving masonry walls are partly recessed in a grassy hill on the north coast of County Antrim.

Although the heyday of the great church-building period of the twentieth century in Ireland would now appear to be over, there has nevertheless been some recent activity. The most interesting example is the Chapel of Reconciliation at Knock,[11] County Mayo (1989-90) (fig. 12), where de Blacam and Meagher have achieved an elegant simplicity of form and plan in a return to rectangularity. Elsewhere in the 1990s a number of architects have turned yet again to the circular plan,[12] a formal preoccupation that seems to underline the enduring element of insularity that has ultimately dominated so much church architecture in Ireland over the course of the twentieth century.

12   de Blacam and Meagher
Chapel of Reconciliation,
Knock, 1989-90

Notes

1   The development of Hiberno-Romanesque Revival architecture over the course of the nineteenth and twentieth centuries is described in detail in Paul Larmour, 'The Celtic Revival and a National Style of Architecture', unpublished PhD thesis, The Queen's University of Belfast, 1977. For Irish Revivalism in general, including architectural aspects, see Jeanne Sheehy, *The Rediscovery of Ireland's Past: The Celtic Revival 1830-1930* (London, 1980).
2   Although Romanesque in style with some Celtic details in the fittings, the church at Spiddal has a square tower and a semi-circular chancel, neither of which is a native Romanesque feature.
3   Edward Martyn, 'The New Parish Church for Spiddal', *The Leader* 6:16 (13 June 1903), pp. 248-9.
4   The Honan Chapel and its furnishings are described and illustrated in detail in Paul Larmour, *The Arts and Crafts Movement in Ireland* (Belfast, 1992).
5   *The Irish Builder and Engineer*, 21 Nov. 1931, p. 1018 ('A Breakaway from Convention').
6   The scheme was illustrated in *Architectural Design* 17:7 (July 1947), pp. 209-10. According to the report on it, a church of similar design was subsequently built in Germany, though it has not been possible to confirm this.
7   This and other post-war Catholic churches are illustrated in Richard Hurley and Wilfred Cantwell, *Contemporary Irish Church Architecture* (Dublin, 1985).
8   The result of a controversial competition in 1954 in which the prize-winning and commended entries, all of a modern type, were set aside in favour of a traditional design.
9   Culminating, in the Catholic church, in the directives of the Second Vatican Council as published in the *Constitution on the Sacred Liturgy* in December 1963.
10 It should be noted that the plan of Burt consists of not one circle but two, one placed tangentially inside the other, an arrangement for which there was a precedent at St John Capistrano, Munich (1960), by Sep Ruf.
11 For which see John Olley, 'The Redemption of Meaning', *Irish Arts Review* 10 (1994), pp. 100-2.
12 As in the case of the Roman Catholic churches at Dunloy, County Antrim (1990), and Coagh, County Tyrone (1992), both by Tracey and Mullarkey; and Holywood, County Down (1995), by Laurence McConville.

1   Holy Cross Abbey, Tipperary, 15th century;
Before renovation

2   Thomas Cooley and James Gandon
The Four Courts, Dublin, 1776-1802;
restored late 1920s

3   Sir William Robinson
Royal Hospital, Kilmainham,
begun *c.* 1684

Remembering and Forgetting

Building Conservation as an Essay on the Fate of History

LOUGHLIN KEALY

Within the present generation, Irish society has been transformed, sometimes in paradoxical ways. It is no longer a society based predominantly on rural settlements and small towns, but a first-generation urban society with a discernible urban/rural divide. From being almost a confessional State, Ireland has become deeply secularised, while underlying religious affiliations exercise continuing influence. It has become focused on Europe rather than on the United Kingdom and America, where most of its expatriate people dwell. Above all, it has 'modernised', pursuing the idea of development through economic growth and generating a transition from a culture of tradition to a culture of progress.[1] The persistence of traditional interests in music, literature and sport has to be seen against these underlying transformations.

The contemporary experience of violence and social and political dissonance in Ireland has made it difficult to put faith in traditional versions of the past. Recent revisionist writings, which have led to a progressive elaboration in the understanding of Irish history and a fragmentation of an inherited consensus, now command fairly wide acceptance.

Given this new complexity in our obsession with history, what do we expect of the buildings inherited from the past? They are popular in a way that few modern buildings could hope to be. It has

been remarked that the buildings of the past help us to 'ground a shaken identity'.[2] That proposition implies that historic buildings are a force for cohesion: that in the appreciation of their historical, architectural and cultural importance, there is a factor that draws society together in the face of the fragmenting dynamics of present-day living. As the final quarter of this century has unfolded, interest in the architectural heritage has deepened and resources devoted to its conservation have substantially increased.

Treatment of architectural heritage in this period provides an insight into shifting social consciousness and is, perhaps, a parable of value for the future. Some thirty years ago in Ireland, the great pre-Reformation and pre-Plantation monuments, the early Christian churches, the monasteries and castles, were maintained as ruins by the State, respected in their antiquity as part of the pre-colonial past. Low-key maintenance and repair meant that the ruin remained a ruin, with its place in the physical and mental landscape intact. In contrast, buildings of the eighteenth and nineteenth centuries were generally seen as the remnants of a colonising power and as obstacles to progress. They were accorded ineffectual protection under the planning acts and were not regarded as national monuments or seen as the responsibility of the State. Public funds were not available to support

4 Christ Church Cathedral, Dublin; restored in 1878 by George Edmund Street

their maintenance or repair. In urban development throughout the 1960s and 1970s their destruction was defended on the grounds that the buildings were redundant and unsound, and that their removal made way for modern buildings, which by definition, and despite their frequent shoddiness, were the architecture of progress.

Today the situation is different. New legislation for the protection of the architectural heritage has been enacted, although anomalies remain and protection under planning laws is still uncertain. Deficiencies in the regulatory environment are being recognised and debated and are the focus of revision within Government departments. Important buildings of the eighteenth and nineteenth centuries have been conserved by State action, while at local level historic buildings are routinely recycled for new uses. Deficiencies in knowledge and skill are becoming recognised and moves are under way to tackle shortcomings through training institutions and industrial initiatives.

A Tale of Two Projects

Some of the lineaments of deeper change can be illustrated by reference to two major projects: Holy Cross Abbey, a fifteenth-century reconstruction of a late twelfth-century foundation, which had survived for three hundred years as a ruin (fig. 1); and the Royal Hospital, Kilmainham, Ireland's most important seventeenth-century secular building, which had been unused for years with its future undecided.

The project to restore the Abbey to use as a church began in the 1960s, whereas the Hospital's restoration was begun in the mid-1970s. Both restorations were welcomed, although the passage of time has seen a more qualified response. Beyond the question of correctness of approach or detail, there are points of similarity and difference in these projects that illustrate changing times.

Each building has established two important issues. Their restoration helped to establish the architectural heritage as a resource for the present, and they offered a clean-cut completeness as the model for

such undertakings. This essay is concerned with the first, with what one might call the utility principle. Providing new and compatible uses for historic buildings is a key requirement for successful conservation. There had been some precedents. The fledgling Free State had restored the great eighteenth-century monumental buildings of the capital damaged during the rebellion of 1916 and the later civil war, and restored them to use in the service of State institutions, albeit with a vigour that would be challenged today (fig. 2). The motivation was complex, but in any case the restorations could be taken as evidence of continuity.

The dominance of this utility principle today rests on different grounds. The Abbey and Hospital projects demonstrate changing social consciousness and cultural values.

The Abbey: The Return of the Dispossessed

The impetus to restore the Abbey had its roots in the previous century, at a time when the works of the past became a means of underwriting cultural identity. The Enlightenment of the eighteenth century had laid the foundation for the development of antiquarian interest in the built relics of the past, an interest later overlaid with the aesthetic sensibility of the picturesque. Medieval buildings acquired a quasi-moral status, representing an age to which aspirations for social and religious cohesion could be ascribed. This status was expressed in the adoption, by the newly disestablished Church of Ireland, of the medieval style for new church building, as well as in the restoration of existing churches, most notably the great Dublin cathedrals, St Patrick's and Christ Church (fig. 4). For its part, the Catholic majority celebrated its emancipation in the triumphal adoption of the architecture of the Roman Renaissance. However, with the passing of time and the Anglo-Irish political order, priorities changed. Perhaps the simplistic and romantic nationalism that came to dominate political discourse in the Free State had something to do with it. The restoration of Holy Cross had been preceded by the restoration of Ballintober Abbey in the 1960s and was followed by that of Graiguenamanagh. These projects were seen as repossessions, resumptions of occupancy that had been interrupted by alien intervention. In the case of Ballintober, the continuity of worship was explicitly invoked.

The ecclesiastical restoration projects, nineteenth- and twentieth-century alike, had in common the fact that they fitted into a comprehensible narrative, one that was underpinned by opposing understandings of history, but united by the imperatives of establishing continuity and identity. Thus the symbolism of restoration was clear and immediate, to whichever side one belonged.

The Hospital: The Emergence of High Culture

With the restoration of the Royal Hospital at Kilmainham one enters different territory (fig. 3). Built *c.* 1684, at a time of immense turbulence in Irish society, it catered for soldiers of the English crown. Today it seems to bear no clear and unambiguous political message. Its patron, James Butler, the first Duke of Ormond, occupies an uncertain position in popular history, and appreciation of his contribution has never fully taken hold of the public imagination. He is credited with the impetus for major civic works in Dublin, notably the creation of the quays along the capital's river banks and of the Phoenix Park. But understanding the man and his political position requires a grasp of the complex relationships between the ruling élites of this country and those of England and the Continent in the seventeenth century. Allegiances and loyalties were already complex before the religious upheaval of the Reformation. The young James was reared a Protestant at the English Court, although the rest of his family, in Ireland, were Catholic. The least one can say is that the story of these relationships undermines simple narratives of conquest, religion and the unremitting struggle for freedom. The Royal Hospital was the largest and earliest of those purpose-built secular institutions which, by virtue of their very existence, expressed the demise of the medieval way of life in Ireland. Its architecture announces the participation of its patron and the society

he represented in the wider scene of the Renaissance in Europe. It is a complex, 'high culture' icon.

But these complexities played little part in public debate about its conservation. The building was subject to two restoration campaigns. In the 1970s the decision rested on the grounds of its importance in Irish architectural history, yet the interventions undertaken were justified by reference to its state of repair. Any reservations that might have been felt were subordinated to the fact that the building had been saved from becoming a ruin. In the 1980s the Royal Hospital was adapted for use as the Museum of Modern Art (pp. 158-9). Again, the arguments were fought on altered conceptual grounds. The protagonists were, on the one side, those who argued against the adaptation on grounds of the building's architectural importance and, on the other side, those who argued that the new use would bring life to an otherwise dead building – one whose previous alterations reduced its claim to be preserved as it then was. The claims of the building itself as a historical document were seen as inconclusive, and its historical context hardly entered public debate.[3]

Whereas the restoration of Holy Cross Abbey rested on its place in cultural consciousness, the Royal Hospital depended on its place in Irish architectural history and opportunistic inspiration. In neither case have the technical decisions taken with respect to the building fabric been subjected to serious critical review. To do so might have led to discussion of the competing values to be addressed in the process of intervention. The answer to what we expect of historic buildings is that they earn their keep while maintaining a representational value, even if that value is sometimes at variance with the building's history. This sentiment is underlined by the fact that the assistance given by the State to the repair of historic buildings in private ownership comes in the form of tax relief against income rather than as a grant. Consistent with this, modifications are frequently introduced in order to comply with consequent functional requirements. While the principle that the best protection for a historic building lies in its being used for purposes that are compatible both with its fabric and its significance is accepted, re-use is becoming the dominant goal of conservation. One consequence has been a pervasive sloppiness in the language used to portray interventions in historic buildings: terms such as 'restoration' and 'refurbishment' are employed to describe projects that amount to reconstruction.

Resources, Evaluation and Critical Interpretation

The years since the Royal Hospital project have been almost a 'golden age' for the conservation of buildings in Ireland. The flowering of interest extends beyond buildings of major architectural importance to include redundant churches, schools, almshouses, gatehouses and such early industrial buildings as mills and warehouses: hardly a small town or village has not attempted to bring some redundant building back into community use. There has been a continuing development in the skill and expertise brought to bear on major undertakings, and such projects as the repair of Dublin's Custom House facade, the conservation of Cormac's Chapel at Cashel and the restoration of the Casino at Marino demonstrate the advances (figs. 5-7). But there are clear shortcomings in expertise and skill when one looks at the broader picture.

There is a question of judgement to be answered: how far should the utility principle extend? A case in point arises with respect to the eighteenth-century Powerscourt House, Dublin (fig. 8).[4] The culture of progress rests predominantly on economic criteria, and much of the impetus for the conservation of the built heritage derives from commercial considerations, such as the creation of a tourism 'product'. But conserving heritage on the basis of its importance for ourselves, and undertaking work in order to present it to tourists, may present conflicting priorities. We should beware of being over-enthusiastic 'restorers' rather than conservators – lest even the economic argument become self-defeating.

There has been little published critical evaluation of conservation, despite the extensive activity in the area. This activity, however, has been somewhat one-sided.

5   James Gandon
Custom House, Dublin, 1781-91; restored 1991

6   Sir William Chambers
Casino at Marino, Dublin, begun 1758; restored 1980

7   Cormac's Chapel, Cashel, 1127-34; chancel fresco

8 Robert Mack
Powerscourt House,
Dublin, 1771; altered 1981
by James Tuomey

While the State has committed substantial resources to the conservation and reuse of the great set pieces, vernacular and industrial buildings, a significant cultural and historical component of the architectural heritage, remain underfunded.[5]

Part of the ideology of conservation is the use of monuments as 'instruments of knowledge and cultural development'.[6] Juxtaposing concepts of 'knowledge', 'culture' and 'historic monument' means that the basis for conservation and interpretation is critical. If not adequately conceived, interpretative programmes are threats to the intellectual integrity of ongoing research and to the monuments themselves. In Ireland, where the experience of struggle for political, economic and intellectual independence has been so close to the public psyche, there is a particular need for thought about the concepts implicitly presented by the acts of conservation and interpretation. The correlation between power, wealth and cultural importance has been the subject of some attention in the critical literature on the preservation of heritage. The fact that this correlation is usually unstated suggests an ideological position that should be addressed. Few conservation projects succeed in tackling this issue well: at Strokestown House the simple juxtaposition of the furnished family house with the Famine Museum in the stables provides an experience that is unique in its capacity to 'empower' the visitor in the exploration of these issues (fig. 9). The role of the conservator and interpreter, whose choices may reflect a value system not familiar to the visitor, thus emerges centre stage.

Notes

1 Richard Kearney and Ronan Sheehan, 'Introductory Note on the Ideological Debate', *The Crane Bag: Final Issue* 9:2 (1985).
2 G. Simmel, quoted in David Harvey, *The Condition of Postmodernity* (Oxford, 1989), p. 272.
3 An exception to this is the article by John Olley, 'Sustaining the Narrative at Kilmainham', *Irish Arts Review* (1991/2), pp. 65-72.
4 Built in 1771-4 to the designs of Robert Mack for the third Viscount Powerscourt, it was one of Dublin's most impressive mansions. Purchased in the late 1970s by Power Securities, it has been transformed into a shopping centre. The issue here is the subjugation of the house itself to the multi-level galleried space at the rear.
5 It should be noted that the adaptation of historic buildings has also been at the leading edge of much contemporary architecture in Ireland. The contrasting fate of two monuments is outlined in William Nolan, 'The Heritage Business: Problems and Possibilties', in W. Nolan (ed.), *Present State and Future Prospects* (Dublin, 1992).
6 Christine Hoepfner, Mark Leone and Parker B. Potter Jr., 'The Preserved is Political', *ICOMOS Information Newsletter*, no. 3 (July-Sept. 1987).

9 Orna Hanly
Famine Museum, Strokestown House,
County Roscommon, 1994

1   Kevin Roche
Oakland Museum, California,
1961-8

2   George Coppinger Ashlin
Monument to Cardinal McCabe,
Glasnevin Cemetery, Dublin,
designed 1888

The Cultural Identity of Ireland in Literature and the Built Environment

SARAH CASSIDY

Culture is a sort of theatre where various political and ideological causes engage one another.[1]

In the memory, a place lies the degree of freedom of self the Irish writer enjoys. If the physical reality of Ireland has stamped itself heavily upon Irish novels and stories, the fiction in turn has put its signatures upon the physical reality.[2]

Kevin Roche, Ireland's most famous contemporary architect, began work in Michael Scott's Office in 1948. After moving from Dublin to London and thence to Chicago, he undertook a course of postgraduate study at the latter city's Illinois Institute of Technology and ultimately entered Eero Saarinen's architectural practice. He later became head designer under Saarinen and, when the maestro died in 1961, Roche formed a partnersip with John Dinkeloo to continue his work (fig. 1).

Roche was born in 1922, the same year as the publication of *Ulysses*, one year after Ireland achieved independence and five after Finland gained hers. Eero was the son of Eliel Saarinen, one of Finland's leading exponents of the national romantic movement in architecture. While it is merely coincidental that Roche worked for Saarinen, the historical similarity between Ireland and Finland is enormous. During the nineteenth century both coun-

tries sought an identity in an effort to assert independence, leading to a kind of cultural nationalism. Both peoples saw themselves as intensely rural. For them, that was the true and untainted spirit of the nation.

The end of the nineteenth century saw the rise and fall of Charles Stewart Parnell, arguably Ireland's most celebrated advocate of Home Rule. However, constitutional agitation subsequently lost much of its appeal and what emerged from the confused aftermath of Parnell was a new kind of nationalism, a cultural nationalism. It was hoped to regain and reassert a cultural identity, an identity independent of British influence.

The Gaelic League was established in 1893 by Douglas Hyde, Fr. Eugene O'Growney and Eoin MacNeill. A non-political organisation, it sought to preserve Irish as the national tongue, to stimulate the study, cultivation and publication of existing Irish literature and to help create a new literature in Irish.

Hyde, together with W. B. Yeats and T.W. Rolleston, founded the Pan-Celtic League, through which they shared their interest in Irish folklore and folktales. Hyde stressed the necessity for 'de-Anglicising' Ireland and inverting the image of 'a nation of imitators'. He did not oppose Anglo-Irish literature. In fact, he used it as a tool for furthering his aim of a return to native conditions. English had been

3   William. A. Scott
O'Growney Memorial Tomb,
Maynooth, 1905

asserted as the language of progress and employment since the early nineteenth century. At the time of the founding of the Gaelic League, the Irish language was considered a symbol of poverty and lack of education – few people outside *gaeltacht* areas spoke it on a habitual basis.

Hyde, an Irish language scholar, began translating folktales from Irish into English, so as to introduce and popularise the national lore. In 1893 *Abhráin Grádh Chúige Connacht* (Love Songs of Connacht), his most famous work, was published. It was enthusiastically greeted by the Anglo-Irish literary movement, to which Yeats belonged.

In its preoccupation with place as a severable aspect of self, Irish Fiction is a descendent of the Irish mythic tale.[3]

The year of Parnell's death, 1891, saw the foundation of the Irish Literary Society in London, which was followed in 1892 by the National Literary Society in Dublin. Later again, the Irish Literary Theatre was established.[4] This group, spearheaded by Lady Augusta Gregory and Yeats, sought to cultivate a public for the literature and legends of Ireland. Their writings contain a romanticised notion of the land and they eulogise the Irish peasant, believing him to be the true Irishman:

> John Synge, I and Augusta Gregory thought
> All that we did, all that we said or sang
> Must come from contact with the soil, from that
> Contact everything Antaeus-like grew strong.[5]

The revivalists sought to provide what was missing in the industrialised world – contact with the soil and tradition. Yeats felt that all good art depended on popular tradition, a fact that he tried to convey to James Joyce on their first meeting. Yeats had turned to peasant plays and dialect, seeking the freshness and sponteneity of the land. What emerged, however, was 'a political image of the countryside which helped to create a sense of social cohesion in a country which was trying to define itself over against England'.[6]

In this period Robert Cochrane, architect and a senior surveyor with the Board of Public Works, was made inspector of national and ancient monuments. He brought his considerable dynamism and archaeological scholarship to bear on fostering popular awareness of Ireland's ancient architectural heritage and consolidated the Board of Public Works' role in preserving that heritage.[7] Other architects involved in the Cultural Revival were William A. Scott, James F. McMullen, George Coppinger Ashlin and James Franklin (fig. 2). Of these, Scott was probably the architect most closely linked to the revival movement. He restored Ballylee Castle (owned by Yeats) and designed a number of buildings in the Hiberno-Romanesque style, including the O'Growney Memorial Tomb, Maynooth, County Kildare (fig. 3), and St Enda's Church, in Spiddal, County Galway (p. 60). Of the buildings McMullen designed, the most notable is the Honan Hostel Chapel, University College Cork, for which Harry Clarke designed the stained-glass windows and Scott the ironwork (fig. 4 and pp. 100-1).[8] Simultaneously, Irish painters, among them Jack B. Yeats (brother of the poet), Nathaniel Hone, Seán Keating and Paul Henry, sought to depict the rural theme (fig. 5).

Successive Irish Governments were also to embrace the rural idyll. Eamon de Valera, who came to power in 1932, had longed for a sovereign Irish republic, Irish-speaking and based on rural small-holdings.[9] Three years previously, a Censorship Act had been introduced that ensured the cultural insularity of the country. The rural represented tradition, and tradition was imbued with cultural identity – 'the true Ireland'. In sharp contrast, the architecture of the city was an *aide-mémoire* of the colonial past. As the capital, Dublin was perceived to be a colonial city.[10] Its Georgian buildings represented a foreign landlord.[11]

This turning from the city became almost inherent in the Irish psyche. Later post-revolutionary writers – for instance, Liam O'Flaherty, Peadar O'Donnell, Patrick Kavanagh, Sean O'Faolain, Frank O'Connor and Kate O'Brien – turned not to the mythic past for things worthy of celebration, but to the heroic in the rural background. 'Place in Irish fiction is essentially fictional and imaginative and packs the power of the individual and communal dream.'[12] That dream is one of

4 Harry Clarke
Stained-glass window of St Declan,
Honan Hostel Chapel,
University College Cork, *c.* 1916

5 Paul Henry
The Potato Diggers, 1912
National Gallery of Ireland, Dublin

rural Ireland. Even essentially urban writers, such as O'Faolain or O'Connor, evoke rural imagery to describe the ideal. The *Sugawn Chair*, a short story by O'Faolain, while set in the city, revolves around the rural memory. The imagery revealed is that of the romanticised rural idyll.

Clare Boylan, also an author associated with the urban, opens her novel *Holy Pictures* with a description of a children's journey from a city centre through villages to the mountains beyond. For reasons of economy, the children are considered too old to celebrate Christmas; they leave behind the prejudice and monetary worries associated with the city, to refind the magic of their earlier years and celebrate it with a winter picnic in the mountains.

The route traced by Nan, Dolly and Mary in *Holy Pictures* is the same as that taken later by 'development' and conurbation. The city offered work, yet it conflicted with the communal dream – the country plot. The expansion from a high-density, tightly built localised city transformed Dublin into a low-density sprawl (figs. 6, 7). The major part of this expansion was accommodated in suburban estates where each house had front and rear gardens. Georgian architecture in Dublin was planned around a square; the single-family house faced onto a communal garden for all the inhabitants of the square and each plot usually contained an individual rear garden. Alternatively, the tenements, for the less well off, contained several families in a single dwelling, usually with a small courtyard to the rear.

The flight to the suburbs was a compromise between urban and rural. An advertisement slogan extolled the virtues of living outside the city and commuting to work: 'Ideal surroundings within easy reach of the city in beautiful countryside.'[13] The suburbs offered independence, freedom and, to a certain extent, land ownership. Unfortunately, the services offered by the original local villages were not enough to sustain this kind of development: a basic service infrastructure was rarely planned with the expanding suburbs, while the surrounding countryside was rapidly overtaken by housing and small individual gardens.

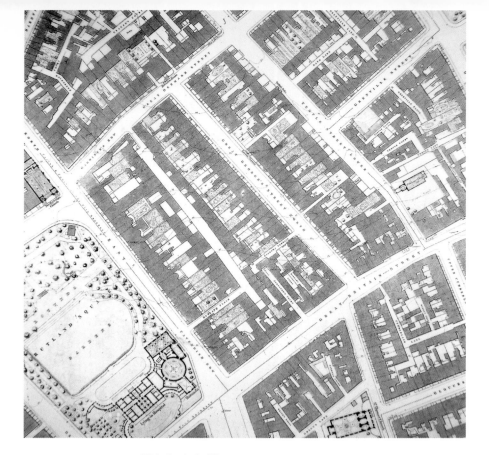

6　High-density building
in 18th-century Dublin

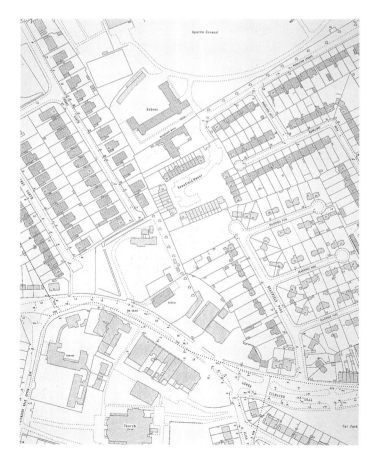

7　Low-density suburban sprawl
in 20th-century Dublin

In May 1899 the young James Joyce closely followed the first performances of the Irish Literary Theatre: *Countess Cathleen* by Yeats and *The Heather Field* by Edward Martyn. (The latter centred around an idealistic Ibsenite hero.) The following year, Joyce's own play, *A Brilliant Career*,[14] was staged there.

Yeats had said that the Irish Literary Theatre would perform plays by Continental as well as Irish dramatists. Joyce was translating Hauptmann with a view to submitting the latter's work to the theatre. Upon learning that the next plays would be 'offensively Irish',[15] Joyce wrote a scathing article condemning the theatre for its parochialism. It was the introspective nature of the plays, and indeed of cultural nationalism in general, that he objected to.

Early in 1902 Joyce presented a paper on the Irish poet James Clarence Mangan to the Literary and Historical Society of University College Dublin. He declared Mangan to be a nationalist poet who had been neglected and misunderstood by nationalists. It was therefore up to Joyce, a self-proclaimed Irishman with European standards, to recover Mangan's name. This paper was published and, as suggested by Richard Ellmann, it helped to clarify that Joyce's quarrel was with bad art and petrified morality, and with his nation only insofar as it condoned these.

Within the year, Joyce had left Dublin for Paris,[16] for in order to 'measure himself and his country he needed to take the measure of a more alien world'.[17] In 1914, in self-imposed exile, Joyce began writing *Ulysses*, the sequel to *A Portrait of the Artist as a Young Man*. *Ulysses* is firmly urban in setting and is the most complete piece of literature on Dublin. 'I want', Joyce declared to a friend in Zurich, 'to give a picture of Dublin so complete that if the city one day suddenly disappeared from the earth it could be reconstructed out of my book.'[18]

Almost seventy years after the publication of *Ulysses*, a celebration of Dublin life, the beloved and yet reviled city of Joyce began an urban renaissance. Tax incentives encouraged people to move back to the centre (fig. 8). The city has started to breathe again. The urban pulse beats after years of draining. The *city* is recognised as part of the Irish identity.

Present-day poet and novelist Philip Casey composed a poem on seeing the Ludwig Mies van der Rohe centenary exhibition, entitled 'Implications of a Sketch', in the New National Gallery, Berlin. In it the author describes the power and influence of a single sketch:

> A sketch of seconds
>> decides
>>> the future
> of thousands,
>> of street and skyline.[19]

City and architecture are no longer the forgotten, the unmentionable, but become an integral part of identity. Robin Walker, Cathal O'Neill and Peter Doyle all either studied or worked under Mies in Chicago. They returned to Ireland with their interpretation of his work and translated it. With others, these architects played a role in enhancing and broadening Irish cultural identity. For, as Oscar Wilde declared: 'It is only by contact with the art of foreign nations that the art of a country gains that individual and separate life that we call nationality.'[20]

Notes

1 Edward Said, *Culture and Imperialism* (London, 1993), p. xiv.
2 John Wilson Foster, *Colonial Consequences; Essays in Irish Literature and Culture* (Dublin, 1991), p. 31.
3 Ibid., p. 30.
4 This would later become known as the National Theatre.
5 Yeats, quoted in Conor Cruise O'Brien, *The Shaping of Modern Ireland* (London, 1960), p. 21.
6 Fintan O'Toole, 'The Country versus the City in Irish Writing', *The Crane Bag* 9:2 (1985), p. 112.
7 Frederick O'Dwyer, 'The Architecture of the Board of Public Works 1831 -1923', in Ciaran O'Connor and John O'Regan (eds), *The Architecture of the Office of Public Works 1831-1987* (Dublin, 1987), p. 25.
8 Jeremy Williams, *Architecture in Ireland 1837-1921* (Blackrock, 1 994), pp. 68-9.
9 Joseph Lee and Gearóid Ó'Tuathaigh, *The Age of de Valera* (Dublin, 1982).
10 Dublin was formerly known as the second city of the British Empire.
11 It was not until February 1996 that an Irish political party published a policy on Georgian architecture in Dublin.
12 Foster (note 2), p. 32.
13 Quoted in Arnold Horner, 'The Dublin Region, 1880-1982: An Overview of its Devolopment and Planning', in Michael Bannon (ed.), *The Emergence of Irish Planning 1880-1920* (Dublin, 1975), p. 37.
14 Joyce destroyed the manuscript in 1902.
15 A play by Hyde was to be performed in the Irish language along with another by Yeats and George Moore based on the Irish legend of Diarmuid and Grannia.
16 On leaving for Paris, Joyce entrusted his sketches, or 'epiphanies', of stories to George Russell, a leading member of the Literary Revival group. This collection later became known as *Dubliners*.
17 Richard Ellmann, *James Joyce* (Oxford, 1983), p. 110.
18 Quoted in Frank Delaney, *James Joyce's Odyssey: Guide to the Dublin of 'Ulysses'* (London, 1977), p. 10.
19 Philip Casey, *The Year of the Knife: Poems 1980-1990* (Dublin, 1991), pp. 83-4.
20 Quoted in Richard Ellman (ed.), *The Artist as Critic* (London, 1970), p. 373.

8 Derek Tynan
The Printworks, Temple Bar, Dublin, 1994

The Cultural Identity of Ireland 77

1   Robin Walker
Walker House, Dublin,
1964

2   Robin Walker
Walker House, Bothár Buí, 1972

Export / Import

The Importance of External Ideas
in Modern Irish Architecture

JOHN TUOMEY

There is no pure indigenous strain of Irish architecture and to seek to establish an exclusive identity in national terms would tend towards an undesirable closure. To deny the creative role of imported experience would be to turn against the continuing tradition of the assimilation of external influences modified to accommodate to an evolving situation.

Robin Walker once introduced a seminar entitled 'Architects' Approach to Architecture' at University College Dublin (UCD) with the words 'I am going to tell you the story of my life'. In this informal discourse he described how he had worked for Le Corbusier on the Marseilles Unité and how fully he had fallen under the influence of the master. Later he had travelled to America, where he studied with Ludwig Mies van der Rohe and changed allegiance to the measured discipline of the Miesian method. He told his audience that the second influence was the more profound and lasting one, and that precise rationality had superseded the subjectivity of the Swiss sculptor. He was able to extrapolate from this experience to inform his current researches into the principles of proportion in the construction aesthetic of Dublin's Georgian streets and squares. He presented his listeners with the proposition that, once the straight and rigorous path of reason has been taken, other instincts have to be put aside. Some years later, when I asked

him to participate in a public lecture series entitled 'Great Buildings of the 20th Century', Walker immediately replied, with a resigned sense of the inevitable, 'you'd better put me down for Crown Hall'.

But such public postures should not obscure the more complex reality that is revealed through Walker's buildings. Separate strands can be disentwined from the apparently singular line of his architecture. In two of his more personal projects, his own house in Dublin and his holiday house in Bothár Buí, County Cork, we can discern a resonant sense of connection between the buildings and the particularity of their location. The mews house is evidence of the negotiation between the ideal type of the courtyard house and the awkward reality of the context (fig. 1). The monopitch frame buildings and converted cottages at Bothár Buí cluster together to make one place, an aggregation of interior containment and a reciprocal relationship with the ocean horizon (fig. 2).

Walker's distinguished series of buildings cannot be read simply as evidence of an external influence brought to bear on an Irish situation. There is a recognisable point of intersection between the zeal of the convert and the contingent cultural reality. These moments of convergence between the irresistible force of an imported value system and the immovable object of the

3 Thomas Ivory
Kilcarty Haus, *c.* 1770–80

4 Sir Edward Lovett Pearce
Houses of Parliament (now Bank of Ireland), Dublin, 1728-9

5 Deane and Woodward
Kildare Street Club in its street context, Dublin, 1858-61

given situation can produce a distinctive and poignant quality in the resulting building. That poignancy is the palpable outcome of the connection between the ideal and the real world, and in the buildings we can sense the effort of the architect to focus the inspiration of acquired experience in order to engage with the innate character of his own place.

Once the phenomenon is recognised it can be seen to characterise many of the defining moments in the story of Irish architecture. The crossbreed represented by Kilcarty in County Meath, the classic Irish house of the middle size, as analysed by Maurice Craig, where Thomas Ivory's Palladian idealism is accommodated to the vernacular tradition, is an eighteenth-century example of the same syndrome (fig. 3). There is a parallel instance in the unusual spatial engagement of Sir Edward Lovett Pearce's Ionic portico of the eighteenth-century parliament building with the medieval delta of the Liffey, its original context on College Green (fig. 4). The Kildare Street Club derives some of its intimate intensity from the constraints placed on Benjamin Woodward's intended expression of his Ruskinian Gothic influence by the plain language and consistent pattern of Dublin's Georgian streetscape (fig. 5).

As students at UCD in the early 1970s, we were taught by Shane de Blacam, who had recently returned to Dublin, direct from the studio of Louis Kahn. His fundamentalist inspiration formed the ethos of our introduction to architecture.

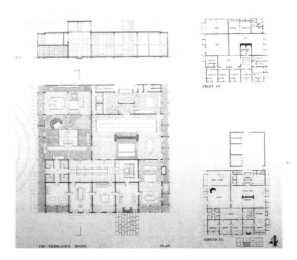

6 de Blacam and Meagher
Entry to the Taoiseach House competition, 1979

De Blacam and Meagher's second-prize entry for the Taoiseach House competition was a poetic expression of the influence of Kahn's tectonics that produced a radical reinterpretation of the plan of the Irish country house. Some of the sense of the material presence of their later buildings is predicted in this unbuilt project (fig. 6).

At that time Cathal O'Neill's work, too, betrayed American influence, for instance in his sketches for a concrete frame house. These pencil-drawn plans on American yellow trace paper show a hierarchical distribution of domestic functions that must derive from O'Neill's postgraduate period in the office of Mies van der Rohe. Such a modern house could not have been constructed in the prevailing social climate without the conviction of his American experiences (fig. 7).

By the mid-1970s the American dimension, which had been such an important influence in modern Irish life, had started to wane and cultural interest began to reflect the political shift back towards European integration and the redefinition of regional identity within a new federal context.

The specific background to my generation's approach to architecture rose from the aftermath of the rejuvenation of the School of Architecture at UCD under the headship of the English architect Ivor Smith. The school was staffed for a period of four years by visiting tutors from London and Glasgow, collectively known as the 'flying circus'. We left college having been introduced to the radical ideas of British practice by tutors who had emerged from the intellectual territory of New Brutalism under the aesthetic influence of Le Corbusier.

Arriving in London anachronistically steeped in the influences of contemporary British architecture, I was lucky enough to be employed in the office of James Stirling, who was at that time fully fed-up with all things English. He was working in a cosmopolitan context, teaching in Yale and Dusseldorf and participating in German and Italian competitions. It was surprising to find the British hero absorbed in overseas activities and my interest in his early elemental red brick buildings was regarded as regressive and unusually out of date. Office conversation was centred on the history of European architecture and its urban tradition. We worked in the basement of 75 Gloucester Place without much reference to the world immediately outside the window.

The tide of influence has again turned east towards Europe. Before the American interlude and the allure of its architecture, consolidated by the setting free of the creative energies of émigré Europeans, Irish eyes had been fixed upon the catalytic effect of another community of émigrés washed up on England's shores. Serge Chermayeff and Erich Mendelsohn offered inspiration to modernism in Britian with their buildings and their involvement with the MARS Group. In turn, this influence crossed the Irish sea in books and journals and through a visit by Mendelsohn to lecture at the Architectural Association of Ireland in Dublin. Shortly after, the two most significant early modern movement buildings in Ireland were conceived, 'Geragh', Michael Scott's own house, and the new terminal building for Dublin Airport by Desmond Fitzgerald (pp. 114-5, 110-3).

The European influence has been a pervasive one for young Irish architects over the past two decades, whether received indirectly from the London circle or, more authentically, via the recent waves of graduates settling in Paris, Barcelona and Berlin. In addition, the Architectural Association of Ireland has invited a steady stream of European architects to lecture in Dublin. Architectural assimilation has proceeded in parallel with Ireland's growing involvement in EU affairs.

In his introduction to the catalogue of the 1980 exhibition 'Sense of Ireland: Traditions and Directions' Edward Jones described his surprise, on first coming to Dublin as a member of the 'flying circus', at finding the calm Miesian campus of Radio Telefis Eireann (RTE) (fig. 8 and p. 123). The Irish work had a distinct quality, discernibly removed from the international corporate character that had become associated with the legacy of Mies van der Rohe. Visitors to the city today remark on the regeneration of Temple Bar, where the principles of European architectural precedents have been employed to provide public space and urban continuity. Just as the RTE complex was seen to represent the apotheosis of American influence on architectural practice in Ireland, so the Group '91 framework plan for Temple Bar marks a particular stage in the inspiration drawn from European contextualism (fig. 9).

7　Cathal O'Neill
Design for a concrete frame house, c. 1974

8　Ronald Tallon
RTE Administration Building, Dublin, 1967

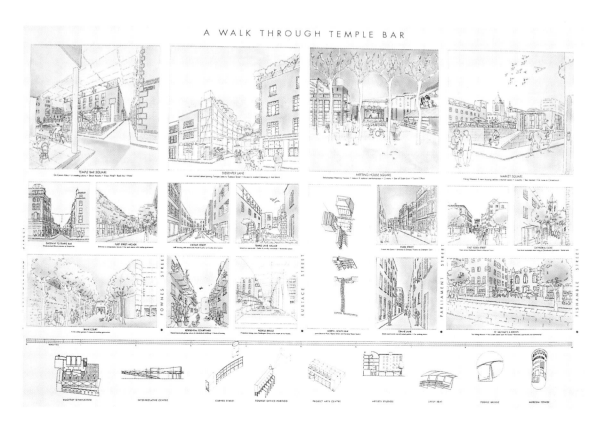

A WALK THROUGH TEMPLE BAR

9　Group '91 Architects
'Architectural Framework Plan' for Temple Bar, Dublin, 1991

1 Seán Keating
Night's Candles are Burnt Out,
1928-9 Oldham Art Gallery, Lancs.;
on permanent loan to the
Electricity Supply Board

2 Hydro-electric power station, Ardnacrusha, 1925-9

3 Hydro-electric power station at Ardnacrusha
during construction

Irish Identity and the Architecture
of the New State

HUGH CAMPBELL

'The character of whole nations, cultures and epochs speaks through the totality of architecture, which is the outward shell of their being', wrote Jacob Burckhardt. Might an examination of the architecture of twentieth-century Ireland provide a biography of the nation? More specifically, what part did building play in shaping the nation's identity following independence in 1922?

The new nation had endured what W. B. Yeats called a 'long gestation', marked by repeated attempts to define Ireland and Irishness. For Irish nationalism, the achieving of independence depended initially on promoting a vision of a free Ireland. While the various versions of this vision all emphasised Ireland's potential, they also sought to 'establish continuity with some suitable historic past'.[1] After 1922 the resultant tension between what the anthropologist Clifford Geertz has described as 'essentialism' – adherence to some shared culture – and 'epochalism' – embracing the spirit of the age – became a defining characteristic of the new state.[2]

Initially, vacillation between historic certainty and projected ideals – between 'essentialism' and 'epochalism' – resulted in inaction. The government provided by Cumann na nGaedheal between 1922 and 1932 has been characterised as a 'holding operation'.[3] In the face of world-wide depression and continuing civil conflict caution, rather than experiment, was the favoured policy. The only significant exception to this prevailing prudence was the massive hydro-electric plant that was constructed on the River Shannon at Ardnacrusha near Limerick between 1925 and 1929 (pp. 104-5).

Seán Keating's allegorical painting of the Shannon scheme, *Night's Candles are Burnt Out* (fig. 1), shows 'Ireland emerging from economic deprivation, enduring the War of Independence and the Civil War, and progressing to economic prosperity'.[4] The destiny of the Irish people is played out in the presence of the power station. An imperious, suited engineer, clutching a folio of blueprints (for the new nation?), confronts a rather tired looking soldier, who has endured the bloodshed of successive conflicts. The forlorn skeleton of 'Ireland past' hangs in the top left-hand corner, while immediately opposite, a young family – 'Ireland future' – points expectantly towards the horizon, which is dominated by the massive concrete dam of the hydro-electric scheme. The electricity generated by the plant will render the priest's candle and the worker's oil-lamp redundant. The painting's message is optimistic: the dark night of Ireland's struggle for independence will be followed by a bright new dawn, ushered in by technological progress. The artist himself is clearly in favour of the development: he is part of the family group looking towards the future.

4   Seán Keating
at work at Ardnacrusha

Energy!

90,000 HORSE POWER

Of energy will be available from the Shannon Electrical Power Station next year for Irish Industry and Irish homes

The American workman is the most prosperous on earth, because he has, on an average, three horse-power, the equivalent of thirty human slaves, helping him to produce.

No wonder he can toil less and be paid more than the workman of other lands. He is not a toiler, he is a director of machinery.

Wages and prosperity are determined by output, and the use of electric driven machinery is the key to the maximum of production with the minimum of effort. It is the secret of successful industrial organisation.

The Shannon is being harnesses to enable the Irish Industrialist and the Irish worker to use that key.

Shannon electricity will lift the heavy work of Industry from human shoulders to the iron shoulders of machines.

The Great Southern Railways are issuing return tickets at single fares (available for 3 days) from all stations to Limerick. Conducted tours daily by I.O.C. buses. Permits for private parties issued on application to The Guide Bureau, Strand Barracks, Limerick.

THE ELECTRICITY SUPPLY BOARD

5   Electricity Supply Board advertisement, 1928

The painting is one of a series commissioned by the Electricity Supply Board to document and celebrate the construction of the plant (fig. 4). The scheme was initiated by an Irish engineer, T. A. McLaughlin, who, while working with Siemens in Germany, had become convinced of the Shannon's potential to generate electricity for the whole of Ireland. His plans eventually gained the enthusiastic endorsement of the Irish Government, in particular of the Minister for Industry and Commerce, Patrick McGilligan. Expert opinion and research was sought throughout Europe and America before the scheme got under way. The project involved the diversion of the Shannon into a head race canal at Parteen weir, which ran a distance of 12.6 km to a huge dam that channelled the water into the turbine hall. The canal then rejoined the Shannon beyond the power station. The scale of earth-moving and construction involved was far greater than anything previously witnessed in Ireland. Siemens was given the contract for the design and construction of the scheme, but an Irish labour force of over 5,000, housed in tents on the site, was principally responsible for its final realisation (fig. 3).

The reinforced concrete buildings, bridges and dams on the Shannon were resolutely modern in appearance, but they also possessed a simple, elemental power, seeming almost to grow out of the surrounding landscape (fig. 2). In contemporary debates, the inspiration for the

Shannon scheme was traced back to Arthur Griffith, D. P. Moran and Padraig Pearse,[5] all of whom had stressed the need for Ireland to exploit its natural resources in order to achieve an independent prosperity. 'A free Ireland', Pearse had promised, 'would drain the bogs, would harness the rivers, would plant the wastes ... Ireland has resources to feed five times her population; a free Ireland will make these resources available.'[6]

For Pearse, Ireland's destiny was inextricably linked to the land. The urge to modernise was not seen as incompatible with his reification of rural life and of the Irish language. Throughout nineteenth-century Europe modernisation had entailed a move away from rural culture. Progress and prosperity became identified with the city. In Ireland, by contrast, the most radical political and artistic achievements of the nineteenth century were rooted in rural areas. The countryside provided the inspiration for a vibrant new phase of nationalism. Initially, decolonisation was achieved simply by portraying the landscape in a new way and thus subverting the coloniser's geography. Much of this imaginative work was done by the writers of the Literary Revival, principally W. B. Yeats. A nation, Yeats felt, could not exist 'without a model of it in the mind of the people'.[7] In his poems and plays he created a social and topographical model of Ireland, using the Irish peasant as his archetype and populating the landscape of Galway and Sligo with figures from Irish myths and legends. Yeats's 'recovery of territory through the imagination'[8] together with Parnell's vigorous campaigns for land reform and the Gaelic League's efforts at a language revival provided the ingredients of a coherent Irish identity. The Irish were presented as a rural, spiritual, ascetic race. Conversely, the English were portrayed as metropolitan, materialist and decadent – providing an ideal foil for Irish virtues.

While opposing the slavish aping of English values, many nationalists none the less favoured progress and modernisation. Within their terms, rural Ireland could provide for Ireland's future prosperity as surely as it formed the well-spring of nationhood. Hence, the radical nature of the Shannon project could be accommodated comfortably within a traditional conception of the Irish nation. Rather than being seen as an imported solution to a practical problem (which, of course, it was), the project was portrayed as a natural phenomenon: something that had emerged spontaneously from the Irish soil, having lain dormant prior to independence. In contemporary Electricity Supply Board advertisements the enterprise was represented by familiar rural images: a stampede of horses; a giant figure bestriding the dam like one of the Fianna finally come to life (figs. 5, 6). Its national status was enhanced by sight-seeing trips form all parts of Ireland to what a local paper dubbed 'the Eighth Wonder of the World'.[9] The project seemed to galvanise the whole nation, inspiring a 'faith ... as steadfast as a religious belief'.[10]

Given that Siemens was responsible for the design of the scheme, it is hardly surprising that some elements – particularly the turbine-hall – are reminiscent of Peter Behrens's work for AEG (fig. 7). Behrens was one of the founders of the Deutscher Werkbund, an association of artists, craftsmen and industrialists that saw industrialised production as 'the manifest destiny of the German nation'.[11] For Behrens, the factory was 'the composite issue of *Zeitgeist* and *Volksgeist*, to which it was his duty as an artist to give form'.[12] After the war, Behrens's ideas permeated the German industrial landscape. Their subsequent translation to the west of Ireland proved appropriate to a nation trying, albeit haltingly, to give form to its own mixture of Zeitgeist and Volksgeist.

The Shannon Hydro-Electric Scheme managed to embrace the future by rooting itself in a geography that evoked the past. However, the Government's cautious approach to spending meant that while the Shannon scheme went ahead, all other building activity languished.[13] It was not until the 1930s that the Irish architectural profession began building on a large scale. Aldo Rossi has written that 'it is precisely at the decisive moments in history that architecture repropose[s] its own necessity to be "sign" and "event" in order to establish and shape that new era'.[14] The Fianna Fail Government, which took power in 1932 under Eamon de Valera's leadership, instigated a hugely expanded

building programme. Architecture was assigned a key role in realising the dream of a 'self-sufficient, bucolic, Gaelic utopia',[15] which formed the cornerstone of de Valera's social policy. That policy was delineated most enduringly in his 1937 Constitution, but perhaps most vividly in his famous St Patrick's Day speech of 1943:

> The Ireland which we have dreamed of would be the home of a people who valued material wealth only as a basis of right living, of a people who were satisfied with frugal comfort, and devoted their leisure to things of the spirit; a land whose countryside would be bright with cosy homesteads, whose fields and villages would be joyous with the sounds of industry, with the romping of sturdy children, the contests of athletic youths, the laughter of comely maidens; whose firesides would be the forums for the wisdom of serene old age. It would, in a word, be the home of a people living the life that God desires that men should live.[16]

De Valera reinforced many of the by now familiar elements of Irish identity – its rusticity, its asceticism and its spirituality. But he knew that, in order to maintain this idyll, substantial improvements needed to be made to the harsh realities of Irish rural life. His strategy of social improvement and economic independence saw Ireland's expansive boglands being used to produce electricity and fuel (fig. 8). A renewed programme of school-building was initiated, and there was a proliferation of new hospitals around the country. The building of the hospitals was

Visit the Shannon Works!

See this Mighty Project in the making

Arrangements have been made with the Great Southern Railway to issue Return Tickets at Single Fares from all stations on its system to Limerick on week-days, available for return within three days including day of issue, from now on until the 29th of September inclusive.

Conducted Tours daily from the I.O.C. premises
Sarsfield Street, Limerick —
1st Tour leaves at 10.30 a.m., returning 1.30 p.m.
2nd   „   „   2.30 p.m.,   „   6.30 p.m.
BUS FARE 4/- (Children Half-price)
Guide's services free.

Those not wishing to avail of these Conducted Tours should apply direct for a permit, giving date of proposed visit.
Conducted Tours on SUNDAYS for large excursion parties ONLY—

Apply to The ELECTRICITY SUPPLY BOARD
GUIDE BUREAU, STRAND BARRACKS, LIMERICK

6   Electricity Supply Board advertisement, 1928

7   Peter Behrens
AEG High Tension Materials Factory, Berlin-Wedding, 1910

8   Turf-powered electricity plant, Portarlington, County Offaly, completed 1950

9 Alvar Aalto
Sanatorium at Paimio,
Finland, 1933-8

financed primarily by the Hospital Sweepstakes – a sort of national lottery – established by the Public Charitable Hospitals Act of 1930. The first new hospital to be built in Ireland since 1904 was opened in Mullingar in April 1936. 'During the next five years 12 new County hospitals ... were completed. During the same period, no less than 30 new smaller hospitals, mainly district hospital types, and 2 mental hospitals were built.'[17]

Vincent Kelly, the architect appointed to oversee the hospitals programme, was sent to study hospital buildings throughout Europe, particularly Aalto's recently completed Paimio Sanatorium (fig. 9).[18] But while his work at Nenagh, County Tipperary, and Portrane, County Dublin, exhibits a thoroughly contemporary appreciation of the benefit to physical and mental health of a clean, well-lit and properly ventilated environment, the building's plain surfaces and organisational clarity could equally be seen to embody de Valera's puritanical vision of Irish society (figs. 10, 12). The more thoroughgoing functionalism of T. J. Cullen's Galway Central Hospital and Michael Scott's Portlaoise Hospital, County Laoighis, invites a similar interpretation (figs. 11, 13). These hospital buildings might be read as a testament to enduring values, as surely as they were symbols of progress. They helped to stabilise de Valera's balancing of a sternly anti-materialist philosophy with the need for material progress. D.P. Moran had previously diagnosed the need for 'making the people sober, moderate, masculine and thereby paving the way for industrial advancement and economic reform'.[19] The stark, utilitarian hospitals, schools and factories of the 1930s gave that prescription a built form.

In his seminal 1908 essay 'Ornament and Crime', Adolf Loos wrote that the 'evolution of culture is synonymous with the removal of ornament from utilitarian objects'.[20] Much of the architecture of the ensuing years pursued and expanded this credo, stripping away non-essentials, emphasising function, eschewing decoration. This process of abstraction was presented as a reaction to the stylistic and materialistic excesses of the nineteenth century.[21] After the First World War, architects began to formulate objective, universal laws from which a pure, modern architecture could spring. For Ireland, this new architecture might confirm the nation's emergence from oppression to freedom. Many of its characteristics – its stark, geometric forms, its emphasis on function and economy, its claims to universalism – made it appealing to an Irish architectural audience eager for new ideas. These same characteristics recommended themselves to a Government beholden to an ascetic tradition, bent on self-sufficiency, but aware of the need for links with the wider world.[22] Champions of modernism in the architectural press portrayed it as a new tradition, specifically linking it to the thatched cottage and the eighteenth-century house.[23] Once again, new ideas were linked to the past in order to gain acceptance.

In the early twentieth century, architecture was seen as a critical practice: aesthetic ideas emerged from penetrating critiques of contemporary society. Social change and the new architecture were inextricably linked. Without this emancipatory aspiration, however, the new architecture was all too easily reducible either to a set of aesthetic motifs or to an impoverished functionalism. Unfortunately, the translation of modern architecture to Ireland succumbed to both tendencies. The former is clearly evident in the Dublin housing schemes, where the language of the Amsterdam School was adopted without any regard to its co-operative procurement and construction system. The latter tendency is revealed in the utilitarian nature of the hospital plans and in contemporary reviews, which were content to dwell exclusively on the programme and construction of the buildings (figs. 14, 15).[24] The Irish architectural profession appeared unwilling or unable to explore in any depth the possibilities of

10 Vincent Kelly
Hospital at Portrane

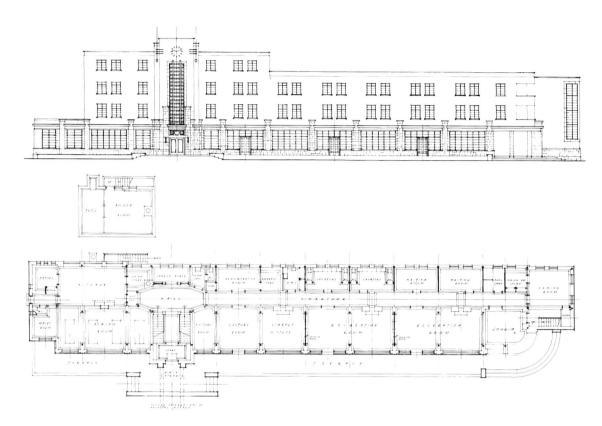

11 T. J. Cullen
Galway Central Hospital, 1933-8

modernism as a cultural critique. For all its improvement of living standards, de Valera's social programme was inherently conservative; despite its modern dress, the architecture of the era mirrored that conservatism perfectly.

The introduction of modern architecture to Ireland did little to alter the accepted Irish identity. Neither did it result in any distinctive manipulation or inflection of the modern idiom. By contrast, when James Joyce exiled himself to the cosmopolitanism of the Continent, he used that experience to continually re-examine and re-invent his native Dublin.[25] In doing so, he found new forms that were as truly Irish as they were modern and universal. Ireland's unstable, peripheral, contingent qualities re-energised the English language and transformed the modern novel.[26] 'It is a symbol of Irish art. The cracked looking-glass of a servant', says Stephen in the opening chapter of *Ulysses*. The Irish were too often content to look at themselves through an imperfect, inherited medium that distorted their image. Instead, Joyce wanted 'the Irish people to have one good look at themselves in [his] nicely polished looking-glass'.[27] To make a distinctively modern, distinctively Irish art required the curiosity to look beyond inherited or imported models and the courage to challenge the prevailing paradigms of nationhood.

Discussing the writer's identification with a particular location, Joan Didion wrote that 'a place belongs forever to whoever claims it hardest, remembers it most obsessively, wrenches it from itself, shapes it, renders it, loves it so radically that he remakes it in his image'.[28] While there have been many Irish artists, like Joyce, whose relationship with their native land was energetic and thorough-going (even from a distance), the Irish architecture of this century has had a far less active engagement with place. Perhaps this is why the independent Ireland has only rarely defined itself by its architecture.

12 Vincent Kelly
Hospital at Nenagh, 1932-6

13 Michael Scott
Portlaoise Hospital, 1933-6

14 J. V. Downes
Hospital at Kilkenny, 1935; ground-floor plan

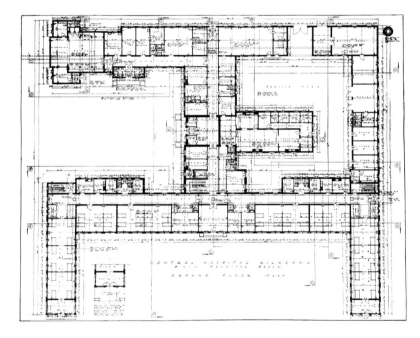

15 Vincent Kelly
Hospital at Cashel, County Tipperary,
completed 1937; ground-floor plan

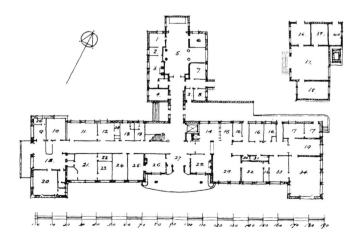

Notes

1   E. J. Hobsbawm, 'Introduction', in idem and Terence Ranger (eds.), *The Invention of Tradition* (London, 1992), p. 1.
2   Clifford Geertz, 'After the Revolution: The Fate of Nationalism in the New States', in idem, *The Interpretation of Cultures* (London, 1975), p. 234. See Terence Brown, *Ireland: A Social and Cultural History* (London, 1981), pp. 181-2, for an application of Geertz's ideas to the Irish situation.
3   Joseph J. Lee, *Ireland 1912-1985: Politics and Society* (Cambridge, 1989), p. 163.
4   Brian P. Kennedy, 'The Irish Free State 1922-49: A Visual Perspective', in idem and Raymond Gillespie (eds.), *Ireland: Art into History* (Dublin, 1994), p. 147.
5   Arthur Griffith (1871-1922) stressed the necessity of economic self-sufficiency, especially in *The Resurrection of Hungary: A Parallel for Ireland* (1904). Denis Patrick Moran (1872-1936) advocated a thorough political, social and economic nationalism in the *Leader*, which he founded in 1900, and later in *The Philosophy of Irish Ireland* (Dublin, 1905).
6   Quoted in Joseph J. Lee, *The Modernisation of Irish Society, 1848-1918* (Dublin, 1973), p. 147. See also D. P. Moran, *Irish Ireland* (Dublin, 1905), passim.
7   William Butler Yeats, *Autobiographies* (London, 1955), p. 493.
8   Edward Said, *Culture and Imperialism* (London, 1993), p. 271.
9   Quoted in Maurice Manning and Moore McDowell, *Electricity Supply in Ireland: The History of the E.S.B.* (Dublin, 1984), p. 40.
10 Editorial in the *Financial Times*, 8 Dec. 1928.
11 Kenneth Frampton, *Modern Architecture: A Critical History* (London, 1985; first published 1980), p. 111.
12 Ibid.
13 The destruction caused by the Civil War necessitated a great deal of reconstruction work, which further mitigated against new building.
14 Aldo Rossi, *The Architecture of The City* (Cambridge, Mass., 1982), p. 93.
15 Lee (note 3), p. 204.
16 M. Moynihan (ed.), *Speeches and Statements by Eamon de Valera 1917-73* (Dublin and New York, 1980), p. 466.
17 J. O'Sheehan and E. deBarra, *Ireland's Hospitals 1930-1955* (Dublin, 1956), p. 24.
18 The building was highly praised by the Minister for Local Government and Public Health, Sean T. O'Kelly, in an address to the Royal Institute of Architects of Ireland in 1933. See Sean Rothery, *Ireland and the New Architecture 1900-1940* (Dublin, 1991) pp. 144-5.
19 Moran, *The Philosophy of Irish Ireland* (note 5), p. 45.
20 Adolf Loos, 'Ornament and Crime', in Ulrich Conrads (ed.), *Programmes and Manifestoes on 20th Century Architecture* (London, 1970), p. 20.
21 Colin Rowe has described how the architects of the early twentieth century saw themselves as the agents of a spiritual renewal after a nineteenth-century fall from grace. See Colin Rowe, *The Architecture of Good Intentions* (London, 1994), pp. 30-43.
22 This sort of double-think is exemplified by de Valera's enthusiastic participation in the League of Nations, while pursuing an isolationist economic policy.
23 See, for example, John O'Gorman's article on the MARS Group exhibition in London, in *Irish Builder and Engineer*, 22 Jan. 1938.
24 See, for example, reviews of hospitals in Kilkenny and Carlow in *Irish Builder and Engineer*, 6 Mar. and 7 Aug. 1937.
25 Similarly, J. M. Synge brought all his Parisian sophistication to bear on the Aran Islands in *The Playboy of The Western World*. See Declan Kiberd's discussion of Synge in *Inventing Ireland: The Literature of the Modern Nation* (London, 1995), pp. 166-89.
26 Joyce wanted to remake the English language primarily because he saw it as inadequate to the expression of his ideas, or to a description of Ireland. 'My soul frets in the shadow of his language', says Stephen in *A Portrait of the Artist as a Young Man*.
27 Richard Ellmann (ed.), *Letters of James Joyce*, vol. I (London, 1966), p. 63.
28 Quoted by Patrick Sheehan, director of the Yeats International Summer School, in his outgoing address; see *The Irish Times*, 10 Aug. 1993.

Buildings

PAUL LARMOUR (P.L.),
ORLA MURPHY (O.M.),
JOHN OLLEY (J.O.),
SHANE O'TOOLE (S.O.)
SIMON WALKER (S.W.)

View of the ward roofs

Royal Victoria Hospital

Grosvenor Road, Belfast 1900–3

WILLIAM HENMAN / THOMAS COOPER

Designed in 1899 by the Birmingham architects Henman and Cooper, the Royal Victoria Hospital was the culmination of their efforts from the mid-1890s to modernise hospital design in the light of advances in both antiseptic treatment in surgery and the successful application of 'Plenum' ventilation. The architectural language was conventional, being a free treatment of English Renaissance in red brick with Portland stone dressings; the building's novelty lay in its layout and technology.

Departing from the long-established 'pavilion'-type plan, the architects placed the wards compactly side by side, on one level, wall to wall, without intervening open spaces, lighted from the ends and by continuous lantern or clerestory windows. Free access to sun and air, one of the usual prerequisites of a hospital layout, was ignored in this scheme. Fresh air was supplied throughout on the Plenum principle, through ducts in the basement. Air coming into the fan house was cleansed by passing through vertical screens of coconut fibre ropes, down which water from sprinkler pipes was poured to remove soot, dust and other impurities. Then the air, warmed in cold weather by a series of heating coils, was forced on into the main duct by two powerful fans or propellers, each ten feet in diameter, manufactured by the Sirocco Works in Belfast. The whole atmosphere in the hospital was changed at regular intervals to keep it perfectly fresh throughout day and night without the need for opening windows.

The innovative design of the Royal represented a revolution in hospital layout, but it has also another claim to fame: humidity control, practised there at an early stage, would appear to make it the first major building in the world to have been fully air-conditioned for human comfort.
P.L.

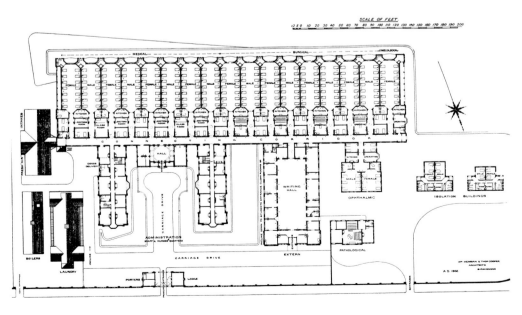

Ground-floor plan

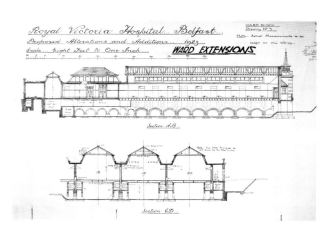

Longitudinal- and cross-sections, including
the extensions of 1923

View from the south

The wash-house

View from the south-west

One of the wards

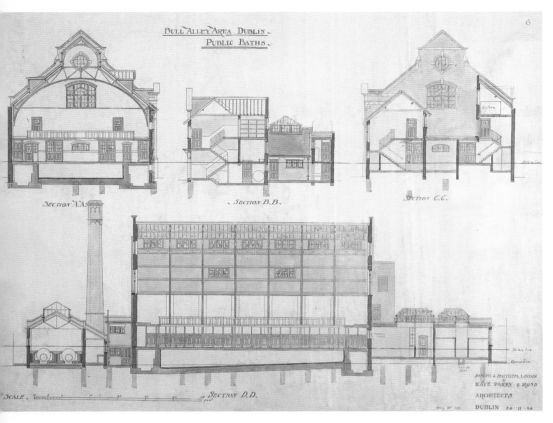

Sections through the Bath Building

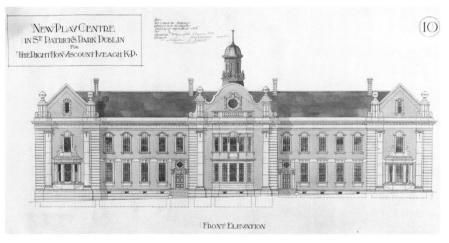

Elevation of the Play Centre

Interior of the Bath Building

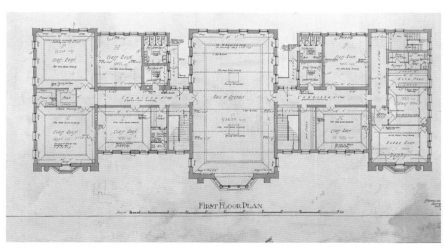

First-floor plan of the Play Centre

The Iveagh-Buildings

Dublin 1900–15

McDONELL AND RIED/JOSEPH AND
SMITHEM/KAYE PARRY AND ROSS

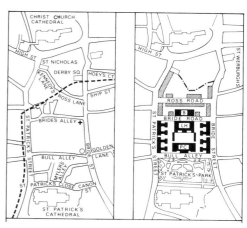

Edward Cecil Guinness, later 1st Earl of Iveagh, founded the Iveagh Trust for 'the amelioration of the condition of the poorer of the working classes' in London and Dublin. In Dublin the Trust created an urban project that aimed to improve the physical and social fabric of the city in the vicinity of one of Dublin's Protestant cathedrals. The ordered collection of new buildings replaced a labyrinthine tangle of streets and courts of tenements. The Guinness dynasty had already restored St Patrick's Cathedral and, more recently, had created a park adjacent to the cathedral, to give the monument more prominence and provide a lung in the city. The latest urban project then stretched from the park northwards to the sister cathedral of Christ Church. The new community of buildings included apartment housing, some of which contained shops on the ground-floor street frontage, a hostel for single home-less men and two recreational buildings, the swimming baths and the Play Centre. The latter was the focus of instructive and improving leisure: it contained class-rooms, a gymnasium and a concert hall.

The architecture of the Iveagh neighbourhood ranged from Edwardian Baroque in the facade of the Play Centre to the freer flowing Art Nouveau that emerged from the Arts and Crafts movement for the Bath Building. Red brick forms the substance of the elevations; it is enriched modestly with pink artificial stone on the Hostel Building, with sandstone and granite on the Bath Building, and, most lavishly and rather pompously, with heavy architectural details in Portland stone on the Play Centre. The facade of the Play Centre was the grandest and fronted on to St Patrick's Park. Two London firms worked on the complex in association with the Dublin practice of Kaye, Parry and Ross.
J.O.

Street facade of the Bath Building

Aerial view

93

Guinness Store House

Market Street, Dublin   1903–4

A. H. HIGNETT

The Market Street Store House was probably designed in the office of the Guinness Brewery's engineer under the supervision of A. H. Hignett, but with some of the steelwork design carried out by the London-based Sir William Arrol. The exterior, in its fortress-like form and detailing, with Victorian Romanesque articulation of the bays and openings and capped with a machi-colated cornice, echoes the Ruskinian 'warehouse' style as filtered through the influence of Chicago and H.H. Richardson. However, this forty-metres-high, styled brick edifice concealed the building's real struc-ture – a steel frame, celebrated on the interior in a Piranesi-like essay in metal. The columns and girder beams of composite bolted construction supported, high above, massive water tanks, which may have served fire protection purposes as well as supplying the fermentation processes which the building housed.

Large uninterrupted floor areas afforded by the approximately ten-metre structural grid allowed for a changing layout of tanks, vats and piping. At the lower level concrete jack-arches supported the floors, where-as above it was steel plates between tertiary structural elements. Deep cruciform galleried lightwells cut through the floors and, together with walls of white glazed bricks, gave this deep-plan building a bright interior.

J.O.

View during construction

General view

Interior view looking along one arm of the cruciform top-lit galleried spaces towards the open-work steel stairs and cage elevators

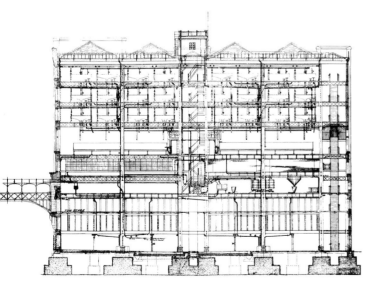

East-west section

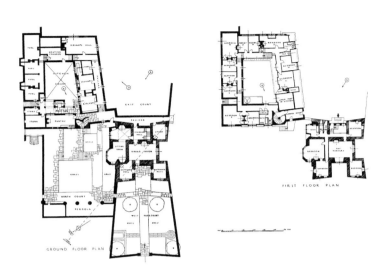

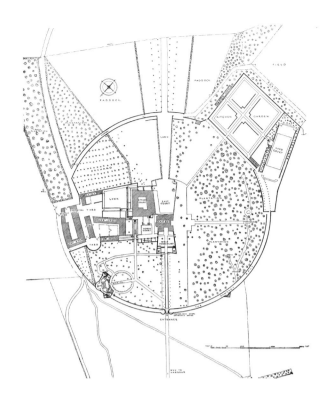

Ground- and first-floor plans

Site plan

View from the sitting room into the east bastion

Aerial photograph of Lambay Island

Lambay Castle

Lambay Island 1905–12

EDWIN LUTYENS

Lambay Castle is an example of the organic evolution of a building and its physical and social context. When Edwin Lutyens was invited to Lambay Island by Cecil Baring in 1905, he found a dilapidated castle and outbuildings that had accrued over four centuries. The brief called for the solution to three problems. Firstly, Baring did not want the proposed extension to detract from the form of the original castle, which had always been the island's historical focal point. Secondly, there was a need to use the topography of the island to create shelter from the easterly winds. Finally, an overall strategy for the site plan was required to unify the existing scattered outbuildings and farmhouse.

In two simple moves, Lutyens solved these problems and created an island oasis for the Baring family. The first move was the design of an extension wing, housing services, kitchens and bedroom. The wing tucks into the contours of the land rising up behind the castle, allowing the emphasis to remain on the older building while producing four sheltered courtyards of individual character. The site plan with its adherence to what is, at first sight, a rigid sense of geometry unites all the buildings within a circular rampart wall. On closer examination, this wall is used subtly to bring together buildings of varying periods, scales and quality into a coherent unit. Stone from the island was used as the main building material, connecting the physicality of building and the land.

On Lambay, Lutyens, through the confident design of new work combined with sensitive remodelling of the old, took on the language and tradition of place and applied his own grammar to it. The richness comes from the reinterpretation of tradition, a deference to the past and aspiration for the future. Above all, Lambay is a cohesive union between man and landscape.
O.M.

North courtyard

View through the circular rampart towards the castle

Mizen Head Footbridge

County Cork
completed 1910
RIDLEY/CRAMMELL

The bridge shortly before completion, 1909

Completed in 1910 on a dramatic site in the south-west extremity of Ireland, the Mizen Head Footbridge was built to give access to the Irish Lights fog-signal station on Cloghnane Island. Spanning fifty-two metres over the ravine with the Atlantic swell forty-two metres beneath, it was at the time the longest-span reinforced concrete bridge in Ireland and Britain. The construction process involved the fabrication on site of two pre-cast concrete ribs made up in sections. These were then built out from the abutments, held in place with the assistance of an aerial ropeway and temporary support of wire ropes, while the remainder of the bridge was cast *in situ* in forms supported by the completed ribs. Owing to the severe weather conditions on this exposed site, the construction was greatly delayed during the winter of 1908–9.
J.O.

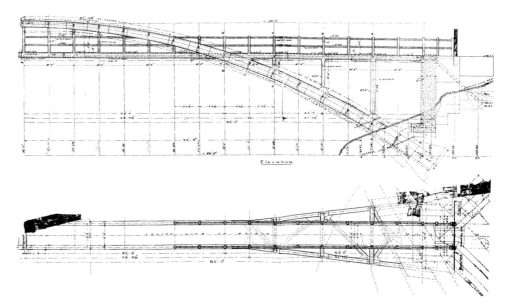

Half constructional section and plan

The bridge today

Aerial view at completion in 1910

West facade

Honan Hostel Chapel

University College, Cork 1915–16

JAMES McMULLEN

Standing in the grounds of University College in Cork, the Honan Hostel Chapel, a fairly restrained example of Irish Romanesque revivalism built of Cork limestone, was the conception of Sir John Robert O'Connell, legal trustee of the Honan family bequest. It was he who determined that the chapel should not only be built in a native style, but also have all its furnishings designed for it as part of a thought-out scheme, in order to make it an embodiment of the best Irish craftsmanship.

All the work, except for the mosaic floor and *opus sectile* Stations of the Cross, was carried out by artists and craft workers from Dublin and Cork. Henry Emery and his apprentices from the Cork Technical School carved the heads of Munster saints around the west doorway, while Oliver Sheppard carved the statue of St Finn Barr placed over it. Professor William A. Scott provided designs for the wrought-iron work made by McLoughlin's of Dublin and also for the silver gilt mon-

strance, sanctuary lamp, candlesticks and other altar plate, which were executed by the firm of Edmond Johnson. The Dun Emer Guild designed and made the sanctuary carpets, the embroidered banner and altar frontal, and the tapestry dossal, while the embroidered vestments were designed and made in the workshops of Egan and Sons. The Celtic ornamental style of most of these furnishings was taken up in the illuminated altar cards by Joseph Tierney and in the tooled missal bindings by Eleanor Kelly. Oswald Reeves designed and made the enamelled tabernacle door. The brilliant stained glass, depicting mainly Irish saints, was the work of Harry Clarke and of the Tower of Glass studio.

The unity of the interior scheme is rare, and all the furnishings and fittings together, despite some differences in style, combine to create a unique record of the best Irish ecclesiastical art of the time.
P.L.

Ground plan

View down the nave with the *River of Life* floor mosaic leading to the altar

Altar and tabernacle

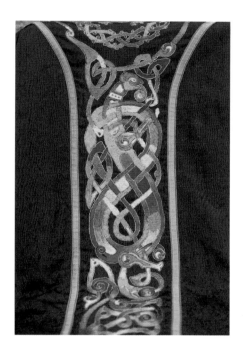

Sanctuary lamp
designed by William A. Scott

Detail of a vestment
designed and produced by
Egan and Sons

Carved oak pews

Stained-glass window of St Gobnait by Harry Clarke

'Dallas'

Malone Road, Belfast 1911–12

CHARLES F. A. VOYSEY

Garden facade

This is a comparatively late work by Charles Voysey of London, his last completed domestic commission and his only building in Ireland. How a major figure of the English Arts and Crafts movement was commissioned to design the house is not recorded, but it may have come about through his brother, who was a Unitarian minister in Belfast the year the building was commissioned. The client was a local linen merchant, Robert Hetherington of the Broadway Damask Company, and the house was named after his wife's home town in America.

Voysey produced a design for the house in January 1911. By April of that year, this proposal had been revised, the principal change being the omission of the projecting porch and hall. Construction began in July, supervised by the local firm of Young and Mackenzie, and the house was finished in May 1912. It comprises two storeys with an attic tucked under a massive, steeply hipped roof of unbroken pitch, except for a tower-like stairwell to the rear. The plan is a rectangular block with a low projecting service return to the rear.

In its abstract vernacular style, it is a typical Voysey design, displaying such characteristic features as white roughcast walls, full-height corner buttresses, stone-dressed windows with iron casements and leaded lights, wide oak-panelled doors and a green Westmorland slate roof. The interior contains brick arched fireplaces set in plain white walls, black Dutch tile paving over the hall floor and a very fine open-well stair with plain slatted balusters, but it does not appear that the rooms were ever furnished to Voysey's designs. Neither is there any evidence that the original proposal for a formal arrangement of flower beds around a central pergola in the garden was ever carried out.
P.L.

Staircase

Entrance elevation on Malone Road

Plans, sections and elevations
(The British Architectural Library Drawings Collection)

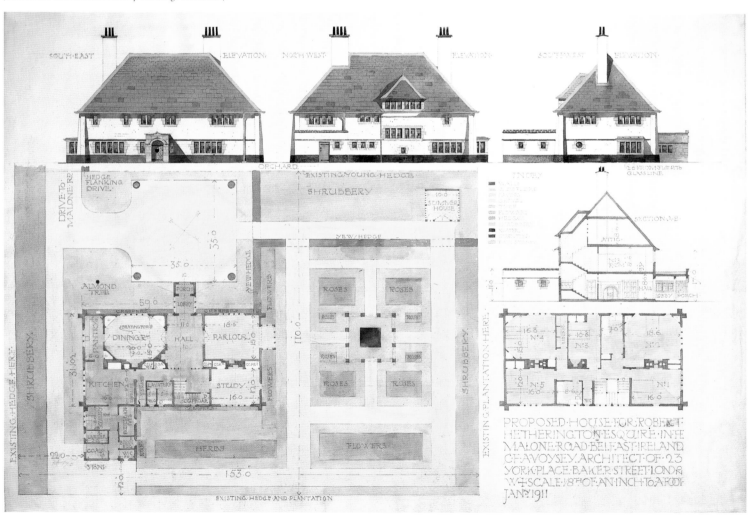

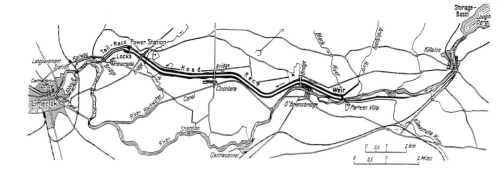

Site plan

Parteen weir

Aerial view

The turbine room in 1929

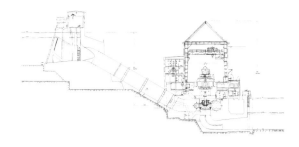

Section through dam, intake, penstocks
and power house

Hydro-Electric Power Station

Ardnacrusha, County Clare 1925-9

SIEMENS SCHUCKERT

Harnessing the waters of the River Shannon at the hydro-electric power station at Ardnacrusha near Limerick, in the west of Ireland, was the largest and one of the first public projects of the newly independent State. It soon became the stuff of heroic myth, interpreted in a series of paintings and drawings by Seán Keating that recorded the construction process. Some images transformed the reality of the works in progress into a romantic landscape setting, whereas others became the stage set for a symbolic tableau representing the modernisation and re-emergence of a nation. Such was the iconic importance of the project that regular trips to visit the station were organised from all over the country.

The project was promoted to the Government by Dr Tommy McLaughlin on his return from working in Germany for Siemens Schuckert. And it was Siemens who were awarded the design and construction contract in 1925. They promptly brought much of the construction machinery and workers from Germany.

The Parteen weir diverted the Shannon into a constructed canal that followed the curving base of the slope of the hills to minimise embankment construction. At the power-station, 12.6 km downstream, the head water is discharged down the 30m-high dam to drive the turbines below. A tailrace canal then takes the water another 2.4 km to rejoin the Shannon just upstream from Limerick.

The 'architecture' of the project is impressive in terms of the landscape, rather than in individual buildings. However, with their elemental forms, the utilitarian components of the scheme, the Parteen weir buildings and those of the dam at Ardnacrusha, demonstrate a progressive modernism. The station itself, on the other hand, bears the imprint of its German origins, with the tall steep-pitched roofs with rows of dormer openings reflecting the pre-First World War industrial work of Peter Behrens.

The project, with its buildings, dams, weirs and bridges, was a celebration of concrete as Ireland's indigenous construction material, which exploited the country's plentiful deposits of limestone for cement and aggregate material.
J.O.

View during construction

View during construction

Parteen weir under construction

Church of Christ the King

Turner's Cross, Cork   1927–31

BARRY BYRNE

Plan

Generally, the patronage of architecture by the Catholic Church in Ireland was fiercely conservative. Forms and styles of the past were restated in order to assert a presence with a precedent. Consequently, the completion of the Church of Christ the King at Turner's Cross in Cork in 1931 was conspicuous in its modernity and was heralded by the *Irish Builder* as the greatest break with convention yet to have occurred.

The American architect of Christ the King, Barry Byrne, had stated that a church should be a practical structure rather than an expression of style. This theoretical stance was validated by the observations of Lewis Mumford: 'Here is an architect who has reconciled tradition and innovation . . . who uses simple and direct methods of construction'. Such sentiments can be found in the letter that accompanied the architect's first sketch design of 1927 for Christ the King.

The plan is a slightly elongated octagon, the main body of which forms a square as it sits beneath the cranked steel trusses spanning the space between reinforced concrete walls and piers. The plaster soffit zigzags to a climax at a linear lantern, which draws a powerful axis of light to the altar. The reredos steps in pyramidal fashion to the same culmination and, behind, the back wall recedes in steps, each marked by a tall slit of light. The facade advances and rises to the central bell tower, beneath which a relief sculpture of Christ the King by John Storrs shows Him spreading His arms to embrace all who enter His church.

With its stepped facade, Christ the King owes a debt to the reinterpretation of Danish tradition that was pursued in expressionist fashion by Peder Vilhelm Jensen-Klint. The church dreams of the exuberance of his Grundtvig Church, Copenhagen (1921-6), but is brought down to earth by Ireland's modest means and Cork's humble suburban site.

J.O.

Interior looking towards the altar

Detail of the front facade

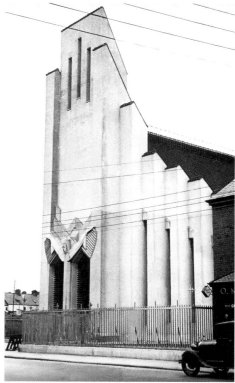

View of the church in the 1930s

Front facade and section

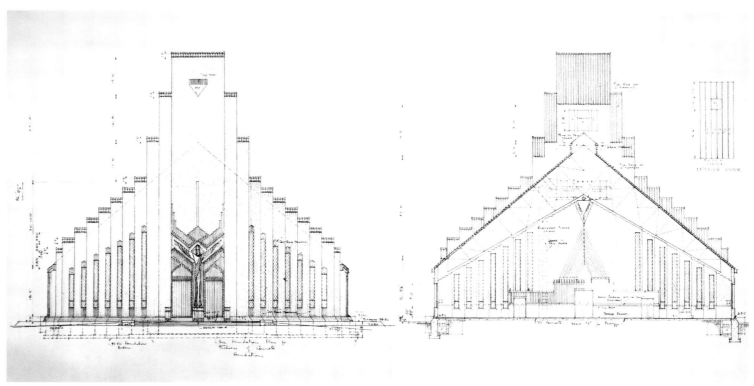

The Regal, Larne, 1935-7, interior view

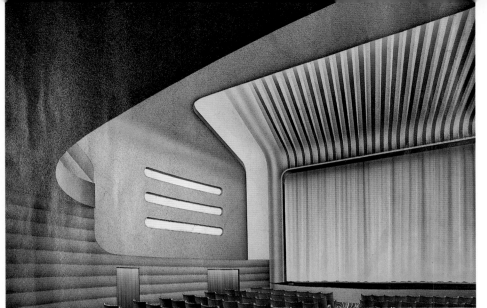

Curzon Cinema, Belfast, 1935-6, interior view

Interior of an unidentified cinema

Curzon Cinema, Belfast

Majestic Cinema, Belfast, 1935-6

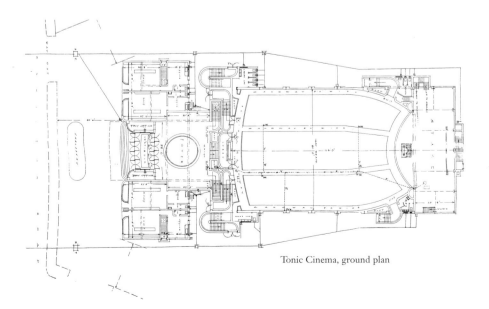

Tonic Cinema, ground plan

The Tonic Cinema

Bangor, County Down 1934
(1992 destroyed by fire)

JOHN McBRIDE NEILL

Tonic Cinema, interior view

Tonic Cinema, perspective view

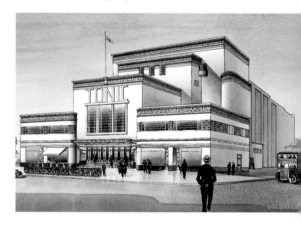

From the great cinema boom of the 1930s, which saw almost every town of any size in Ireland equipped with a building to show sound-track films, one specialist designer emerged: John McBride Neill of Belfast. He was responsible for much of the most characteristic cinema architecture in Ulster, working in an overtly modern or 'modernistic' idiom that moved from Art Deco facades with futuristic details to the more muted language of the International Style.

Neill was particularly successful at carrying through the 'moderne' exterior treatment, which suited the up-to-date image of the new cinemas, to the interiors, where his work was marked by smooth lines and subtle curves, with skilful use of concealed lighting and decoratively treated ventilator and loudspeaker grilles.

The Tonic in Bangor was perhaps the masterpiece of the fifteen or so cinemas that Neill designed; certainly, with a seating capacity of 2,250 it was the largest in

Ulster at the time and the second largest in the whole of Ireland. It was an impressive example of modern architecture, with white cubic masses finished in Snowcrete and streamlined horizontals formed by bands of rustic brick at the top. The design was symmetrical: low wings containing ground-floor shops and first-floor flats flanked a tall entrance block, and the main auditorium rose behind with curved staircase towers and a small balconette for the projectionist to take the air or enjoy a cigarette between reel changes. Inside, the auditorium walls were decorated with sprayed textured metallic paint with bars of colour in futuristic style and the floors were laid with carpeting in grey and black.

The Tonic closed in 1983 and, after standing derelict for nearly a decade, this once magnificent building was finally destroyed by fire in 1992.
P.L.

Tonic Cinema in 1934

Main Entrance

Aerial view

Airport Terminal Building

Collingstown, County Dublin 1937–41

DESMOND FITZGERALD

View from the south-west

The terminal building at Collingswood, County Dublin, was commissioned following the establishment of a national airline in Ireland. Design commenced in 1937, construction began in the summer of 1939 and final fitting out was completed by early 1941. Although the building received little publicity at first owing to the necessity for security in the wartime years, it subsequently became conspicuous among contemporary buildings. It may have owed its originality and modernity to the youth of both the building type and the design team. Within the Office of Public Works the project was the responsibility of a group of young architects headed by Desmond Fitzgerald, himself only a year out of college. This stylish building represented the arrival in Ireland of that spirit of expression and experiment liberated in Britain by the presence there of Erich Mendelsohn and Serge Chermayeff.

The site layout and the form of the terminal building have a simple elegance. The building describes an arc in order to establish the threshold between arrival and departure. The concavity of the landward side gathers the passengers to prepare them for the radiating directions of air travel. It was one of the first airports to establish that functional logic, soon to become the accepted standard, according to which the smallest possible plan serves the maximum number of aircraft lined up along its curving perimeter.

The landward facade is static and earthbound: the symmetry and monumentality of the central element, dominated by a double-height glazed entrance concourse, is contained and anchored by blind piers marking the location of the stairs at either end of the hall. The arms, which curve out from this central pavilion, present a heavy face with a low glazing-to-wall ratio appropriate to the series of service spaces that are accommodated on this side of the plan.

To the airfield, the elevation looks set for flight: generous glazing endows it with lightness and permits enjoyment of the spectacle of the planes departing and landing. A central, roof-top location gives the control room a cockpit appearance. The curving arms of the plan now become wings swept back with tips of open, curving, cantilevered viewing platforms and terraces. All this makes the building much more expressive of flight than the ponderous block-like or tendril airports of today.

J.O.

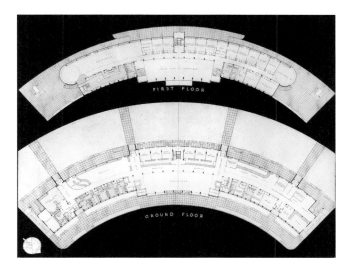
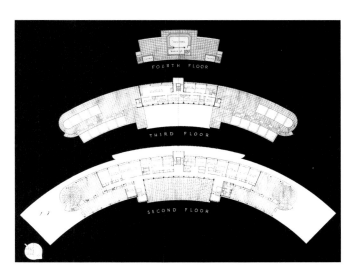

Plans

Three photographs taken during construction, *c.* 1938

View from the south-west

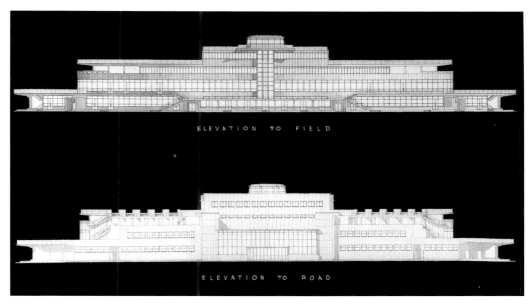

ELEVATION TO FIELD

ELEVATION TO ROAD

Elevations

'Geragh'

Sandycove, County Dublin 1937–8

MICHAEL SCOTT

'Geragh', Michael Scott's own house, was built on a spectacular and prominent site on a hook of rock that encloses the diminutive Scotsman's Bay and Sandycove harbour in the wider sweep of Dublin Bay. This outcrop has been reinforced with a sensuous, curving sea wall and planted with a martello tower. The tower, now the James Joyce Museum, was the fictional location for the opening pages of *Ulysses*. If *Ulysses* is a milestone in European modernism, 'Geragh' has become symbolic of the introduction of modern architecture to Ireland. It gained iconic status partly through the significance and prominence of the site, but more through being the residence of the most extrovert and successful champion of modernism in Ireland.

Not long after Erich Mendelsohn had come to lecture in Dublin, a preliminary sketch sought to emulate the expressive dynamism of the master's graphic flair. The final plan settled to something more static and rigid, but retained the cascading concentric curves that rhyme with the neighbouring lines of enclosure and tower. Scott himself thought of the house as 'a series of descending circles, each one wider than the other. It is my tribute to the tower and to James Joyce.'

The house stood on an undercroft of stores and garage. This formed a plinth, which provides for a semi-circular terrace beyond the grand bay of the living room and for a south-facing terrace adjacent to the dining-room in the angle of the cranked plan. Above, are the bedrooms, where the principal room occupies the bay and makes a terrace on the roof of the sitting room. To the exposed north, the fenestration closes down to a minimum.

The panorama from the bays and terrace is predominantly landward, following the swerve of shore from Sandycove round to Howth Head; in turn, this makes the living spaces of the house easily visible from the shoreline. The conspicuous maritime language of the International Style here gains credence from its context.

J. O.

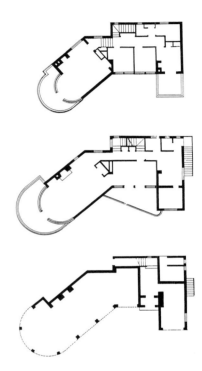

Ground-, first- and second-floor plans

Aerial view from the south east

114

View from the south-west

View from the west

The dining-room, looking towards the terrace

The sitting-room

Site plan

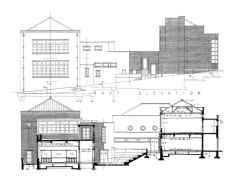

View from the east and north/south section

Botanic Primary School

Agincourt Avenue, Belfast   1936–9

R.S. WILSHERE

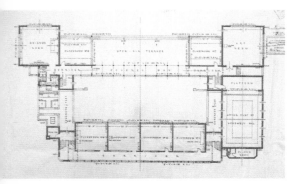

First-floor plan

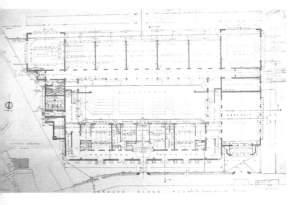

Ground-floor plan

Largely owing to R.S. Wilshere's initiative, school design in Belfast in the 1920s and 1930s was completely transformed: air and light were provided in abundance, while spaciousness and cheerfulness were the dominant characteristics.

In architectural style his schools ranged from neo-Georgian of English origin to a more modernistic idiom derived from German, Scandinavian and Dutch design, with Willem Dudok a particular influence. Most were built in rustic brick with dressings of artificial or reconstituted stone and roofs covered with Roman tiles. Classrooms were frequently finished in varying shades of colour, Wilshere continually experimenting in that field.

Botanic Senior Public Elementary School, as it was titled originally, is a striking example of Wilshere's work. It displays all the usual characteristics of his schools of the 1930s, but in addition it was provided with one unique feature. In the enclosed space between the two main parallel blocks, which in most schools is called a quadrangle or courtyard, Wilshere took advantage of the steep fall of the sloping site to provide five tiers of outdoor seating and create an 'amphitheatre'. It was designed for outdoor classes and as an open-air theatre. The problem posed by the varying levels of the ground and, accordingly, by the blocks that surrounded the amphitheatre was overcome by an ingenious arrangement of the floors and staircases. Another feature of special interest is the terrace at the upper level of the south block, designed to accommodate open-air classes with two flanking classrooms that have two glazed walls and thus provide semi-open-air rooms.

Although there have been later changes to the building, notably the introduction of additional blocks in the amphitheatre, Botanic still remains a striking example of the work of an architect who, in his time, was recognised as having built the first modern schools in Ireland.

P. L.

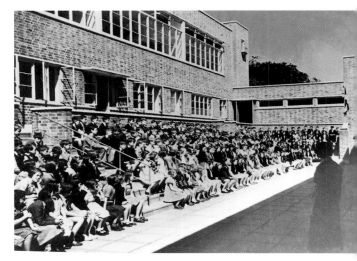

The courtyard auditorium

View from the south-west

'Meander'

Westminster Road, Foxrock, Dublin
1939

ALAN UND MAIRIN HOPE

'Meander', the architects' own house, was built almost contemporaneously with Michael Scott's 'Geragh'. However, in contrast, it pursues an alternative sensibility to that of the heroic abstraction of the International Style. The modernism explored in this building was Scandinavian rather than Mediterranean in origin. In its secluded wooded garden, still a tranquil oasis in the engulfing suburbia south of Dublin, it sought to embody more sensuous experiences of the building and its site than Scott's fashionable statement could offer.

The structure and construction of the house were the result of pragmatism, economical in materials and construction processes. The general construction is of concrete block walls, battened and then clad with cedar boarding on the exterior and lined with butt-jointed plywood sheets on the interior.

'Meander' aimed as much to create the site as to occupy it. The entrance to the plot was through a stone wall boundary and a stand of mature trees. Here, under the shelter of the trees, a shallow entrance court was formed between the house and this northern boundary. The hall and stairs were the only elements originally on this side. The rest of the plan unfurls towards the south and extends the living space onto terraces and into the garden. The house and its garden grew and matured together to make an ensemble appealing more to the senses than to the mind. The approach to detailing and the choice of materials allowed the building to be finished by the family and their friends, giving the house a hand-made, crafted feel and resulting in a warm and tactile environment. J.O.

View from the south-east, looking across the garden

The dining and living space

View from the south-east in 1939

The gallery on the first floor

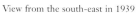

Detail of the south facade

West facade

View from the river

The concourse during construction

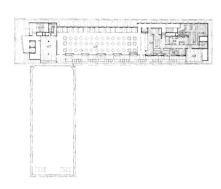

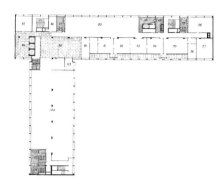

Busáras

Store Street, Dublin 1944–53

MICHAEL SCOTT

Busáras, the Central Bus Station, was begun in 1944, abandoned in 1949, when the Government decided to convert the building into an unemployment exchange, then restarted. The project was shrouded in controversy from its inception. Both Busáras's location, adjacent to the grand eighteenth-century Custom House, and its scale made it a forceful herald of the arrival of modernism in central Dublin. Michael Scott's design team included many young graduates who were later to become prominent in their own right: Patrick Scott, Wilfie Cantwell, Brendan O'Connor, Kevin Fox, Kevin Roche and Robin Walker. Ove Arup, who had set up an office in London after the war, and published articles in Ireland on reinforced concrete construction, was the structural engineer; Jorgen Varming, also from Denmark, was the services engineer. Both set up offices in Dublin that remain to this day.

The project was originally envisaged solely as a bus station but later Coras Iompair Eireann decided to include a new office headquarters in the programme. A double-height hall and concourse protrudes from underneath a six-storey office slab block on the northern part of the site, allowing the free circulation of passengers and buses. Further accommodation was placed in three storeys at right angles to the main block with the bus station concourse in the angle. The two blocks, whose ends are clad in white Portland stone, display a rich diversity of materials, many of which appear now to have a classic 1940s character. The concourse roof construction dispensed with intermediate columns by adopting a system of two-way diagonal beams, intersecting at slender concrete columns positioned at 3m centres along the periphery, whence a 65mm-thick corrugated canopy slab, cast on hardboard shuttering, cantilevers 7m. The air-conditioning plant was designed to be automatically controlled by a compressed air system and a basement vacuum cleaning plant had outlets on all floors.

The design shows many influences, the most prominent being Le Corbusier's Cité de Refuge and Oscar Niemeyer's Ministry of Education in Rio. Even so, Busáras represents many firsts for Ireland, such as double glazing, concrete box-frame construction, automatic air-conditioning and the undulating concrete canopy.
S.W.

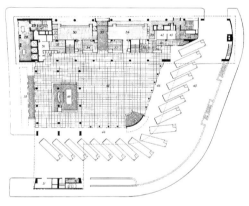

Ground-, third- and sixth-floor plans

View from the staff restaurant

The control room in the concourse

Layout and views of housing at Coill Dubh,
County Kildare

Bord na Mona Housing

The Irish Midlands 1950s

FRANK GIBNEY

The Irish Midlands is a landscape rich in peatlands. These were exploited in the 'Emergency' to provide Ireland with its own indigenous supply of fuel. The turf was cut by hand and thus the sparse population of the area needed to be augmented by outside workers, who had to be accommodated in hostels. After the Second World War, Bord na Mona (the Turf Board) accelerated its development of the bogs for electricity generation and briquette manufacture. Although the process of extraction was now heavily mechanised, the original workers were a valuable asset and in any case were being assimilated into the local community. Thus more than hostels were required. Seven housing schemes were built by Bord na Mona, at Kilcormac, Rochfortbridge, Lanesboro, Cloontuskert, Derraghan, Timahoe and Bracknagh.

Most of the projects depended heavily upon a revised version of the Garden Suburb ideal. In all there was an overriding ambition to establish places with a sense of identity. Various devices were employed: terraces of houses created enclosures, their architectural forms, whether symmetrical, axial or asymmetrical, modulated in order to provide legibility and assert an overall character and create local incident. This was facilitated by the schools, shops and community halls that formed part of the programme of some schemes. Local elements focused on these buildings, which were central to the programme, to generate an unfolding sequence, moving from the entrance to the core of the development. The completeness of the community, and the sense of its identity created, varied with the degree of isolation from, or connections to, existing villages – from Lanesboro in County Longford, where the development of 61 houses engages with the established village, making the existing church spire the axial marker to the central access road, to the largest scheme, at Coill Dubh in County Kildare, with its 160 houses, schools, shops, and so forth creating a totally new village.
J.O.

Layout of housing at Rochfortbridge, County Westmeath

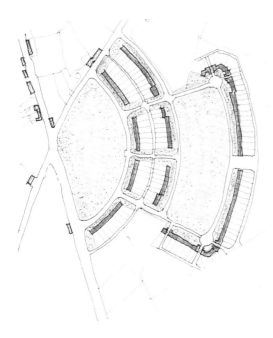

Layout of housing at Kilcormac, County Offaly

Layout of housing at Lanesborough, County Longford

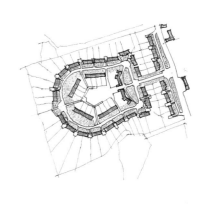

Layout of housing at Cloontuskert, County Roscommon

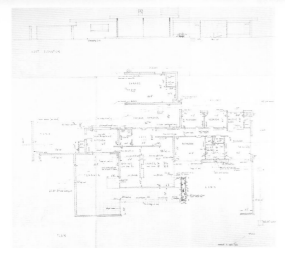

Plan

'Scandia'

Brocklamount Park, Ballymena, County Antrim 1953–6

NOEL CAMPBELL

Approach from the west, showing a wall with a mosaic by Colin Middleton

With its slick form and sophisticated detailing, this luxurious house is probably the best of a series of innovative designs produced by Noel Campbell during the 1950s and early 1960s that broke new ground in domestic architecture in Ulster.

Designed in an uncompromisingly modern style, of international provenance, it is essentially a composition of horizontal and vertical planes, laid out on an asymmetrical plan with a cruciform arrangement of overlapping flat roofs. The materials are varied and comprise rubble stone walling, smooth white-painted render, vertical timber boarding and large areas of glazing. The latter include all-glass walls around the lounge and dining area, detailed with such precision that floor and roof planes can pass from inside to outside without interruption. Superb corner glazing details, unmatched perhaps in any other house in Ireland of the time, accentuate the abstract qualities of the composition, as does the highly polished finish of the terrazzo paving around the all-glass bay.

The view from the house looks out to beautifully landscaped gardens in front and over a large terrace to one side; this originally incorporated a small swimming pool, its enclosing walls still bearing mosaic murals of abstract patterns and female figures by the well-known Ulster artist Colin Middleton. Another Ulster artist, the sculptor James McKendrie, was commissioned to design the large abstract metal sculpture placed near the front of the house.

The architect's inventive approach to design, and the richness of detail, were carried through to the interior. A cascade of water was designed to flow down the polished marble face of a rubble stone chimney breast in the lounge, and the walls were covered with Corbusier wallpaper.

The house has been extended and altered by other hands in recent years, but the changes have largely been sympathetic outside, except for the insertion of a 'porthole' window on the garden front.
P. L.

The enclosed court, once the swimming pool, with mosaic mural by Colin Middleton

Part of the west facade with the sculpture by James McKendrie

Interior view

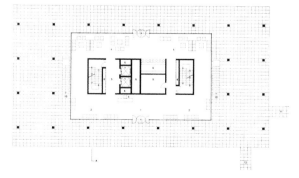

View from the north-east

RTE Administration Building

Donnybrook, Dublin
completed 1967

RONALD TALLON

The Administration Building, completed in 1967, formed part of the Stage 2 development of the Radio Telefís Éireann complex, following on from Tallon's original Television Studios of 1962. In the Administration Building glass and steel enclose a three-storey block over a ground-floor colonnade. The building reads very powerfully within the complex of other buildings, the increased verticality still finely balanced by its horizontal length and by the emphatic horizontal bands at floor levels and the shadow of the recessed ground floor. Yet the facade is not a curtain, nor is it infilled structure – it is a seamless, welded grid in itself comprising flat steel bands at the floors and continuous vertical steel mullions to the outer face, the glass fixed behind the inner face. So although it has a certain depth of section, its effect, when placed over the three-storey structural frame, is a two-dimensional, flattening one.

Grasping the immediacy of the effect of Miesian buildings in an Irish context – small, in a landscaped setting, proportionally sound, well detailed but not over-elaborated – Tallon quickly succeeded in producing a recognisable, easily identifiable style for modern Irish architecture. Typical of this potential, the Administration Building became another element in the composition of the RTE Campus. The relationship between buildings is defined by a series of rectilinear pathways that respects the orthogonality of the site layout.
S.W.

View from the north-west looking along the spine of the RTE complex

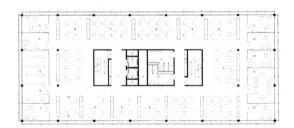

Second-floor plan

Ground-floor plan

The entrance elevation sitting between eighteenth- and nineteenth-century buildings

South facade

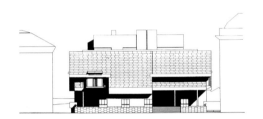

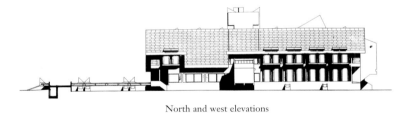

North and west elevations

Ground-floor plan

East facade

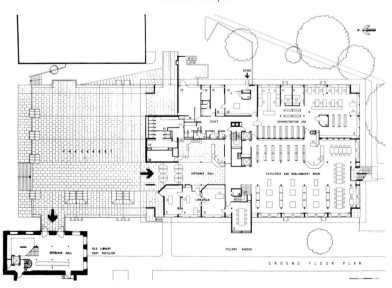

Berkeley Library

Trinity College Dublin   1961–7

AHRENDS BURTON KORALEK

The Berkeley Library was the subject of an architectural competition in 1961. The winning design underwent extensive refashioning to become the superbly built essay in concrete that now takes its place among some of the most distinguished eighteenth- and nineteenth-century buildings of Dublin in the rich architectural ensemble of Trinity College.

The new library pushes a raised terrace into the break between the quadrangular form of the eighteenth-century College buildings and the object like buildings of the nineteenth century. Thus sited, the entrance facade of the new library is framed, to the right, by its neo-classical predecessor with its sublime long room on the first floor and, on the left, by the museum building by Deane and Woodward, which embodies the doctrines of John Ruskin.

The basement plans extend beneath the raised entrance plaza, providing large stack storage for this 'copyright' library. At entrance level you are introduced to administration and catalogue before climbing to the *piano nobile* with its open stacks and reading spaces, many of which occupy the generous curved plate-glass window bays with their framing sheet-bronze ventila-

tors. This first-floor level provides open general and periodicals reading, whereas the second floor is reserved for specialised and postgraduate reading. This upper level is an introverted space where skylights provide the only illumination of the book-lined interior. Beneath the most generous of the skyward openings the space and light cascades down to the floor beneath, and elsewhere natural illumination trickles down the 'light tubes' to supplement lumen levels on the lower floor. To add to the bright feel of the interiors, extensive use of *in situ*, fair-faced concrete work employs white cement and the lightest coloured local sand. The exterior also has exposed *in situ* concrete, but in places is wrapped around with Wicklow granite in homage to its monumental neighbours.

This building established the architects' reputation and demonstrated a youthful exuberance and enthusiasm for the plastic potential of concrete, even though criticism censured the 'tendency to grasp every opportunity of dramatic and plastic expression in such secondary elements as light shafts, reading desks, book stacks, viewing windows and ventilation outlets'.

J.O.

Conceptual sketch

Reading room

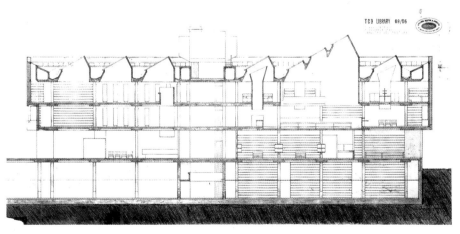

Section

Aerial view

Exterior view

Interior of the rotunda

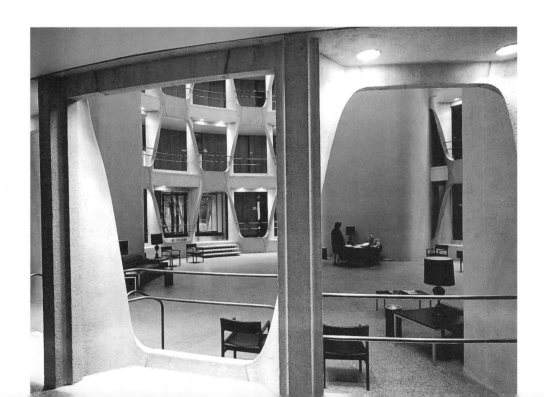

American Embassy

Elgin Road, Dublin 1962–4

JOHN JOHANSEN

Designed by the American John Johansen, his country's embassy in Dublin sits on an acute-angled site at a prominent road junction and is surrounded by large nineteenth-century villas. Prompted partly by the nature and location of the site, the building took a prominent rotunda form. Although Celtic Early Christian round towers are often cited as the inspiration for its form, the edifice, with its squat proportions and encircling moat, bears far closer affinity with the Martello towers that were built around Ireland's coastline in response to the Napoleonic threat.

An annular plan on three storeys encloses a central rotunda with galleried spaces that give access to the rooms at each level. A basement houses service plant, a semi-basement and lunchroom, which look into a moat that is bridged at two points to give access to the ground floor. At this level rooms for consular activities surround the 16m-diameter rotunda, which becomes a grand galleried reception room lit by a continuous band of clerestory glazing. This space's

theatrical potential is attenuated by the intrusive bulk of three vertical circulation towers.

The structure is an assembly of pre-cast concrete elements with double curved forms that compose the three storeys of the exterior elevation and are repeated in the interior galleried facade. The complex curving and twisted pre-cast elements were a major fabrication and constructional challenge, thought to be beyond the expertise and experience of the Irish or British building industries. The 1,600 individual pre-cast members were made by Kampen of the Netherlands and shipped to Dublin from Rotterdam.

Initially, most of the sharp corner site was given over to a paved public terrace dotted with trees, from which the building was separated by the planted moat. Today, in the age of international terrorism, this rather romantic notion of security has been rendered redundant. The site has now been reconfigured by railings and other definers of territory.
J. O.

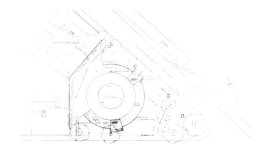

Lageplan

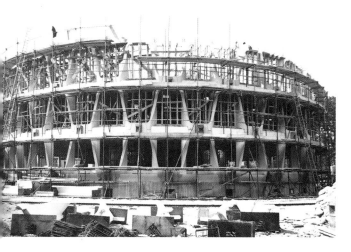

During construction, 1963

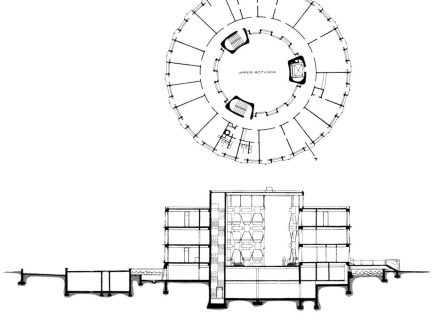

Second-floor plan, section

The monastery church, looking towards the altar

Our Lady of Bethlehem Abbey

Portglenone, County Antrim
1962–71

PADRAIG MURRAY

This large, three-storeyed and multi-gabled monastic complex by the banks of the River Bann was built for the Cistercian order in the grounds of an eighteenth-century house. It is an impressive example of modern architecture, intended to accommodate an anticipated community of over seventy monks; numbers, however, have never exceeded thirty.

Although uncompromisingly modern in style, it was arranged in a traditional layout, with conjoined blocks grouped around a central landscaped cloister garth. The abbey church, which occupies the north side, with a seven-stage open-work concrete campanile to the east, dominates the view of the complex from the public area. The church consists of a long, timber-roofed, aisleless nave lit by clerestory windows, with a high cage-like sanctuary from which projects a 'public church', or chapel, in a transeptal position. Standing on pilotis and reached from below, this is arranged to overlook the high altar but not the monks' choir.

Construction throughout the complex is of reinforced concrete and grey concrete brick, with hyperbolic paraboloid roofs of timber covered with copper. Unusually, the roofs are arranged in groups of four to each square bay, so that they appear as a series of shallow gables along the eaves line. The architectural idiom of grid-like exposed frames with closely spaced mullions is used throughout, and the severely rectilinear character of the main elevations is softened only by the encroachment of ivy along the west elevation of the monastery.

Inside, finishes are mainly plain, with some left as board-marked concrete. The only decorative effects are on floors, in the form of patterned parquet on landings or PVC tiles in the cloisters, where the monks stipulated coloured symbols, such as the shamrock and St Brigid's Cross. Otherwise, the Cistercian ethos prevails and an appropriately austere appearance is maintained throughout.
P.L.

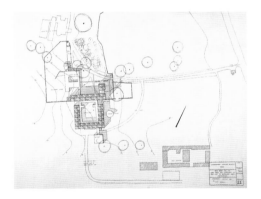

Site plan

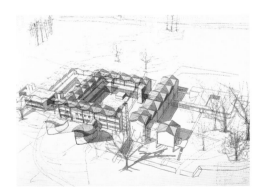

Project drawing

View from the north, showing the chapel

The cloister

View from the south-west

First-floor plan

View along the east facade towards the bell tower,
showing the lantern over the church altar

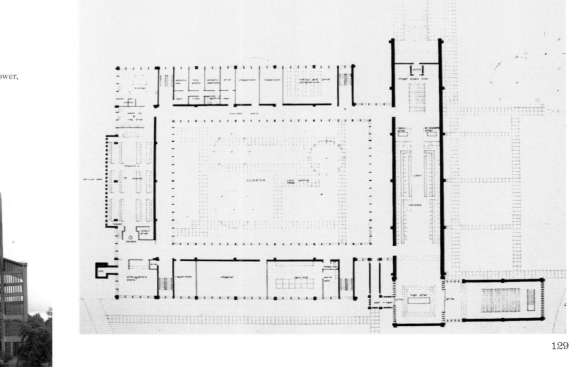

View from the north-west

Carroll's Building

Grand Parade, Dublin 1962–4

ROBINSON KEEFE DEVANE

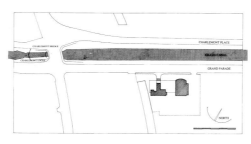

Site plan

Built early in the period in which Ireland's economy was modernised, Carroll's Building (since 1996 the headquarters of the Irish Nationwide Building Society) is immediately distinguished by the rare generosity of spirit that motivated and characterised its development. Occupying a site on the south side of the Grand Canal, the main floors of the building, which houses a bonded warehouse for cigarettes, with offices above, were raised on an encased steel frame, allowing sunlight to penetrate right through to the street and offering a range of facilities for public use on both the open ground floor and the suspended mezzanine. Two thirds of the ground plan was given over to a 'sculpted' formal garden that included pools (now dry), platforms and benches. The recessed mezzanine comprised a reception area, a gallery for paintings, pottery, glassware and other facets of the cultural and artistic life of the country, and an auditorium that became the city's premier venue for public lectures.

These public facilities are not currently in use, but Carroll's Building retains unique value as the best of very few Irish examples of a universal modern building type, 'the building in the air, far from the soil, with gardens stretching beneath'. The cool, abstract elegance of the overall building form, with its 'elongated windows', is heightened by the smaller-scale elements: curved brick wall, garden and glazed entrance bridge. The external materials are few and noble: dry Portland stone, aqueous plate glass in stainless steel frames, soft yellow 5cm brickwork pointed in crushed Portland stone, and ceramic mosaic.
S.O'T.

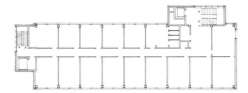

View from the north-east

Ground-, first- and fifth-floor plans

Interior view towards the altar

Church of St Aengus

Burt, County Donegal 1964–5

LIAM McCORMICK

This rural church stands on an open hillside overlooking Lough Swilly in County Donegal, its sculpturally treated, asymmetrical form integrating perfectly with the mountainous setting. The circular stone-built walls of an ancient fort, Grianan of Ailech, on a hilltop above provided the inspiration for the design.

Two circles, one placed tangentially within the other, form the plan, the crescent of space between the walls being used to house the baptistery and subsidiary offices, so that the church appears circular both inside and outside. It is built with a barrel-like squared rubble stone wall on the exterior; inside, the wall consists of concrete blocks with a plaster finish and a steel and timber roof is supported on an inner ring of steel columns. Above a continuous glass clerestory the copper roofing, with up-turned overhang, sweeps up eccentrically to form a conical spire, which contains a lantern light placed directly over the altar. Surrounding the base of the church is a moat with four small circular pools formed of granite cobbles, while the brown brick path leading up to the church is laid in circular patterns. Inside, the shallow steps that encircle the altar and the layout of seating comply with this curvilinear theme.

The work of various artists is a distinctive and pleasing feature of the building. It includes stained glass by Helen Moloney; the crucifix, altar and font by Imogen Stuart; the bronze and enamel tabernacle by Patrick McElroy; candlesticks by Brendan Friel; and a sculptured free-standing wall outside depicting the history of the site in cast concrete by Oisin Kelly. All was skilfully co-ordinated by the architect, whose brilliant initial concept and choice of site combined to produce an outstanding example of modern church architecture that thoroughly deserved the award of the RIAI Triennial Gold Medal in 1971.
P. L.

Detail of the exterior

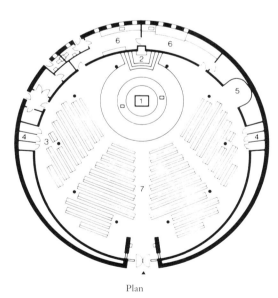

Plan

View from the south-west

131

Carroll's Cigarette Factory

Dundalk 1967–9

RONALD TALLON

View north along the pool towards the entrance bridge

In Carroll's Cigarette Factory, completed in 1969, the industrial programme has been complemented by a machine-like aesthetic to make this the most glamorous of Ronald Tallon's many factory buildings. The best elements of Tallon's work are clearly demonstrated here – a finely drawn form with an elegant skin set in careful landscaping, all controlled by an ordering grid. The complex overlay of differing grids seen at the RTE Campus is replaced here by a single matrix, to allow for the addition of further repetitive units, or cells.

The building consists of thirty-five cells occupying a flat area of four acres on an irregular plan, with one isolated cell, the boiler-house, appearing like the key to the system of construction. Two of the units rise up to two storeys, marking nodal points. A trussed steel space-frame roof stretches across the entire building, sheltering all the services below and supporting a constant standing depth of water above in order to maintain constant humidity levels. Yet the greatest success of the building lies in its external expression. The roof truss can be seen clearly behind a continuous band of dark-tinted glazing, either as the top section of a full-height glazed wall with dark-patinated steel framing or as a clerestory above infill silver-grey brick panels. The panels themselves are further delineated by subtle expansion joints that correspond to the increments of the truss above, emphasising the two-dimensional nature of cladding.

The appearance of the building in the landscape is bold and striking, encompassing a mysterious, dark presence in the morning mist, a magical reflection in the pool at the entrance, with its giant three-fingered chrome sculpture by Gerda Frommel, and a gleaming sharpness on sunny days, when the building's pure good looks exude a happy serenity.
S.W.

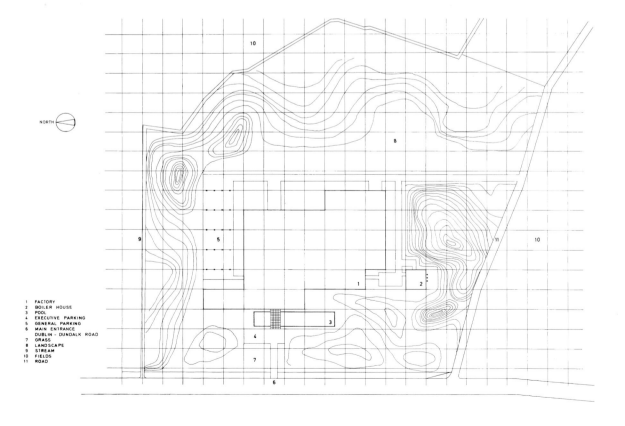

NORTH

1 FACTORY
2 BOILER HOUSE
3 POOL
4 EXECUTIVE PARKING
5 GENERAL PARKING
6 MAIN ENTRANCE
7 DUBLIN - DUNDALK ROAD
8 GRASS
8 LANDSCAPE
9 STREAM
10 FIELDS
11 ROAD

Site plan

View from the north-west

Corner detail

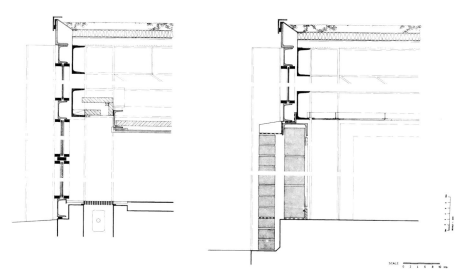

Wall sections

Entrance foyer

Ground-floor plan

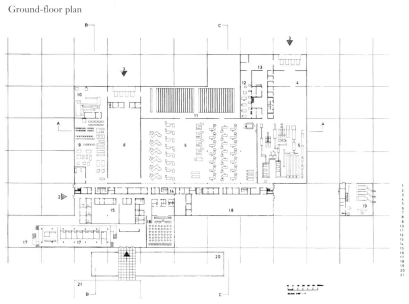

1 PUBLIC ENTRANCE
2 STAFF ENTRANCE
3 LOADING
4 TOBACCO STORE
5 TOBACCO PROCESS
6 CIGARETTE MAKING
7 CIGARETTE PACKING
8 DESPATCH STORE
9 PIPE TOBACCO MAKING
10 PIPE TOBACCO PROCESS
11 MATERIAL STORE
12 TOBACCO DUST FILTER
13 OFFAL
14 FACTORY DEPT OFFICE
15 FACTORY STAFF LOCKERS
16 CANTEEN
17 ADMINISTRATION
18 WORKSHOPS
19 BOILER HOUSE
20 POOL
21 EXECUTIVE CAR PARK

133

O'Flaherty House

Kinsale, County Cork   1967

ROBIN WALKER

The O'Flaherty House explores the Miesian idiom in concrete in an attempt to give clarity to the idea of structure. A single-storey square plan is raised on eight piers, set back from the corners in a 1:4:1 relationship to optimise the distribution of bending moment. The visual depths of roof and floor slabs are in proportion to their respective loadings. The columns pass outside the plan and support the floor with triangular concrete fillets, added to transfer the load from the chamfered edge of the underside of the waffle slab; at the roof slab, a primitive capital is formed as the column spreads out to collect the loads.

The single space occupying the plan is glazed on all four sides with large sliding glass panels, opening the interior to the landscape and affording spectacular views of the coast and Kinsale. Beneath the windows, a concrete upstand beam forms a continuous window seat. Respective corners of the plan contain living, dining,

bedroom and study spaces, with two asymmetrically positioned pieces separating the bedroom and study from the rest – a plywood core containing bathroom and kitchen, and a masonry wall containing storage space and fireplace.

The siting of the building on the side of a slope, rather than on the nearest piece of flat ground, shows sensitivity to the lateral sweep of the countryside. The purity of the form is unaffected – floating just above the ground, it is joined to the site only by a small foot-bridge on the rear side. The tiny guest bedroom structure built near the main house is cut into the hillside, revealing only the glass front and the small paved forecourt between the two ends of the retaining walls emerging from the ground. The integration of such a radically modern building into the landscape provides a welcome alternative to the pastiche holiday bungalows that have proved so destructive to the Irish landscape. J.O., S.W.

Dining area with view across the bay

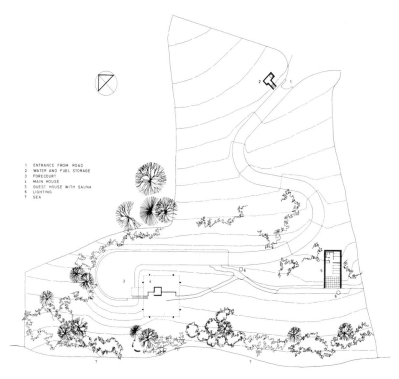

1 ENTRANCE FROM ROAD
2 WATER AND FUEL STORAGE
3 FORECOURT
4 MAIN HOUSE
5 GUEST HOUSE WITH SAUNA
6 LIGHTING
7 SEA

Site plan with basement plan

View from the south-east

Detail of concrete construction

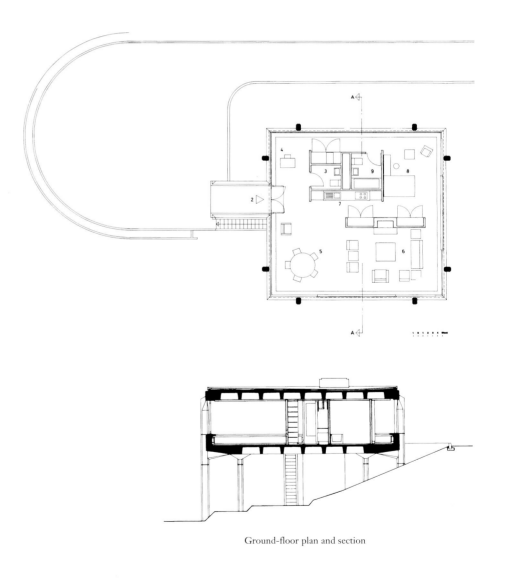

Ground-floor plan and section

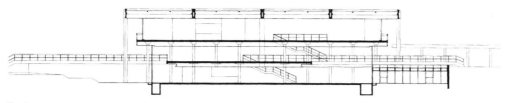

Section

Restaurant Building

University College Dublin 1967–70

ROBIN WALKER

The Restaurant Building at UCD was completed in 1970 and awarded the RIAI Toenail Gold Medal. It resembles, and doubtless was influenced by, Mies van der Rohe's New National Gallery in Berlin, which had been finished just two years before. However, instead of burying the programme in a basement plinth, leaving a clear field of outwardly radiating space on top and surmounting the whole with a structurally pure canopy, the Restaurant adopts a more complex and sensitive attitude to the issue of section, roof and horizontal space. The section is brought alive by the interaction of the building both above and below the naturally undulating ground level and by the development of basement courtyard spaces around the building that form an almost continuous moat.

Three individually supported concrete slabs telescope together. The ground floor, or table, sitting on slender legs in the centre of the basement court, is connected to the surrounding lawns by bridges across the moat and to a double-height, glass-enclosed volume created by the projection of the mezzanine level over-

head. This second table, in turn, becomes a glass-enclosed *piano nobile* beneath the projecting roof canopy.

The slabs are trimmed at the edges with prestressed concrete beams, articulated almost as trusses with recessed panels. These beams have a blonde, acid-etched finish that looks today almost as it did nearly thirty years ago. They stand proud of the continuous glazing, which is set in black steel frames whose proportions emphasise the uncompromising horizontality of the whole building.

Inside, the delicate articulation of structural increments continues in the plywood panelling that surrounds the central service core. This core, containing all the toilets, kitchens and service counters, is positioned to one side of the central column in plan, the corresponding space on the other side being cut through to allow two cascading staircases to connect all levels.

S.W.

Detail of north-east elevation

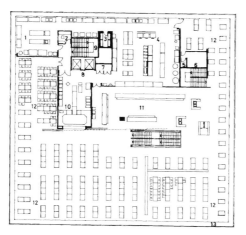

First-floor plan

Detail of south-west elevation

View from the north

Ground-floor plan

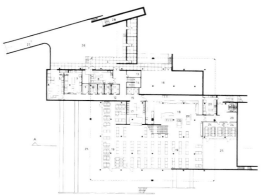

Mezzanine plan

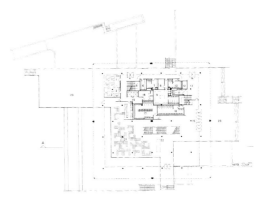

View from the south-west

Detail of north wall

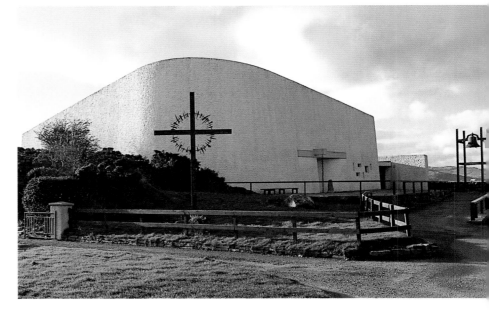

View from the east

View from the interior towards the west

St Michael's Church

Creeslough, County Donegal 1970-1

LIAM McCORMICK

St Michael's Roman Catholic Church stands on a ridge outside the village of Creeslough in a landscape dominated by Muckish Mountain, whose distinctive profile it echoes. The church is laid out on a fanshaped plan with immensely thick walls, built of concrete blocks finished with white-painted roughcast, which comprise two skins, the outer one battered, the inner one ver-tical. Diaphragm walls connect the two skins at intervals and, in the deep cavity thus formed, are placed the steel columns that support the roof trusses.

The roof itself is suppressed, allowing the walls to dominate. To the front they present a strong, battered, almost solid face with very small windows and a deep-set entrance. Away from the road, a carefully positioned full-height window in the sweep of the wall allows a limited view over rough pastures to the mountain beyond.

Ingeniously housed in the space between the two walls at the front are a sacrament chapel and a baptistery, both with curved ends and lit from above. A curvilinear theme is present inside, too: curved pews with curved lighting units above them focus attention on the rectangular altar, which stands on two circular platforms and is lit by a circular rooflight. In an interior otherwise pervaded by rural simplicity, stained glass in the chapel and various altar furnishings add effective notes of brilliant colour, while the clever use of flowing water serves a symbolic function in the baptistery. The various art-works were contributed by Helen Moloney, Veronica Rowe, John Behan and Ruth Brandt.

Outside, the sensitive landscaping, combined with such restrained adjuncts as a painted steel-frame bell tower and steel cross, provide an effective setting and foil for the sculptural form of the building.
P .L.

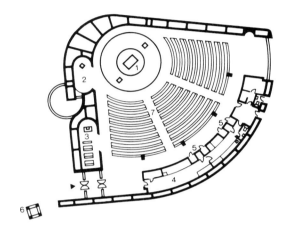

Plan

Stained glass windows

second floor level

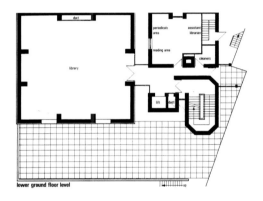

upper ground floor level

lower ground floor level

Plans

Institute of Advanced Studies

Burlington Road, Dublin 1969–71

SAM STEPHENSON

Essentially an annexe accommodating the School of Theoretical Physics, the new element sits in the garden at the side of the existing Institute. The building is conceived as two distinct elements - a tall cluster of enclosed load-bearing brick towers, containing the stairs, lift and ancillary 'servant' spaces, and an open raised cube, framed in reinforced concrete, providing the bulk of the accommodation, including the larger spaces of the library and conference room. The library is located at the lower ground-floor level, shaded from direct sunlight. The main entrance is at upper ground-floor level, approached by a flight of steps, following the pattern established by the older houses on the road. The upper floors are private and contain study rooms for professors and scholars. The design of the windows distinguishes between the functions of viewing and ventilation.

Owing not a little to the laboratory towers of Louis Kahn's Richards Medical Research Building in Philadelphia, the structure of the Institute of Advanced Studies (also a building for scientists) has eight perimeter columns placed at points one third and two thirds along each side. The *in situ* columns support the floors and roof, which are a series of coffered concrete trays whose exposed soffits form the ceilings.
S.O'T.

View from the north

General view from the north-west

Science Laboratories, St Columba's School

Rathfarnham, Dublin 1971

ROBIN WALKER

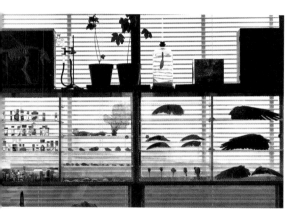

View through the glass display cabinet
in the biology laboratory

St Columba's, a purpose-built teaching laboratory building, consists of a steel space-frame lattice truss roof, with some of the load being taken in the centre of the plan by block walls. The rest of the structural support becomes integrated in the construction of a highly original double-skin glass wall that stretches round the entire perimeter. This upper, single-storey volume sits on a lower exposed concrete structure consisting of a small central core and a deep perimeter beam elevated on piers, which allow the undulating garden site to flow through under the building. The skin, or glass curtain, sits on top of, and protrudes over, this beam, enclosing and following the edge of the L-shaped plan, stepping out at the inside corner where the L intersects with the core and marks the entrance at the lower level.

The construction of the skin comprises an inner glass wall incorporating minimally sized steel T-stanchions, which support the space-frame, and an outer glass wall free of structure, divided only by the slimmest vertical mullions. The two are spaced apart at the increment of the triangulation of the trusses – the outer skin therefore being suspended from the top chord of the truss, allowing plenty of space for cleaning and maintenance. Behind the outer skin run continuous horizontal venetian blinds, while the mediating and enriching of the glass envelope is fully achieved by the display of scientific specimens in glass jars on glass shelves running continuously around the inside skin, through which the interior is flooded with light.

The building demonstrates clarity of structure in the separation of the upper and lower volumes, while the skin, although semi-opaque, intuitively and necessarily implies the existence of a space-frame roof. The original and masterly detailing exploited the best from the construction industry during an era that, perhaps ironically, was marked by the surviving presence of so many traditionally trained craftsmen. This building, Robin Walker's best, could be considered the high point of the modern architecture in Ireland that emerged and evolved from Miesian influence.
S.W.

General view from the east

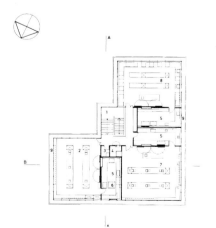

Wall section

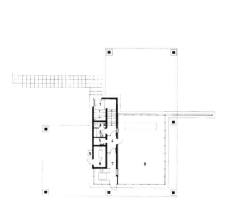

Plans

Irish Management Institute

Sandyford Road, Sandyford, County Dublin   1971–4

ARTHUR GIBNEY

Nestling at the foot of the Dublin mountains, the Irish Management Institute (IMI) has a dual role as the corporate headquarters of an organisation with a large membership and a specialised training centre for managers. To begin with, the site was more or less flat; but the placing of the accommodation has turned it into the semblance of a hill. A terraced podium, moulded to conceal a large dining room, library and courtyards, connects the constituent parts of the complex.

Those elements of the project that figure as 'ground' are of grey *in situ* concrete to invite lichen, weather stains and a general earthiness, while the parts that figure as 'building' are of gleaming, white, precast concrete. Arranged around a two-storey courtyard, the management accommodation is conceived as an immutable square temple. Portal frames, with a peristyle of paired white columns, form a protective *brise-soleil* to the offices. The training accommodation comprises precast U-frames, laid out to an irregular plan that follows the contours of the site in an accretive, cubic composition, anticipating future expansion.

An elegant, timeless duet is played out at IMI by abstract white forms on a constructed green landscape, giving us, in the words of the March 1977 issue of *Architectural Review*, 'the joys of monumentality without the usual attendant pomps'.

S.O'T.

View from the west into the sunken library court with the Teaching Block behind

Teaching Block from the north-west

Looking north-east along the Library
Podium past the Teaching Block

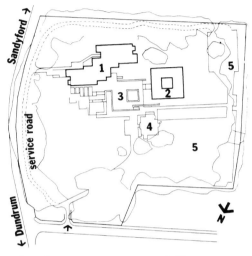

Site plan

site plan : key
1, teaching block
2, offices
3, library
4, existing house
5, car park

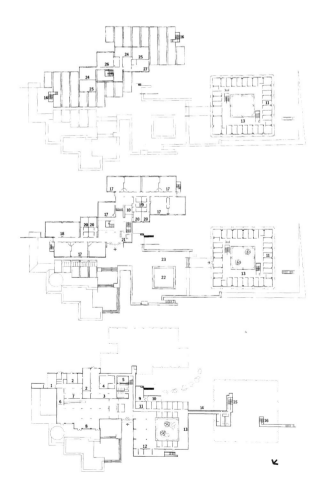

Plans

143

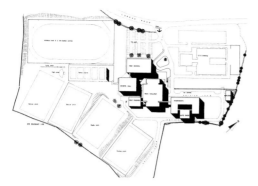

Site plan

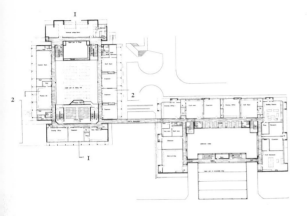

Plan of Level 4

Technical College

Portadown, County Armagh
1972–6

J.B. KENNEDY

This impressive and uncompromisingly modern structure is a *tour de force* in concrete and glass that imposes a strong but somewhat alien form on its gently sloping site. A multi-level complex, it consists of a number of separate, clearly defined blocks placed at various levels to suit the contour of the site but linked to each other by underground and overhead corridors.

The general construction of the buildings is mainly in reinforced concrete, supplementary steelwork being employed in the large workshop, sports hall and assembly hall roofs. Externally, the buildings are finished in board-marked *in situ* concrete, handled with exemplary skill and with evident care in the arranging of patterns. There are also some areas of exposed aggregate in the ribbed walls around the concourse. Internal finishes are mainly fair-faced brick to walls, with concrete coffer-moulded roofs left as finished ceilings both inside and outside. Windows are generally in galvanised steel or aluminium patent glazing.

The central focus of the entire complex is the College Block, where a large internal assembly hall forms the core, with classrooms and laboratories, library and administration offices, grouped around all sides at five different levels.

The whole complex is characterised by highly modelled forms, with deep recesses and angled planes. The central block is the most boldly treated, with cantilevered masses towering on the entrance front and tall thin columns along the sides, through which canted bays in purple brick and square oriels give expression to various rooms.

The landscaped pedestrian walkways and courtyards between and around the various blocks add to the spatial quality, which, combined with formal inventiveness, is one of the chief merits of the building. It is a highly complex but well controlled design that shows a mastery of sculptural form.
P.L.

Sections

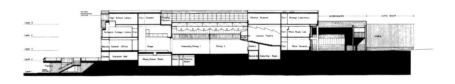

1:1

2:2

South-west and north-east elevations

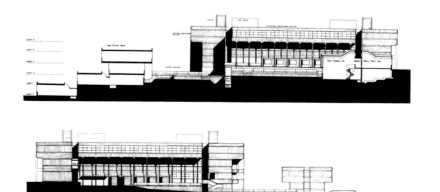

High School Block

College Block

The Assembly Hall

View from the west

View from the north

Goulding House

Enniskerry, County Wicklow 1975

RONALD TALLON

Plan and section

The Goulding summerhouse is situated on a steeply wooded riverbank site in the Dargle Glen at the foothills of the Wicklow Mountains. The simple single-storey steel cantilever structure protrudes over the river from the steep bank. The structural box is about ten metres long and divided into five bays; it has a width of three bays. The interior contains one large open-plan space, with a small free-standing core for kitchen and bathroom. The last two bays of the structure, over the river, are entirely glazed; the others are filled with horizontal timber siding. The dark umber-painted steel frame is expressed on the exterior by a single stanchion descending on either side to the water's edge. The resultant three-bay cantilever, with only two bays anchoring it to the hillside, gives the form an uneasy visual stability. Each bay is diagonally braced on the exterior and, where the I-stanchion intersects with floor and roof I-beams, Tallon has inserted fillets in the webs in the classical Miesian style.

The exposed underside of the floorboarding, clearly seen from below, runs longitudinally, mirroring the timber boarding in the side walls. The clarity and crispness of the form and its daring attractiveness exemplify the very best in Tallon's work, which seems particularly suited to this scale. The immediate hightech aesthetic, softened by the use of timber, makes this a very inviting and desirable building, and it has an open, bold relationship with its outdoor surroundings that is refreshing in an Irish context.
S.W.

View from the river

Elevation drawings and site plan

Workshop at New Dock

Galway 1976–7

NOEL DOWLEY

View from the east

This small office building and workshop, measuring 14 by 7 metres, was constructed in 1976–7 in the industrial area of the port of Galway. It represents a conspicuous exploration of an architecture of minimal means, seen as part of a tradition of Irish building. A modest vocabulary of low-cost materials and construction exploits self-supporting roof sheeting, pre-cast concrete pipes, industrial translucent cladding, stock windows, doors and joinery, and load-bearing concrete block walls. The building is painted white, except where bright colours highlight the points at which the skin is penetrated.
J. O.

Stairhall

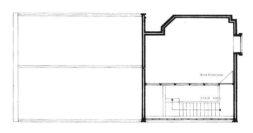

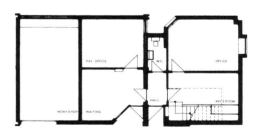

Plans

View from the south

Our Lady of Mount Carmel

Firhouse, County Dublin 1976–8

SHANE DE BLACAM/JOHN MEAGHER

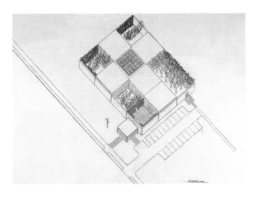

Axonometric view

Entrance courtyard

The church at Firhouse is built as a paradise garden. Behind its enclosing walls the quadrant plots are divided by the cruciform body of the church. The building becomes a sanctuary in a desert of suburbia, revealing little of its interior, bright and verdant, on its protective blank concrete blockwork boundary, except where an increase in height marks the position of the arms of the church's plan.

At the western end of the south face, and standing detached from the walled enclosure, a tetrastyle portico announces the entrance. Passing through the simple opening you enter a warmer world. Now in the first courtyard garden, the entrance to the church proper lies ahead. A timber panelled facade is organised into three portals; central tall double doors are accompanied by framing side doors. To the right the transparency of the garden/church ensemble is revealed as the light timber and glass walls allow garden and church to become almost one. The four gardens with their groves of trees also mark out the four quarters of the year in their seasonal change: the blossom of spring; the lush, leafy summers, shedding a cool green light to the church the interior; the warm glow of autumnal colours; and the leafless winter.

The body of the church is supported by a modular structure that takes its dimensions from the crossing. Each unit, a free-standing tetrastyle construction of reinforced concrete with edge and diagonal beams, supports its covering of timber joists and boarding. An exception occurs at the crossing. The configuration of beams changes to a cross, which divides the ceiling into four squares, each with a skylight. Now illumination floods onto the altar directly from the heavens.

As the building matures, the blank grey concrete blockwork is being clad in the green vestment of ivy and the four garden groves gain external presence as they raise their leafy canopy above the walls, giving subtle articulation to the cruciform body of the church that lies behind the mute mask.
J.O.

View of the interior, looking towards the altar

Detail of nave wall

Large tree court

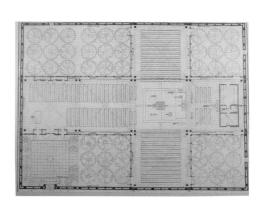

Plan

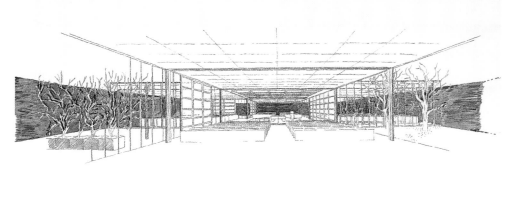

Interior view across the transepts towards the altar

The school from the south-west

Connecting spaces

One of the courtyards

Section

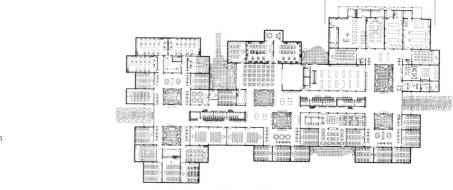

Plan

Community School

Birr, County Offaly 1976–9

PETER AND MARY DOYLE

The Department of Education held a competition in 1974 to find a generic solution to school building. This was to provide an alternative to the current standardised form, which, pinched by budgetary constraints and misguided by a fashion imported from Britain, took on a deep-plan, compact form to minimise construction costs but with consequent dependence on indirect and artificial lighting. The winning project from Peter and Mary Doyle was a *tour de force*; every element within the plan could enjoy direct daylight and a sense of openness – and this was achieved within a minimal budget.

The strategy of the design was embodied in the organisation of the plan and the adoption of a structure derived from an industrial building system. A pleasant environment offering community and identity was achieved by forming clusters of classrooms, often associated with a discipline within the curriculum, attached to the armature of a 'street'. The street runs north-south and is so arranged in relation to the town of Birr to allow the two polar entrances to segregate those arriving by bicycle or on foot from those brought by car or bus. The street broadens and narrows, providing both circulation and spaces for people to stop and meet. It becomes a linked sequence of large covered spaces, generously high and open, with planted courtyards connected to the classroom clusters, each with its own social space that can be extended into the sheltered courtyards, weather permitting.

The structure is a series of portal-framed sheds with their axes reinforcing the orientation of the street, and a variety of heights and spans appropriate to articulating the different functions housed. The rather bland industrial building system is greatly enhanced by the imaginatively conceived and conscientiously applied detailing. The end result is a legible, rich and bright school for a remarkably low budget.
J.O.

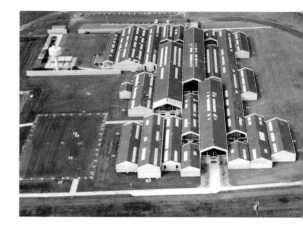

Aerial view

The school under construction, revealing the skeletal framework

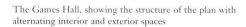

The Games Hall, showing the structure of the plan with alternating interior and exterior spaces

Interior

Ailwee Caves Visitors' Centre

Burren, County Clare   1977—9

A & D WJECHERT

Aerial view looking south

The visitors' centre forms an entrance and ante-space to the dramatic Ailwee caves, which were carved by water seeping from the depths of the strange limestone landscape of the Burren in County Clare in the west of Ireland.

A large terrace had been cut into the hillside to provide car parking. Here the building forms a kind of organic growth from the wounded slope. This naturalistic allusion is reinforced by the building's curvilinear forms and its cladding in the same limestone as that of the hillside. The construction's ambition to meld with the terrain initiated a reticent approach to building in the Irish landscape, one that sought a precedent in Neolithic passage tombs, rather than in the proud assertiveness of the primal forms of medieval tower houses and their successors. This structure was also one of the first examples in Ireland of a new building type, the visitors' or interpretative centre, invented to serve the tourist industry.

In form and plan the building resembles an ear. Listening to the landscape, awaiting the arrival of tourists, it first channels the visitors into a kind of acoustic chamber - the reception and tea-room - before conducting them down the narrowing cochlear passage to the cavities beneath the cranium of the mountain. In contrast, from the mezzanine level in the main space, a route leads onto a terrace and, echoing the line of the passageway that leads to the concealed depths below, forms a path that then climbs the mountainside in the open air.

J.O.

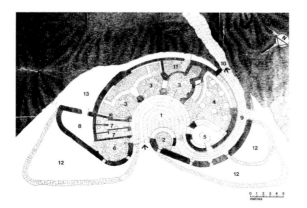

Ground plan

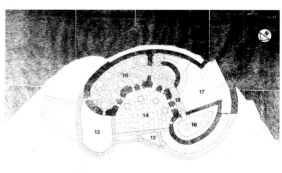

Upper-level plan

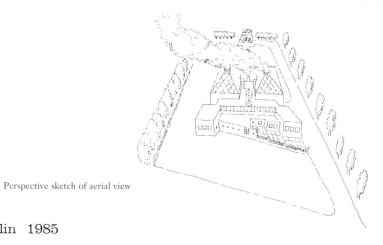

Perspective sketch of aerial view

Laboratory

Abbotstown, County Dublin 1985

JOHN TUOMEY (Office of Public Works)

The building is a meat testing station, a unit of the State Laboratories sited on the Abbotstown Estate. Primal, hut-like forms boldly occupy the agricultural landscape, contrasting with venerable, ancient, ivy-covered oaks. The built shapes are wrapped with facades that embody a contemporary reinterpretation of the traditionally severe neo-classicism of Ireland.

This austere tradition also invades the plan. A strict symmetry, its axial orientation aligned to the orthogonal field pattern, breaks open only at the entrance, in order to engage the approach road. Thus the form and facade of the entry front do not celebrated the axis, but lead the visitor to discover it.

The three-dimensional forms of the ensemble articulate the plan. The axis, as if an expression of some ritual programme, leads from the administration offices through a decontamination zone of changing rooms with central celebratory 'font' before entering a pair of pavilions. Here the laboratories are found beneath their hipped roofs. The large roof space provides for the elaborate ventilation and service systems and rises to 14 metres to enable the spent air to be expelled safely. J.O.

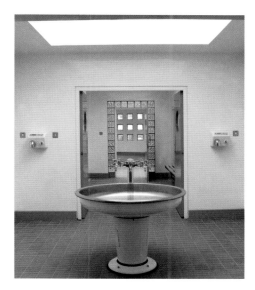

The decontamination area, between laboratories and offices

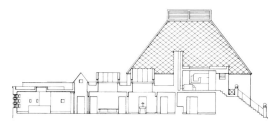

Sections

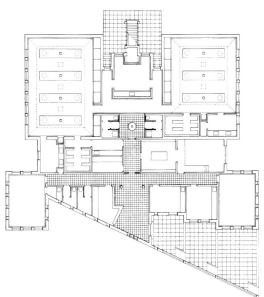

First-floor plan

Laboratory building from the south-west

The Atrium

Trinity College Dublin   1987

SHANE de BLACAM / JOHN MEAGHER

Detail of the west side of the atrium

The atrium is the centre-piece of the replanning and rationalisation of three centuries' accretions around the splendid eighteenth-century dining-hall at Trinity College Dublin. Ironically, this remodelling was aided by a disastrous fire that gutted the Great Hall and adjacent spaces. It cleared a path through at least part of the warren of buildings, and through the perception of both architect and client of the potential for replanning. Circumstances and design triumphed in the production of the atrium, a superb galleried space that rediscovers the volume of the eighteenth-century kitchens. It now forms a fitting twentieth-century counterpart to the restored old dining-hall, with which it is paired in the section; together they form the twinned focus of the building around which each of their functions unfolds, dining and student activities.

The galleries around the atrium space become, on occasions, rooms that are turned to a multitude of uses. A double-height gallery exploits the original tall windows to the west and becomes an exhibition space or a reception room on being isolated from the atrium by its shutters and doors. To the north and south, the uppermost galleries can be made into private meeting or dining rooms behind additional internal glazed shutters. It is the natural theatricality of the central galleried space that is the atrium's triumph and, with its resonances with the form of Elizabethan and Spanish Renaissance theatres, it has been a natural set for plays.

The primitive monumentality of the atrium facades, with their storeys of superimposed abstracted orders, the square columns successively decreasing in width, reveals the influence of Louis Kahn. It successfully establishes a contemporary language of classicism appropriate to the surrounding buildings of Trinity College, which form the most impressive ensemble of neo-classical architecture in Dublin. This work at Trinity demonstrates an approach to the reuse of existing buildings, allowing the new to exploit and discover the particular qualities and exigencies of existing fabric. J.O.

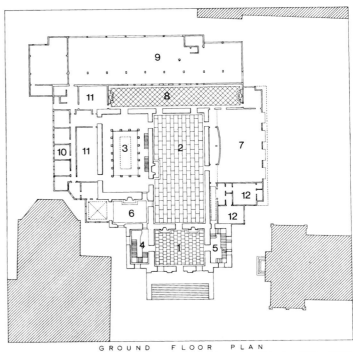

GROUND FLOOR PLAN
1 ENTRANCE HALL 2 DINING HALL 3 ATRIUM 4 ATRIUM STAIRS 5 SENIOR COMMON ROOM STAIRS 6 UPPER LUNCH ROOM 7 EAST DINING HALL 8 FOOD HALL 9 KITCHEN 10 SOCIETY ROOMS 11 MEETING ROOMS 12 TOILETS AND BATHROOMS

Plan of the dining-room complex

Gallery space on the west side of the atrium

View of the atrium from the first gallery

CROSS SECTION
1 ATRIUM 2 DINING HALL 3 BUTTERY BAR 4 SOCIETY ROOMS 5 NEW COMMON ROOM

Section through the atrium
and the adjacent dining-hall

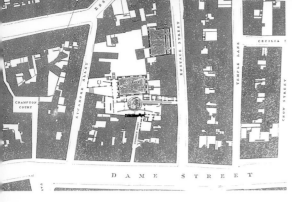

Site plan

Irish Film Centre

Temple Bar, Dublin   1987–92

SHEILA O'DONNELL / JOHN TUOMEY

Entrance from Eustace Street

As a project the Irish Film Centre had a long gestation period, five years from the purchase of the site to the commencement of construction. During that period, the time in which it took to secure funding, the brief matured and expanded along with the development of the design. The IFC became a precedent and an exemplar for the subsequent interventions in the Temple Bar refurbishment, both in its nature as a cultural institution and in the way it represented an approach to urban design embodied in a single building. The complex of spaces — foyer, restaurant, café and bar, two cinemas and an archive — involves the stitching of new fabric into the existing, as the ensemble weaves its way into the circumstantial spaces and buildings within the centre of an urban block. The site was a collection of buildings of the Quaker Meeting House and school, which had already inhabited part of the backlands of the block. The outside spaces adjacent to the buildings became the front of house areas, glazed over and tidied up with new elements of construction.

The main entrance to the Centre is from Eustace Street with little more than a pedimented doorway and a small neon sign to announce its presence. Through this door a lighted strip along the floor leads you frame by frame, like a film unwound, down the passageway to join the foyer. This is the hub of the IFC's functional and physical plan. Here also new meets old. A steel and glass roof transforms a back yard into a protected urban public space. In this space a new curved facade houses a restaurant that looks down through the unglazed windows onto the activity beneath. Under the restaurant is the ticket office and information kiosk. The plane of the facade is carried through into the old school room to form the bar. The two small cinemas inhabit existing hall-like spaces with a minimum of intervention. Beyond, the space leads through to the bookshop and then moves outside, beneath a new loggia that supports the projection box for both cinemas. Here also is a new brick building for the archive that gives the IFC a front onto Sycamore Street. The IFC is a public institution that also provides a pedestrian route through the city block and now connects into the new Meeting House Square as part of the Temple Bar Project.
J.O.

Ground plan

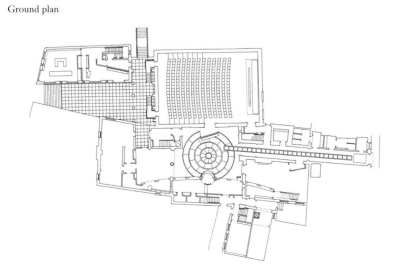

The Archive Building
with the Projection Room on pilotis

The foyer

Exploded axonometric of the architectonic
elements

The Archive
Building

Interior of the small cinema

Approach across the courtyard of the Royal Hospital to the entrance to the Irish Museum of Modern Art

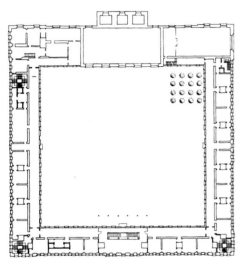

First-floor plan

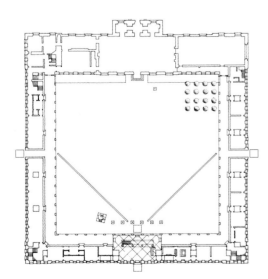

Ground plan

Site plan

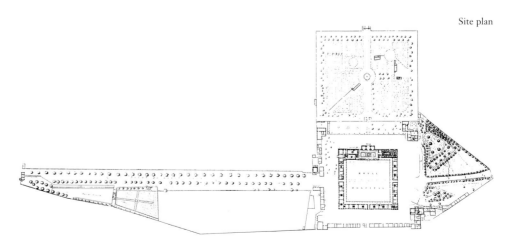

Irish Museum of Modern Art

Royal Hospital, Kilmainham, Dublin 1991

SHAY CLEARY

Originally built in the 1780s under the patronage of the Duke of Ormond, the Royal Hospital, Kilmainham, is a four-square courtyard building. Its north flank contained the large-scale elements of the plan: the chapel, great hall and master's lodging. This wing was emphasised by the spired tower that rises over the great hall, defining one of the axes of the courtyard. Around the other three sides of the courtyard were ranged the pensioners' rooms; units of mirrored room and cabinet, they opened onto the continuous arcade at ground level and onto wide corridors on the upper floors. Each of these wings presented a long repetitive classical range of building relieved at its centre by a five-bay pavilion in low relief.

It is behind the central pavilion of the south range that a bright modern entrance foyer for the Irish Museum of Modern Art was created. This space looks out through five bays of the arcade, now glazed in, to frame a view of the grand architectural range of the north wing. The courtyard was transformed into an impressive urban-like space by replacing the quadrants of grass with a hard-rolled gravel floor. This now becomes the first 'room' of the museum, for display or performance or just to stroll in to take in the grandeur of the space and its architectural frame.

From the entrance lightweight glass and steel stairs lead to the first floor, where the main collection and temporary exhibitions are located. Here the ensemble of spaces that comprised the original plan of the hospital provides a variety of exhibition environments. The wide corridor that overlooks the courtyard has the proportions of a long gallery in a grand seventeenth-century country house, with which it shares a similar typological origin. The collection of apartments is reconfigured to give a rhythm of enfilade spaces and ante-spaces that facilitate a variety of divisions and interconnections within the sequence of display, or provide distinct rooms for special installations. The project has provided a rich medley of spaces, all discovered and reawakened within the building's typological ancestry with minimal intervention in this culturally important historic building. J.O.

View from the entrance hall into the courtyard

Approach along the south arcade to the entrance to the museum

Entrance hall

159

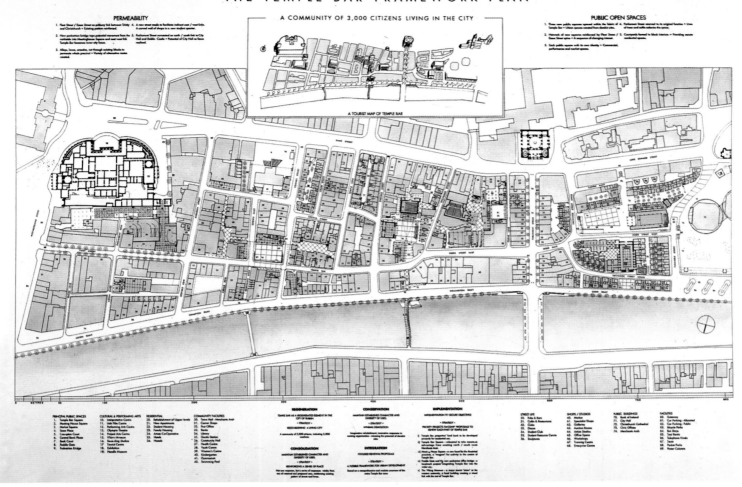

Framework plan

Site plan

Temple Bar

Dublin 1991–6

GROUP '91 ARCHITECTS

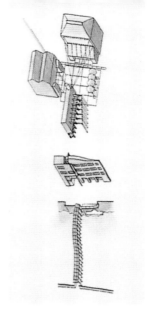

Temple Bar is a prominent quarter of Dublin. It stretches between two historic centres, the medieval and the eighteenth-century Georgian city. The axis joining their nodal points from Christ Church Cathedral to Trinity College and the eighteenth-century Parliament building forms Temple Bar's southern boundary. To the north, the limit is the watery boulevard of the River Liffey and its quays, which bisects the city.

Dublin succumbed to that twentieth-century urban disease which leaves the core to rot while the periphery breaks out in a rash of suburbs. The inner city fell victim to road building programmes to serve the daily influx of commuters, an action that tore apart the urban fabric, communities and culture alike. Temple Bar became a prime target. It was designated for a massive transportation interchange. Planning blight was the pathological consequence, making the area an urban purgatory. Lack of economic means for execution and then growing public concern protracted and finally halted redevelopment. Neglect of the building fabric was favoured and short-term leases demanded. Rents sank sufficiently to allow a fortuitous infestation of fringe and alternative cultural and commercial activities: second-hand and specialist shops, cheap and ethnic restaurants, alternative theatre and cinema, and practice spaces and recording studios for Ireland's burgeoning pop music industry. The streets were animated with activity and decaying buildings brightened up with colourful and creative decoration. All this became the trajectory towards salvation.

Appropriately, in 1991, Dublin's year as European City of Culture, the vibrancy of this area was established as State policy. A development company, Temple Bar Properties Ltd, was set up to nurture 'what has been taking place in the area spontaneously and to create a living, bustling cultural and tourist quarter which people will visit in sufficient numbers and in which many more will work and live'. The challenge was not to extinguish the vitality through real estate speculation and redevelopment, but to provide a structure for encouraging creative evolution on a path to prosperity. Temple Bar Properties held an urban design competition to produce an architectural framework plan. The winning entry was by a consortium of young Dublin-based practices, Group '91. Over the previous decade, individually and collectively, through exhibitions, proposals, research and publications, they had done much to create awareness of Dublin's distinguished urban heritage. Their aspirations for the city became public policy with the Government's initiatives and ambitions for Temple Bar. Both promoters and architects favoured 'Going with the grain of history by recognising, respecting and building on traditions, accents and local heritage'. Group '91 seized the opportunities provided by dereliction and its circumstantial distribution to create a variety of places that become punctuations, points of arrival and settings for the various amenities, existing and projected.

The idea has become a reality through a combination of tax incentives and support from the EU for par-

ticular projects and for upgrading the public domain of streets and new public spaces. Cultural buildings, part sponsored, part commercial, have been the most conspicuous architecture to invade the quarter. They have been executed by the individual practices of Group '91 and include the Irish Film Centre, Photographic Gallery and Archive, the Multi-media Centre, the Music Centre and the Ark, a children's cultural centre. The majority of these are the materials for two urban design interventions. A new curved street carved from circumstantial dereliction facilitates east-west pedestrian movement within Temple Bar and focuses on the seven-teenth-century facade of the Ark. Here an archway passes into Meeting House Square, a new public place moulded from the decaying interior of an urban block.

The cultural institutions assert their presence by new, sober, white or monumental brick facades that contrast strongly to the riot of styles, colours and encrustations that has come to characterise Temple Bar. However, private development of commercial and residential mix follows and enjoys this indigenous character.

In Temple Bar the fabric of the city is being recycled, whether in its standing form or by the reuse of its materials. The interventions of Group '91 are stitching new uses and activities into the spaces and buildings of the existing fabric. The urban tapestry is enriched while its material worth is conserved and an ecological alternative is formulated to suburban expansion and the process of destruction and rebuilding.

J.O.

A walk through Temple Bar

161

Temple Bar Square and Temple Bar Building

GRAFTON ARCHITECTS

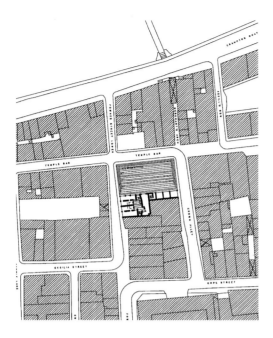

View of Temple Bar Square

Interior of an apartment

End facade, detail

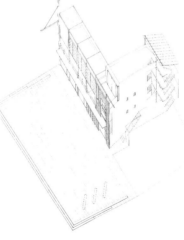

Axonometric view

Second-floor plan

First-floor plan

General view from Temple Bar Square

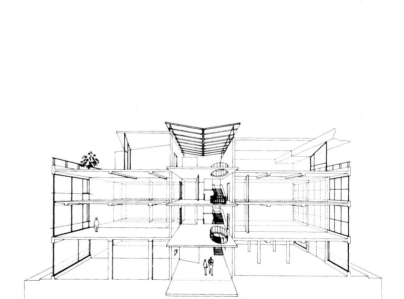

Studio

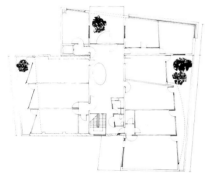

Third-floor plan

Ground-floor plan

South/north section

Street facade

The Printworks

DEREK TYNAN ARCHITECTS

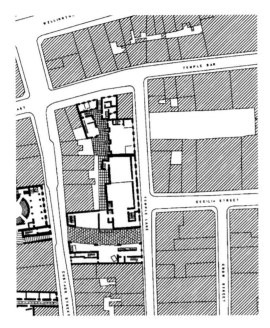

Site plan showing The Printworks, Temple Bar
Music Centre, and Arthouse

First-floor plan

Ground-floor plan

Facade to Temple Lane South

Brick facade to Essex Street East

Interior of a Design Studio.
View from reception towards entrance

Facade of the apartments to the courtyard

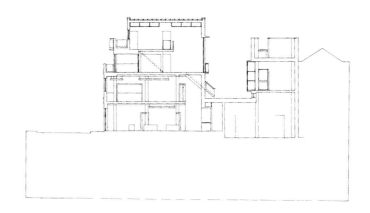

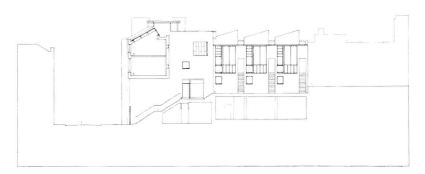

East/west section
North/south section

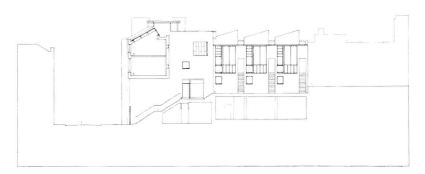

Courtyard with entrance from Essex Street

Temple Bar Music Centre

McCULLOUGH MULVIN ARCHITECTS

View from Cecilia Street

View from Eustace Street along the facade
in Curved Street

Plan

Interior

Stairwell

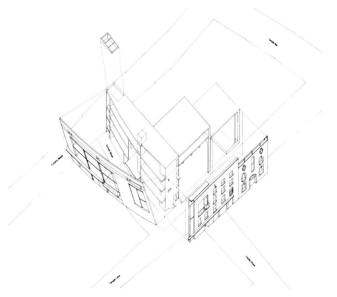

Axonometric

Facade to Curved Street

North/south section

Café

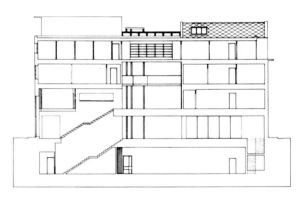

East/west section

Detail of the entrance facade

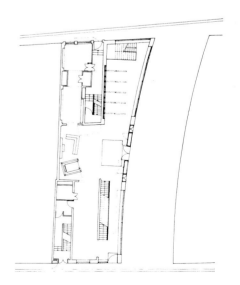

Ground-floor plan

Gaiety School of Acting
PAUL KEOGH ARCHITECTS

Part of the facade to Sycamore Street

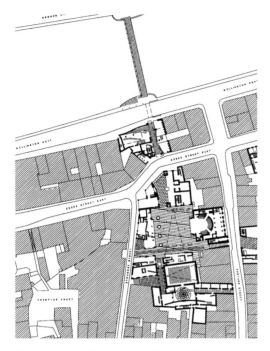

Site plan showing Gaiety School of Acting, The Ark, and
Photography Centre Buildings

View from the square during a film showing

Plans

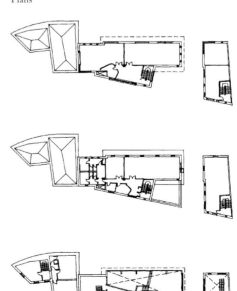

Entrance between the two parts of the building on the square

View from the square

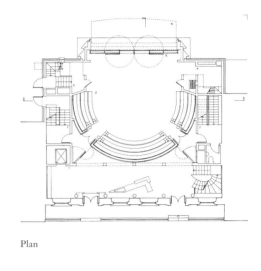

Plan

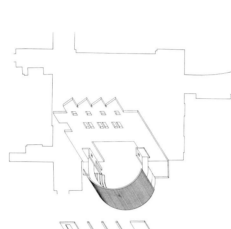

Axonometric

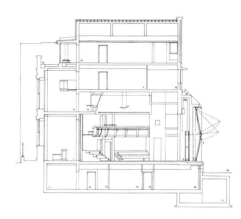

East/west section

The auditorium

The foyer is reminiscent of the long hall of the old
Presbyterian Meeting House

The theatre during a performance,
with gate open to the square

169

Photography Centre Buildings
O'DONNELL TUOMEY ARCHITECTS

Plan

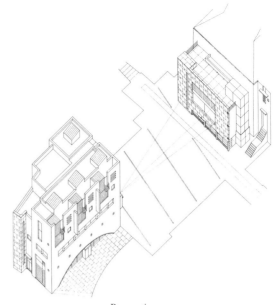

Perspective

Section

Interior, Gallery of Photography

View from the square of the Gallery of Photography

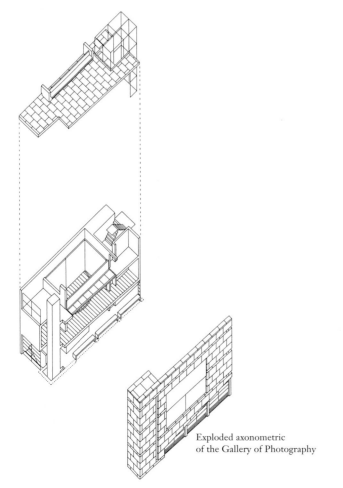

Exploded axonometric
of the Gallery of Photography

National Photography Archive, view from the square

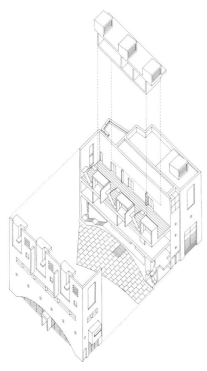

Exploded axonometric

National Photography Archive, entrance hall

National Photography Archive, front view

Aerial view of the Civic Park

Tourist Information Office

Civic Park, Limerick   1991

HUGH MURRAY / SEÁN O'LAOIRE

General view

Commendably, this is one of the few buildings in Ireland that dares to adopt a high-tech pose. It was conceived as a gateway to the new Civic Park in Limerick, created on land reclaimed from the River Shannon estuary. The ground, laid out in symmetrical, geometric fashion, draws a diagonal line from the city centre to the water's edge. Standing astride this axis, a structural pylon gives greater visual presence to this small building while defining the park's entrance. From the mast's apex stretch tension cables to support two flat elliptical booms – one a transparent umbrella

sheltering a gathering space, the other roofing the Tourist Information Office. The office has a transparent enclosure for the customer space, which then becomes opaque to house the service part of the plan in the 'stern' of the building.

Strong nautical associations reside within the building's form and rigging and in the asymmetry of its plan, which gives it a direction, its 'bow' heading off downstream. However, it is beached, drawn back from the quayside, blocking its own view of broader horizons.

J.O.

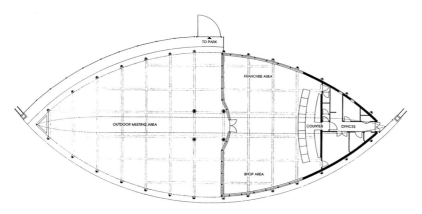

Plan

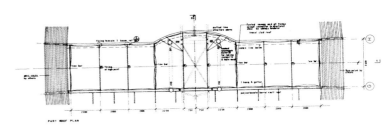

Detailed plan of the roof

View of the mast from below

Entrance

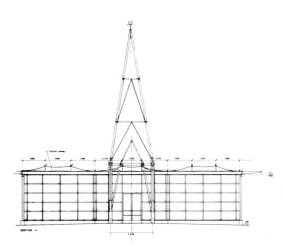

Section

View from the north, with the nineteenth-century Charge House of the Mills in the foreground

Gunpowder Mills Visitors' Centre

Ballincollig, County Cork 1992

TOMÁS DE PAOR/EMMA O'NEILL

A national competition in 1991 produced this fine building from two very young architects within a year of their graduation. The building forms the entrance and introduction to a heritage landscape. The site and structures of the disused gunpowder milling complex, dating from 1794, have been restored to become a regional park outside Cork city.

Between an existing line of beeches, a cranked steel canopy announces the entrance to the building and leads to the door. Inside, the hall expands into an exhibition space, where the history of the landscape to be visited is told and the landscape itself then revealed, framed by a strategically positioned window. From here a clerestory lit gallery leads past the audito-

rium, which bulges timber-clad from the building. Cut into the gallery wall, spy-hole openings peep through to other parts of the building and add further frames of the landscape and its objects. Beyond, outside, begins the journey in the park, where the as yet unbuilt steel and timber bridge will offer a route.

The route returns back over the canal by way of a stone bridge, across the paved terrace, through a glass screen to end in the tea-room. This refreshment space opens from beneath its butterfly roof, pushing its paviour floor out across the terrace to the canal's edge and providing a broader and reflective prospect of the landscape visited.
J.O.

The exhibition corridor

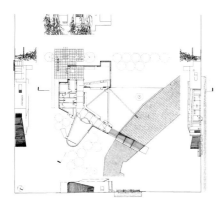

Plan and elevations

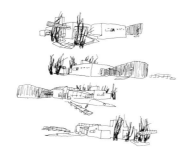

Perspective sketches

Site plan

View from the exhibition corridor through to the tea-room and the landscape beyond

Entrance to the Visitors' Centre

The timber-clad form of the auditorium, with the nineteenth-century Charge House of the Mills beyond

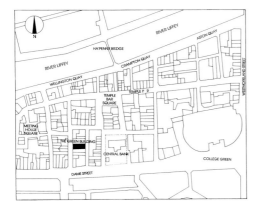

Site plan

Green Building

Temple Bar, Dublin 1992

HUGH MURRAY / SEÁN O'LAOIRE

Temple Lane facade with its sculptural elaboration using recycled materials

Roofscape with the paraphernalia for renewable energy collection

The 'Green' building is one of the show-case projects of the recent regeneration of the Temple Bar area of Dublin. It is a self-conscious exploration of the possibilities of 'greening' the urban fabric. Financial assistance for the novel ecological and environmental investigation and realisation of this building came through the Thermie Programme of the European Union. Its site, measuring 26 by 11 metres, was the vacant lot stretching across a city block between two parallel streets. The building covers the whole plot and consequently has two front facades, one to Crow Street, the other to Temple Lane. It accommodates a mix of uses: two floors of commercial space, an office level and then, stacked above this, eight apartments of differing size.

An atrium sits hard against the southern boundary of the site to bring light and ventilation into the deep plan and to be central to the building's integrated approach to energy performance and ecological concern. The light penetration into the section is maximised by light-coloured surfaces, glass-block floors to the access galleries and the use of a glass-enclosed lift. Air for ventilation is drawn from the streets, filtered and re-oxygenated by the basement winter gardens, with additional oxygenation to be provided by the proposed hanging gardens suspended from the balconies. The mode of circulation of the ventilation in the atrium is orchestrated to fit conditions and season by means of a heat exchanger and an air mixing fan equipped with an accompanying fabric funnel device for times when natural convection fails to provide adequate air movement. To augment the energy performance, apartments have sun spaces that can be incorporated into the living space when conditions are appropriate. There was a self-conscious attempt to maximise the use of recycled or green materials as far as budget and availability would allow.

Even though the building, typologically, is not unusual in such an urban situation, it has made a polemic out of its response to the ecological imperative. Bedecked with the paraphernalia of renewable energy sources, windmills, solar collectors and photovoltaic cells, it is encrusted with reused and recomposed objects and scrap in the form of commissioned sculptural decoration.
J.O.

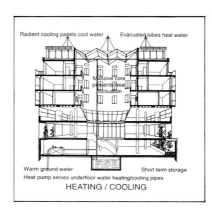

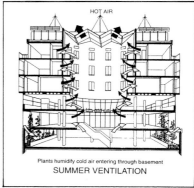

174

Sitting room and sun space of an apartment

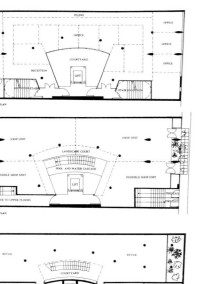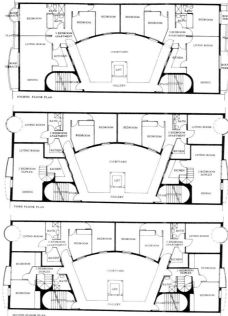

Plans

The atrium

Sections showing ecological control processes

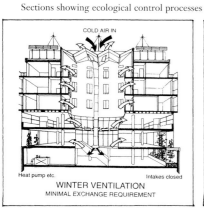
WINTER VENTILATION
MINIMAL EXCHANGE REQUIREMENT

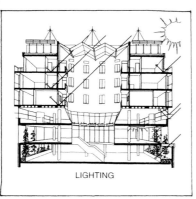
LIGHTING

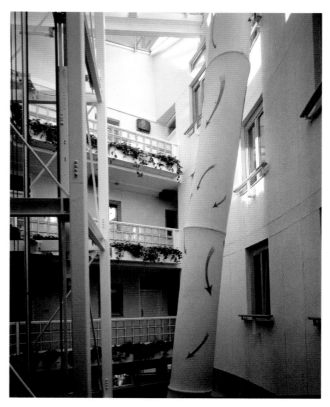

Museum shed

Railway Transport Gallery

Cultra, County Down 1992–3

IAN CAMPBELL AND PARTNERS

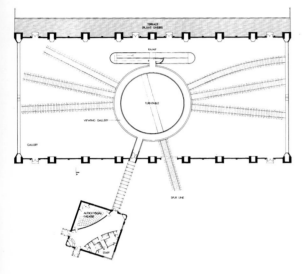

Site plan

Built on a steeply sloping site in pleasant countryside not far from Belfast, this elegant and functional building was designed to house the Ulster Folk and Transport Museum's comprehensive 'Irish Railway Collection', which covers the whole of Ireland.

The building consists of a large exhibition space or gallery linked by an angled bridge to a reception block on a higher level. The barrel-vaulted shape of the gallery, with its soaring gables and radiating members, was consciously influenced by the great Victorian railway stations of the past. Construction is of curved tubular space frames, which spring from a base of blue engineering bricks to span thirty-five metres and support the roof of embossed aluminium panels, which were profiled and curved on site and crimped into position.

Inside, the V-shaped space frame trusses are used to carry flexible air ducts across the roof and support the soaring hoops of gable glazing, which provide a strong dramatic element and welcome relief in an otherwise artificially lit space. Demountable connections between the gable trusses and the radial posts at each end of the building allow for future extensions. The elevated link from the entrance building connects with a circular gallery, permitting views down over the trains as if from a railway bridge; from here a ramp descends to the gallery floor level. Bridge, viewing gallery and ramp were all constructed of cast *in situ* reinforced concrete with an exposed aggregate finish.

With its hangar-like space and structural display, this building recaptures some of the grandeur of nineteenth-century engineering achievements, while its crisp precision and some of its details recall the heyday of the modern movement.

After the Railway Transport Gallery opened in October 1993 another building, the Road Transport Gallery, also designed by Ian Campbell, was added to it. This opened in 1995.
P. L.

Entrance building

Interior of the museum shed

Aerial view

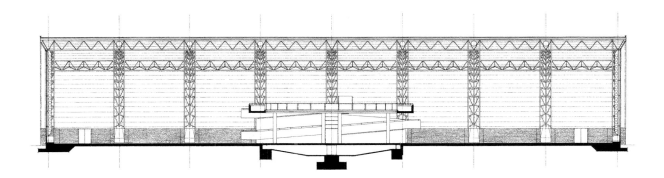

Longitudinal section

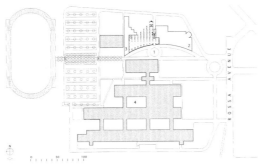

Site plan

Detail of the entrance hall with reflection of reading hall

Reading hall

Reading hall, looking towards the bookstack halls

North facade

Library, Regional Technical College

Bishopstown, Cork   1994–6

SHANE DE BLACAM/JOHN MEAGHER

This new library, along with a second complex, containing lecture theatres and a centre for information technology, will form a new central focus to the campus of the Regional Technical College, Cork. The new building's south and entrance facade, a monumental curved brick wall, describes an all but symmetrical arc to define an outside gathering space.

Passing from the entrance hall into the library is like emerging from the spine of a book into the space of its open pages. The 'front cover' of the building curls back, as the interior of the library fans out from the information desk to create a grand, lofty space in which to read. On its flyleaf is written the latest knowledge held by the library – the south wall is spread with current journals like words upon the page – and to the right the books tight-packed in the deep bays are like the pages yet to be opened to divulge their stories. As one paces down the central axis towards the tall end window, the slender piers of brick and block mark the rhythm of the structural bays. To the right, within the discipline of this structure, a wall of books is folded into deep bays like quires, the volumes on the shelves like lines of print. The text is then divided into columns and stanzas as the post and beam construction frames up tiers of galleries.   These stanzas *are* like rooms, spaces made almost of a single natural material, harmonising in its various forms – the paper of the books, the beechwood of the structure and the sisal floor covering, each a joy to touch – a warm place, where footfalls and noise are hushed. Here is a place to pause, to sit on the floor or lean on the balustrade while leafing through volumes in order to choose which to take to the margin, where daylight floods in through the lofty north-facing windows that terminate each galleried bay.

The ethos of the library design is reader-centred and one that could assimilate information technology and its impact upon teaching.
J.O.

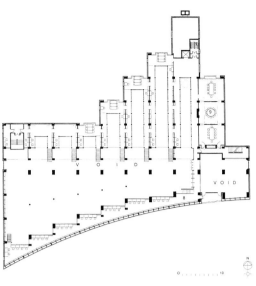

First-floor plan

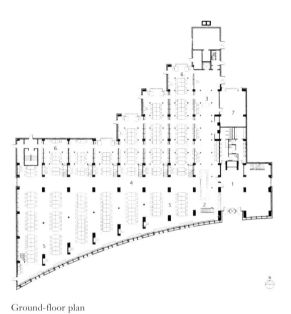

Ground-floor plan

Curving south facade with entrance to the library

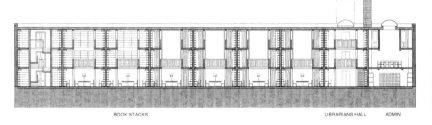

BOOK STACKS   LIBRARIANS HALL   ADMIN

Sections through librarians' hall and bookstacks

BOILER   LIBRARIANS HALL   DESK   PERIODICALS GALLERY

179

British Embassy

Merrion Road, Dublin 1995

ROBERT ALLIES/GRAHAM MORRISON

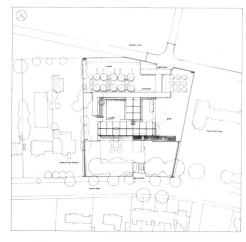

Site plan

The British Embassy was built in the Dublin suburb of Ballsbridge, on land acquired from the adjacent Royal Dublin Society. It is an area where many embassies occupy grand nineteenth-century suburban villas, the larger ones on substantial plots of grounds with generous mews that have been adapted for offices. This was the typology emulated by the new British Embassy, chosen with a view to the particular security problem posed for the British Embassy in Ireland and the concomitant desire not to appear too assertive. The use of the site in this fashion allowed the building to be set back and, as gently as possible, to arrange the security lodge and curtilage as a natural attribute of the adopted typology.

The embassy presents a sober classical form to the street, a reference, perhaps a little inappropriate, to the eighteenth-century neo-classical heyday of British ascendancy in Dublin. The facade is a mask, revealing little of the spatial or organisational order behind this precisely measured face. However, it does allow itself to articulate the separation between the formal embassy and the consulate and visa departments. The eight-bay elevation splits into two facades: one of five bays, formal and symmetrical; the other for the consulate, asymmetric and informal as the Wicklow granite verneer is peeled away to reveal a steel cladding beneath, which otherwise appears on the facade only as extended framing around window openings.

The main entrance leads not to some grand hallway, but through the convolution of security control to emerge in the notional core of the building – a stair hall that becomes the pinwheel centre of the T-shaped plan and of the departmental organisation of the building.

This building represents quality in its design detail and its material realisation, and, as elsewhere in the architects' oeuvre, it seeks to make the very construction articulate.
J.O.

Entrance in Merrion Road

North-east facade of central courtyard

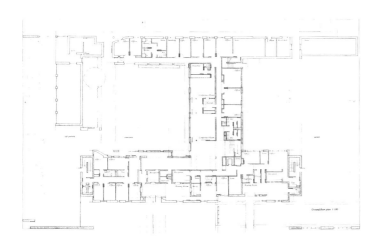

Ground-floor plan

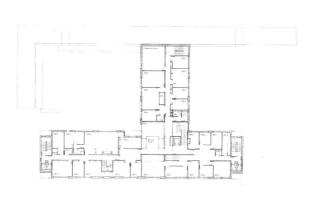

First-floor plan

Entrance hall

Planes of Wicklow granite and brickwork form the enclosure of the courtyard

The layers of the facade revealed in
the central courtyard

View along the moat

View across the river from the north-east

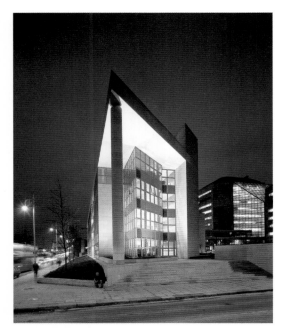

View from College Green

The main entrance

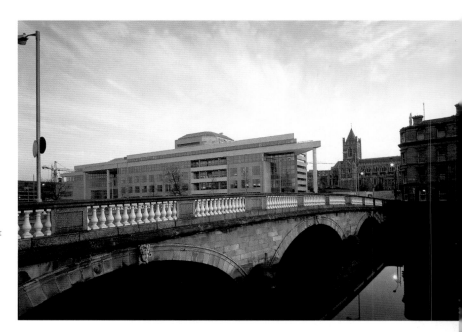

View across the river from the north-west

Section

Civic Offices

Wood Quay, Dublin   1992–4

RONALD TALLON

The completion of this complex for municipal administration marks a triumphant conclusion to the redevelopment of the most controversial site in Dublin — the city's Viking birthplace and, within memory, the focus of angry marches, occupations and court cases. Among the more important urban design problems successfully resolved by the project are the correct relationship of the new buildings to Christ Church Cathedral and the city quays, their architectural and functional integration with the pre-existing towers, the position of the site as the termination of the Temple Bar area and connections made to the surrounding city.

The new composition works particularly well on the incidental, urban scale. From within the city blocks on the north side of the river, we sense an abstract white datum against which three taller objects (the two original towers and the Cathedral tower) may be read. But the most pleasant surprise is the view from College Green: from here the prismatic, glazed atrium brilliantly completes the asymmetrical composition framed by two stone towers of different height, subtly expressing a concealed bend in the street. The intelligible urban whole created by the Civic Offices is a far cry from the dismayed comment of the *Architectural Review* in November 1974 that 'discontinuity is the chief mark of modern intervention in Dublin'.
S.O'T.

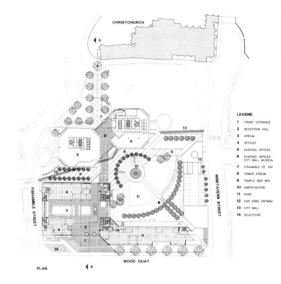

Plan

Looking along the south facade

Staircase on the upper floors

Blackwood Golf Club

Clandeboye, Bangor, County Down
1992–4

SHEILA O'DONNELL / JOHN TUOMEY

The architects describe their project as a 'constructed landscape' in which the buildings are integrated with their pastoral surroundings by means of terraces, gardens, hedges, embankments and cuttings. Sited on a mound at the edge of woodland, the working parts of the brief are arranged in a series of buildings grouped around a raised courtyard-promenade that completes the circuit from 1st tee to 18th green and overlooks the landscape beyond the driving range.

Drawing on an international language of traditional forms, each element of the programme is individually expressed, so that even the ordinary becomes extraordinary. The collagist planning of the project brings to

mind aspects of the 'ancient and sacred acropolis of Cashel', with its complex ordering of castle, cathedral, side chapels, tower and Cormac's Chapel: *urbs in ruris*.

The central pile of masonry gives way to a lighter timber construction, creating a sense of movement towards the woodland, marking a diminution from the collective facilities to the natural landscape and creating what has been described as 'a painterly, cinematic and dreamy effect', best seen, fragmented and flickering, through the trees. This project contributes to re-establishing confidence in, and sensitivity to, building in the Irish landscape.
S.O'T.

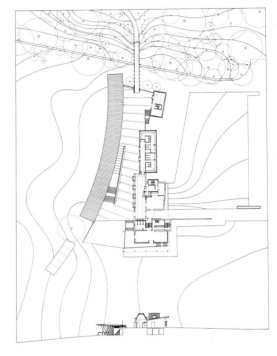

Plan

South elevation

186

General view from the west

General view from the east

The Club Room

Detail of south facade

Entrance

187

Appendix

Selected Bibliography

Books, Exhibition Catalogues
and Articles

Aalen, Frederick H.A. 'The Rehousing
of Rural Labourers in Ireland under
the Labourers (Ireland) Acts,
1883- 1919'. *Journal of Historical
Geography* 12, no. 3 (July 1986),
pp. 287-306.

Aalen, Frederick H.A. *The Iveagh
Trust: The First Hundred Years,
1890-1990.* Dublin,1990.

Abercrombie, Patrick, Sydney Kelly
and Arthur Kelly. *Dublin of the Future:
The New Town Plan.* Liverpool and
London, 1922.

Abercrombie, Patrick, Sydney Kelly
and Manning Robertson. *Town
Planning Report: Sketch Development
Plan.* Dublin, 1941.

Adam, Peter. *Eileen Gray, Architect -
Designer: A Biography.* London, 1987.

Airport Terminal Building *Irish Builder*
(11. August 1945), pp. 372-377

Architects' Journal 89 (22 June 1936),
pp. 1074-87. Special issue on Dublin.

Architects' Journal 144 (7 Sept. 1966),
pp. 563-644. Special issue on Ireland.

Bannon, Michael J. (ed.). *A Hundred
Years of Irish Planning: The Emergence
of Irish Planning, 1880-1980.*
Dublin, 1985.

Beckett, J.C., and R.E. Glasscock
(eds.). *Belfast: The Origin and Growth
of an Industrial City.* London, 1967.

'Bord na Mona Housing' *Irish
Architect* 11.Oktober 1995, pp.41-45

'Botanic Primary School' *Irish Builder
and Engineer* 13. Mai 1939, pp.387-388

Boyd, Brian. *A Heritage from Stone: A
Review of Architecture in Ulster from
Prehistory to the Present Day.*
Belfast, 1986.

Buckley, Eoghan. 'Exhibition of
Modern Architecture'. *Ireland Today* 2,
no. 2 (1937), pp. 130-59.

Butler, A.S.G. *The Architecture of Sir
Edwin Lutyens.* Vol 1, London, 1950

Butler, Rudolf Maximilian. 'Sixty
Years of Architecture in Ireland'.
Irish Builder and Engineer. Jubilee
edition (June 1919), p. 46ff.

Cahill, Gerry. *Dublin City Quays: Projects by the School of Architecture, UCD.*
Dublin, 1986.

Cahill, Gerry, and Niall McCullough.
'Irish Renaissance'. *Architects' Journal*
180 (31 Oct. 1984), pp. 31-49.

Campbell, Hugh. 'Interpreting the
City: Dublin and the Culture of
Nationalism'. M.Arch.Sc. thesis,
University College Dublin, 1994.

Casey, Christine, and Alistair Rowan.
The Buildings of Ireland: North Leinster.
London, 1993.

Chidlow, Rachel et al. (eds.). *Figurative
Architecture: The Work of Five Dublin
Architects.* Exh. cat. London, Architec-
tural Association,1986.

Colquhoun, Alan. 'Library, Trinity
College Dublin'. *Architectural Review*
142 (1967), pp. 264-77.

Colquhoun, Alan. 'Michael Scott and
Partners'. *Architectural Design*
38 (March 1968), pp. 106-25.

Constant, Caroline. 'E.1027: The
Non-heroic Modernism of Eileen
Gray'. *Journal of the Society of Architec-
tural Historians* 53 (1994), pp. 265-79.

Constant, Caroline, and Wilfred
Wang (eds.). *Eileen Gray: An Architecture for All Senses.* Exh. cat. Frankfurt,
Deutsches Architektur-Museum,
1996.

Cullinan, Eve-Anne (ed.). *Development
Programme for Temple Bar.*
Dublin, 1992.

Cuffe, Luan P. *Architectural Survey.*
Dublin, 1953.

Dal Co, Francesco. *Kevin Roche.*
New York, 1985.

Davies, Colin. 'Footsteps of a National
Hero' (Scott Tallon Walker). *World
Architecture,* no. 30 (1994), pp. 80-7.

DeCourcy, John. *A History of Structural
Engineering in Ireland, 1908-1983.*
Dublin, 1983.
Delany, Patrick M. (ed.).
Dublin: A City in Crisis. Dublin, 1975.

'Eileen Gray'. *Archithese* 21
(July-Aug. 1991), pp. 1-76.

Evans, David. *An Introduction to Modern
Ulster Architecture.* Belfast, 1977.

Field, D.E., and O.G. Neill. *A Survey
of New Housing Estates in Belfast.*
Belfast, 1954.

Figgis, Darrell. *Planning for the Future.*
Dublin, 1922.

Fraser, Murray. *John Bull's Other
Homes: State Housing and British Policy
in Ireland, 1883-1922.* Liverpool, 1996.

Garner, Philippe. *Eileen Gray.*
Cologne, 1993.

Graby, John (ed.). *150 Years of Architecture in Ireland: RIAI, 1839-1989.*
Dublin, 1989.

Graby, John (ed.). *Building on the Edge
of Europe.* Dublin, 1996.

Graby, John, and Deirdre O'Connor
(eds.). *Dublin.* London, 1993.

Graeve, Jobst. *Temple Bar Lives! A
Record of the Architectural Framework
Competition.* Dublin, 1991.

Group '91 (eds.), *Making a Modern
Street: An Urban Proposal - The Work
of Eight Irish Architects.* Exh. cat.
Dublin and Zurich, 1991.

'Green Building' *Irish Architect*
(September/Oktober 1994), pp. 25-33

Henman, William, and Henry Lea.
'Royal Victoria Hospital, Belfast: Its
Initiation, Design, and Equipment'.
*Journal of the Royal Institute of British
Architects,* 3rd ser., 11 (Dec. 1903),
pp. 89-113.

Hurley, Richard, and Wilfrid
Cantwell. *Contemporary Irish Church
Architecture.* Dublin, 1985.

Hussey, Christopher. 'Lambay Island'.
Country Life, no.1696 (20 July 1929),
pp. 86-94, and no.1697
(27 July 1929), pp. 120-6.

'Institute of Advanced Studies'. *The
Brick Bulletin. Journal of the Brick
Development Association (Windsor)*
Vol.10, No. 1/November 1973, pp.16-19

'Ireland 1947'. *Architectural Design* 17
(July 1947), pp. 172-210.

Johnson, J. Stewart. *Eileen Gray,
Designer.* New York, 1979.

Kamen, Ruth H. *British and Irish
Architectural History: A Bibliographical
Guide to Sources of Information.*
London, 1981.

Larmour, Paul. 'Celtic Revival and a
National Style of Architecture'. Ph.D.
thesis, The Queen's University,
Belfast, 1977.

Larmour, Paul. *Celtic Ornament.*
Dublin, 1981.

Larmour, Paul. *Festival of Architecture,
1834-1984.* Belfast, 1984.

Larmour, Paul. *The Arts and Crafts
Movement in Ireland.* Belfast, 1992.

Larmour, Paul. 'The Father of
Church Design: Liam McCormick,
1916-1996'. *Perspective* 5, no. 2
(Nov.-Dec. 1996), pp. 30-43.

McCullough, Niall. *Dublin: An Urban
History.* Dublin, 1989.

McCullough, Niall. *Palimpsest.*
Dublin, 1994.

McCullough, Niall, and Valerie Mulvin. *A Lost Tradition: The Nature of
Architecture in Ireland.* Dublin, 1987.

McDonald, Frank. *The Destruction of
Dublin.* Dublin, 1985.

McDonald, Frank. *Saving the City:
How to Halt the Destruction of Dublin.*
Dublin, 1989.

McDonald, Frank. 'Recreating the World: Recent Irish Architecture'. *Irish Arts Review* 12 (1996), pp. 171-81.

MacDonald, Suzanne, and Antonello Vagge. 'Temple Bar: The Left Bank of Dublin'. *Casabella* 58 (May 1994), pp. 28-39, 70-1.

McKinstry, Robert J. 'Contemporary Architecture'. In *Causeway: The Arts in Ulster*, pp. 27-42. Belfast, 1971.

McNarnara, Shelley. 'Blackwood Golf Club'. *Bauwelt* No. 38/1995, pp.2186-2189

Manning, Maurice, and Moore McDowell. *Electricity Supply in Ireland: The History of the ESB*. Dublin, 1984.

Murphy, Orla. 'Three Islands: A Reading of the Cultural Landscape of Ireland'. M.Arch.Sc. thesis, University College Dublin, 1996.

O'Beirne, Tomas. *A Guide to Modern Architecture in Dublin*. Dublin, 1978.

O'Connell, John R. *The Collegiate Chapel, Cork*. Cork, 1932.

O'Conner, Ciaran, and John O'Regan (eds.). *Public Works: The Architecture of the Office of Public Works, 1831-1987*. Dublin, 1987.

O'Donovan, Donal, and Alan Powers. *God's Architect: A Life of Raymond McGrath*. Bray, 1995.

O'Kelly, Michael J. *The Honan Chapel, University College Cork*. Cork, 1966.

Olley, John. 'Rebuilding in a Classical Tradition'. *Architects' Journal* 185, no. 24 (1987), pp. 37-51.

Olley, John. 'Dublin Courts: Urban Tradition Revived'. *Architects' Journal* 187, no. 28 (1988), pp. 32-48.

Olley, John. 'Sustaining the Narrative at Kilmainham'. *Irish Arts Review* 8 (1991-2), pp. 65-72.

Olley, John. 'The Theatre of the City: Dublin 1991'. *Irish Arts Review* 9 (1993), pp. 70-8.

Olley, John. 'Redemption of Meaning: Chapel of Reconciliation at Knock'. *Irish Arts Review* 10 (1994), pp. 100-2.

Olley, John. 'The Art of Reading: A New Library and Image for Cork Regional Technical College'. *Architectural Research Quarterly* 1 (Winter 1995), pp. 30-41.

O'Regan, John (ed.). *The Architecture of Peter and Mary Doyle, 1970-1990*. Dublin, 1990.

O'Regan, John (ed.). *The Irish Pavilion*. Dublin, 1992.

O'Regan, John, and Nicola Dearey (eds.). *Michael Scott, Architect: In (Casual) Conversation with Dorothy Walker*. Kinsale, 1995.

O'Sheehan, J., and E. DeBarra. *Ospideil na hEireann/Ireland's Hospitals, 1930-1955*. Dublin, 1956.

O'Toole, Shane (ed.). *Collaboration: The Pillar Project*. Dublin, 1988.

O'Toole, Shane 'Irish Architect'. *Journal of the Royal Institute of the Architects of Irland* 104 (November/Dezember 1994), pp. 25-33.

O'Toole, Shane (ed.). *The Architect and the Drawing*. Exh. cat. Dublin, 1989.

Quinn, Patricia (ed.). *Temple Bar: The Power of an Idea*. Dublin, 1996.

Rothery, Sean. *Ireland and the New Architecture, 1900-1940*. Dublin, 1991.

Rowan, Alistair. *The Buildings of Ireland: North West Ulster*. Harmondsworth, 1979.

Scott, W.A. 'A University School of Architecture in Ireland'. *Studies* 1 (Dec. 1912), pp. 621-30.

Sheehy, Jeanne. *The Rediscovery of Ireland's Past: The Celtic Revival, 1830-1930*. London, 1980.

Simms, Herbert. 'Municipal Housing Activities in Dublin'. In *Centenary Conference Handbook of the Royal Institute of Architects of Ireland*, pp. 47-56. Dublin,1939.

Stollard, Paul. 'The Architecture of No Man's Land'. *Architects' Journal* 180 (1 Aug. 1984), pp. 24-39.

Tuomey, John. 'Work in Progress'. *Transactions of the Royal Institute of British Architects* 5, no. 2 (1987), pp. 72-85.

Williams, Jeremy. *A Companion Guide to Architecture in Ireland, 1837-1921*. Dublin, 1994.

Wilson, T.G. *The Irish Lighthouse Service*. Dublin, 1968.

Wright, Lance, and Kenneth Browne. 'A Future for Dublin'. Special issue of *Architectural Review* 156 (Nov. 1974), pp. 267-330.

Wright, Myles. *The Dublin Region: Advisory Plan and Final Report*. Dublin, 1967.

Irish Archtectural Journals and Annuals

Architectural Association of Ireland: Greenbook (1903-75)

Irish Architect, no.1 (1987) –

Irish Architecture: RIAI Regional Awards (1993) –

Irish Arts Review 1 (1984) –

New Irish Architecture: Architectural Association of Ireland Awards, no. 1 (1986) – . An annual exh. cat. of the AAI awards competition.

Perspective: Journal of the Royal Society of Ulster Architects 1 (1992) –

Plan: Magazine of the Construction Industry 1 (1969) –

RIAI Bulletin 1 (1972) - 13 (1987)

Royal Institute of the Architects of Ireland: Yearbook (1839) –

Ulster Architect: Journal of Architecture and Building Economics in Northern Ireland (1986) –

Selected Descriptions of Individual Buildings and Projects in Ireland in International Architectural Journals

Architects' Journal

'Bus Terminus and Offices in Dublin'. 119 (15 April 1954), pp. 453-66.
'Abbey Theatre Building Illustrated'. 144 (31 Aug. 1966), pp. 529-40.
'Centre for the Physically Handicapped'. 152 (7 Oct. 1970), pp. 829-42.
'Dining in at University College Dublin'. 153 (Feb. 1971), pp. 228-31.
'St. Columba's College'. 160 (24 July 1974), pp. 186-9.
'Riverside Theatre, New University of Ulster'. 166 (9 Nov. 1977), pp. 899-912.
'Reflecting on Dublin: The Bord Na Mona Building, Dublin, Ireland'. 169 (25 Jan. 1979), pp. 156-7.
'Trinity Triangles: Holy Trinity Church, Grangemore, Dublin, Ireland'. 169 (21 March 1979), pp. 570-2.
'Building Study: Community School, Birr, Offaly, Ireland - Architects: Peter and Mary Doyle'. 172 (24 Dec. 1980), pp. 1235-44.
'Dublin's Quay Development'. 189 (22 March 1989), pp. 34-47.
'Designing a Special Needs School'. 197 (31 March 1993), pp. 45-54.
'Space to Display Rolling Stock' [Ulster Rail and Transport Gallery, County Down]. 198 (14 July 1993), pp. 35-45.
'Blackwood Golf Centre'. 201 (25 May 1995), pp. 25-36.
[British Embassy]. (23 Nov. 1995), pp. 43-52.

'British Embassy.' (23. November 1995), pp. 43-52

Architectural Design

'Radio Eireann Television Studios at Montrose'. 33 (Feb. 1963), pp. 90-4.

Architectural Review

'Bus Terminus and Offices in Dublin'. 115 (1954), pp. 242-57.
'United States Embassy, Dublin'. 136 (1964), pp. 420-5.
'Berkeley Library'. 142(1967), pp 264-277
'Roman Catholic Church, Burt, Co. Donegal'. 143 (1968), pp. 361-2.
'Miesian in Eire: Tobacco Factory and Offices, Dundalk, Ireland'. 149 (1971), pp. 45-54.

'Church at Creeslough, Co. Donegal, Ireland'. 151 (1972), pp. 180-4.
'Banker's Acropolis: Bank of Ireland Headquarters in Dublin'. 153 (1973), pp. 85-97.
'Science Buildings and Library' [University College Galway]. 157 (1975), pp. 327-37.
'College, Booterstown, Dublin' [St. Andrew's College]. 159 (1976), pp. 355-9.
'Management Institute, Sandyford, Co. Dublin'. 161 (1977), pp. 166-71.
'Two Ulster Churches'. 163 (1978), pp. 171-4.
'Arts Faculty, Trinity College, Dublin, Ireland - Architects: Ahrends, Burton and Koralek'. 166 (1979), pp. 35-43.
'Central Bank, Dublin, Ireland'. 166 (1979), pp. 347-55.
'Into the Past' [Irish Museum of Modern Art]. 189 (1991), pp. 62-6.
'Dublin Renaissance'. 192 (1993), pp. 42-9.
'Wild in the West: Visitors' Centre, Co. Kerry, Ireland'. 193 (1993), pp. 58-60.
'King of the Castle' [Visitor Centre, King John's Castle, Limerick]. 194 (1993), pp. 54-7.
'Campus Chutzpah: Student Theatre, Dublin' [Samuel Beckett Theatre]. 194 (1993), pp. 62-5.

Architecture and Urbanism

'Eileen Gray: Two Houses and an Interior', no. 95 (Aug. 1978), pp. 97-106.
'Ahrends, Burton and Koralek: St. Andrew's College, Booterstown, Dublin, Ireland', no. 106 (July 1979), pp. 103-10.
'Ahrends, Burton and Koralek: Trinity College Arts Building, Dublin, Ireland', no. 109 (Oct. 1979), pp. 83-95.

Architektur und Wohnen

'Ein Stück Filmgeschichte', no. 5 (Oct.-Nov. 1990), pp. 48-52.
'Ein Märchen in Nordirland', no. 4 (Aug.-Sept. 1991), pp. 70-7.
'Dialog in Dublin', no. 2 (April-May 1994), pp. 38-44.

Lotus International

'Residence of the Irish Prime Minister: Competition for the Housing of the Irish Prime Minister . . .', no. 25 (1979), pp. 15-24.

World Architecture

'Town and Gown' [Scott Tallon Walker], no. 40, pp. 112-17.

Biographies

Compiled by
Paul Larmour, John Olley, and Tom Russell

AAI = Architectural Association of Ireland;
RIAI = Royal Institute of Architects of Ireland;
RIBA = Royal Institute of British Architects

ALLIES AND MORRISON ARCHITECTS

Robert Allies b. 1953

Studied at Edinburgh University, 1971-7. Rome Scholar in
Architecture, 1981-2. Worked for Peter Collymore and Associates,
Martin Richardson Architects, Michael Brawne and Associates and
Michael Glickman before forming the practice of Allies and
Morrison in 1984 after their success in the competition for the
new public square in front of the National Gallery of Scotland in
Edinburgh. Lecturer at Cambridge University (1983-7) and
George Simpson Visiting Professor at the University of Edinburgh
(1994-5).

Graham Morrison b. 1951

Studied at Cambridge University (1969-75). Worked for Keïjo
Petajä, Cambridge Design, Eric Lyons, Martin Richardson and
YRM before founding Allies and Morrison in 1984.
A director of the RIBA Journal, he is also a member of the Archi-
tecture Advisory Committee of the Arts Council of Great
Britain.Works in Britain include: Manor Farm Housing,
Farningham, Kent (1985); Brown House, Amersham; The Mound,
Edinburgh (1990); conversion of the Clove Building, Butler's
Wharf, London (1990); Scott Howard offices and showrooms,
London (1991); Morrison House, Blackheath (1992); Admiral
Court, Blandford Street, London (1993); Underground Station,
Hanover Square, London (1994); Sarum Hall School, London
(1995); Pierhead,f Liverpool (1995); Student Housing, Newnham
College, Cambridge (1995); Student Union Building, Southampton
University (1995); Gallery and Shop, Contemporary Applied Arts,
London (1996). In Ireland: British Embassy, Dublin (1995).

JAMES M. BRENNAN b. 1912, d. 1967

Studied at University College Dublin, graduating 1938. Began to
practise privately in 1937. Collaborated with Michael Scott on the
Chassis Factory at Inchicore, Dublin. In the early 1950s he was
appointed Housing Architect with Cork Corporation, and in 1953
he was elected Fellow of the RIAI.

Works include: 'Church Experiment' (drawings; 1935); Dolphin
Bar, Essex Street, Dublin (1939); Workshop, Rathdown Road,
Dublin (1949); Bohemian Bar, Phibsboro, Dublin (1950); Housing,
Trim, Meath (1950); Housing, Kells, Meath (1951); Housing,
Navan, Meath (1951); School, Navan, Meath (1953); House, 102
Merrion Road, Dublin (1954); De La Salle Monastery, Navan,
Meath (1954).

RUDOLF MAXIMILIAN BUTLER b. 1872, d. 1943

Studied in Dublin and in continental Europe before being
apprenticed to Walter Doolin, eventually establishing the partnership Doolin, Butler and Donnelly before practising privately. A
fluent writer, he contributed extensively to Irish and British professional and technical journals and was editor of the Irish Builder and
Engineer for forty years. President of the AAI (1906-7) and Fellow
of the RIBA (1906). Held the Chair of Architecture at University
College Dublin (1924-42).

Works include: Carnegie Library, Enniskerry, Wicklow (1912);
University College Buildings, Earlsfort Terrace, Dublin (1914-18);
Church, Newport, Mayo (1915-18); Church, Westport, Mayo;
Church, New Ross, Wexford; County Hospital, Castlebar, Mayo;
County Sanatorium, Rathdrum, Wicklow; Maternity Hospital, the
Coombe, Dublin; Richview Press Offices, Clonskeagh, Dublin;
Gorevan Store and Offices, Camden Street, Dublin (1925-27);
Church, Killanny, Monaghan (1925-31); Church, Ardoyne, Belfast;
Templeton Carpet Factory, Navan, Meath; Irish Artistic Engraving
Company Factory, Dublin; Convent Chapel, Holyhead, Wales.

FRANCIS BARRY BYRNE b. 1883 in USA, d. 1968 in USA

Studied under the apprentice system in the Oak Park Studio of
Frank Lloyd Wright in Chicago (1902-9). Worked in Seattle
(1909-13) before taking over the practice of Walter Burley Griffin
in California. In 1922 formed his own construction company,
which was dissolved after the stock market crash in 1929. Practised
privately in New York (1932-45) before returning to Chicago.
Contributed extensively to architectural publications, on general
topics and on church architecture in particular.

Works include: Clark House, Seattle, Washington (1909); Francke
House, Fort Wayne, Indiana (1914); St Thomas the Apostle
Church, Church of Chicago (1922); St Patrick's Church, Racine,
Wisconsin (1924); Christ the King, Turner's Cross, Cork, Ireland
(1927-31); Williams House, Westport, Connecticut (1936); Sts Peter
and Paul Church, Pierre, South Dakota (1939); St Francis Xavier
Church, Kansas City, Montana (1949); St Benedict's Abbey, Atchi-
son, Kansas (1951); St Procopius College Library, Lisle, Illinois
(1962).

WILLIAM HENRY BYRNE b. 1844, d. 1917

Studied as an apprentice with J. J. McCarthy before establishing a
partnership with John O'Neill in Belfast in 1869. After the death
of O'Neill in 1883 he practised alone until 1902, when he took his
son, Ralph Byrne, into partnership. Elected Fellow of the RIAI in
1885, he was responsible for the construction of some of the
largest buildings in Dublin, including the South City Markets on
South Great George's Street, the Mater Hospital and the
Children's Hospital on Temple Street.

Works include: Christian Brother's Novitiate, Marino, Dublin
(1900); 35-38 Belvedere Place, Dublin (1903); Archbishop House,
Tuam, Galway (1903-4); Church, Greystones, Wicklow (1909);
Town Hall, Ballinasloe, Galway (1913).

GERRY CAHILL b. 1951

Studied at University College Dublin and the Architectural Association, London. Prior to returning to Ireland in 1979, he worked
with the London Borough of Camden, Levitt Bernstein Associates
and the Royal College of Art Project Office. Established Gerry
Cahill Architects in 1984 and has specialised in social housing and
in building conservation and restoration. Active in many areas of
community development, he has produced several publications on
urban renewal in Ireland, including Back to the Street (1980). He
has been involved with architectural education at University
College Dublin and at colleges in continental Europe and America.

Works include: Housing at Stanhope Green, Dublin (1991);
McCleans Lane, Dublin (1994), Raheny, Dublin (1995), Mulhud-
dart, Dublin (1995), Balbriggan, Dublin (1995), Swords, Dublin
(1995), Ballyogan, Dublin (1995), Queen Street, Dublin (1995),
Seán McDermott Street, Dublin (1995), Allingham Street, Dublin
(1996), George's Hill, Dublin (1996).

ROSS CAHILL O'BRIEN

Studied at the University of Hull, England, graduating 1984.
Worked in the offices of A & D Wjechert, Dublin, and Chapman
Taylor Partners and CZWG, London, before setting up a private
practice in 1989.

Works include: Camphill Housing, Gorey, Wexford (1991); Taylor
Galleries, Dublin (1992); Tosca Restaurant, Suffolk Street, Dublin
(1992); Purty Loft Night Club, Monkstown, Dublin (1994);
Kitchen Night Club, Essex Street, Dublin (1994); Restaurant, Bal-
lina, Mayo (1994); Café Bar, Dun Laoghaire, Dublin (1995);
House, Bofara, Mayo (1995).

IAN CAMPBELL

Studied at the Belfast Royal Academy and was apprenticed to John MacGeagh in Belfast (1944-7) before continuing his studies at the School of Architecture, Belfast College of Art. Member of the Royal Society of Ulster Architects' Design Team, who were responsible for the Festival of Britain Exhibition in Belfast (1951). Elected member of Modern Architecture Research Group (MARS) in 1955 and attended the CIAM Summer School in Venice in 1956. Assisted J. V. T. Scott of Belfast on the design of schools before establishing his own practice in 1958. Partnership with David J. Allardyce formed in 1978. Elected President of the Royal Society of Ulster Architects (1971, to 1973), he has received numerous architectural awards and commendations for his work.

Works include: Campbell House, Holywood, Down (1959-60); McCabe's Bar, Portadown, Armagh (1959-60; now remodelled); Ulster Folk and Transport Museum, Cultra, Down (1965); Teahouse, Tollymore Forest Park, Down (1979); Health Centre, Poleglass, Belfast (1986); Recreation Centre, Loughside, Belfast (1986); Bar, Wellington Park Hotel, Belfast (1992); Railway Transport Gallery, Cultra, Down (1992-3); Road Transport Gallery, Cultra, Down (1993-5); School, Abbots Cross, Belfast (1996).

NOEL CAMPBELL

Apprenticed to H. V. and R.E. McCaughan of Belfast (1938-40) before working with John McGeagh. Joined the Works Branch of the Northern Ireland Ministry of Finance in 1942 and the Republic of Ireland Health and Local Government Hospitals Department in 1947. In 1948 he was appointed County Education Architect for the Londonderry Education Committee at Coleraine. Established the Dalzell and Campbell Partnership with Crofton Dalzell in 1961. Now retired, he continues to work as a consultant.

Works include: Schools in County Derry at Garvagh (1951-2), Coleraine (1953-7), Eglington (1954-6), Magherafelt (1954-6), Limavady (1955), Faughan Valley (1955-9), Coleraine (1956), Dungiven (1958-61); Houses at Broclamont Park, Ballymena, Antrim (1953-6), Dhu Varren, Portrush, Antrim (1959), Strand Road, Portstewart, Derry (1959), Larkhill Road, Portstewart, Derry (1960); Sheltered Housing, Moneymore, Derry (1964); McKinney Offices, Mallusk, Antrim (1971); Russell Court Hotel, Belfast (1972; now remodelled).

WILFRED CANTWELL *b.* 1921

Studied at the Dublin Institute of Technology, graduating in 1944. Worked with Michael Scott (1944-5) and J. N. Kidney (1946-7) before practising privately (1947-75). Since 1976 he has specialised as a consultant in church design and in the legal aspects of building. Founder member and Chairman of the Irish Branch of the Chartered Institute of Arbitrators and former President of the RIAI (1966-7). He has taught architectural design at the Dublin Institute of Technology and liturgical design at St Patrick's College, Maynooth, All Hallows College, Dublin, and the Irish Institute for Pastoral Liturgy, Carlow.

Works include: Church of the Holy Spirit, St Leonard's, Ballycullane, Wexford (1971).

SHAY CLEARY *b.* 1951

Studied at University College Dublin, graduating 1974. Worked with Marcel Breuer and Candilis Josic Woods in Paris and with Neave Brown at the Camden Borough Council in London before returning to Dublin in 1976. Worked as a partner with Grafton Architects (1977-80) and Cleary and Hall (1981-6) before establishing Shay Cleary Architects in 1987; also a member of Group '91 Architects. In addition to having been published extensively internationally, the work of the practice has received numerous awards. President of the AAI in 1980. He has taught at University College Dublin and Princeton University, New Jersey.

Works include: Apartments, Chapelizod, Dublin (1980); Houses, Swan Place, Dublin (1983); Bars and Restaurant, Point Depot, Dublin (1989); Irish Museum of Modern Art, Kilmainham, Dublin (1991); Apartments, Beggars Bush, Dublin (1989); Foyer and Conference Facilities, Agriculture House, Dublin (1994); Arthouse, Curved Street, Dublin (1995); Teacher's Centre, Blackrock, Dublin (1996); Project Arts Centre, Essex Street, Dublin (1996-); Municipal Library, Waterford (1996-); Civic Offices, Donegal (1996-); Housing, Queen Street, Dublin (1996-); House, Sandymount, Dublin (1996-); House, Grand Canal Quay, Dublin (1996-); School, Dungarvan, Waterford (1996).

THOMAS JOSEPH CULLEN *b.* 1880, *d.* 1947

Apprenticed to Ashlin and Coleman in Dublin before practising privately from 1908. Worked on several projects in Dublin for Matthew J. McCabe in the early years of the practice before specialising in work for public and religious bodies. In 1922 he was appointed architect with P. H. McCarthy for the reconstruction of Cork city. Elected Fellow of the RIAI in 1922, he also served on the governing body of University College Dublin.

Works include; Loreto Convent, North Great George's Street, Dublin (1920); St Patrick's Basilica, Lough Derg, Donegal (1926); St Peter's Seminary, Wexford (1931-2); St Mary's Hospital, Cappagh, Dublin (1932); Central Hospital, Galway (1933-38); Technical School, Carnew, Wicklow (1934); St Peter's Hospital, Castlepollard, Westmeath (1938-41); Hospital, Loughlinstown, Dublin (1945).

DE BLACAM AND MEAGHER ARCHITECTS

Shane de Blacam *b.* 1945

Studied at University College Dublin (1963-8) and at the University of Pennsylvania (1969-70). Worked in USA with Chamberlain Powell and Bon before joining Louis I. Kahn for three years, leaving in 1973 to return to Ireland to teach at University College Dublin. Established de Blacam and Meagher Architects in 1976. President of the AAI in 1975.

John Meagher *b.* 1947

Studied at the Dublin Institute of Technology School of Architecture (1966-71) and at Helsinki University of Technology School of Architecture (1971-2). Worked in Dublin, Germany and the USA before establishing de Blacam and Meagher Architects in 1976. President of the AAI in 1977. Served in various roles on the boards of ROSC (1975-83), the Municipal Gallery of Modern Art (1985-90), the Dublin Graphic Studio (1989-92), the Irish Museum of Modern Art (1989-95) and the Black Church Print Studio (1994-).

Works include: Church, Rowlagh, Dublin (1977); Firhouse Chapel, Dublin (1979); Taoiseach's House, Phoenix Park, Dublin (unbuilt; 1979); Shelbourne Hotel, St Stephen's Green, Dublin (renovation; 1981); Psychogeriatric Hospital, Clonkeagh, Dublin (1983-7); Housing, Trinity College-Pearse Street, Dublin (1984-90); School, Jobstown, Dublin (1985-91); Atrium and Dining Hall, Trinity College Dublin (renovation; 1987); Aer Lingus Offices in Dublin, Cork, Manchester, Düsseldorf and London (1988); Chapel of Reconciliation, Knock, Mayo (1989-90); Campus Buildings, Graduate School of Business, Blackrock, County Dublin (1990-3); Campus Buildings, Regional Technical College, Cork (with Boyd Barrett Murphy O'Connor; 1991-); Stack B Offices, Custom House Docks, Dublin (1993-5); Entrance Landscape, University of Limerick (1996-); Housing, Mayor Street, Dublin (1996-); Restoration of Lyons Estate, Kildare (1996-).

TOMÁS de PAOR *b.* 1967

Studied at the Dublin Institute of Technology and University College Dublin, graduating 1991. Has practised privately since 1991, often working collaboratively with other architects and artists, including Emma O'Neill, Dominic Stevens and Éilis O'Connell. Has taught at University College Dublin since 1992.

Works include: Visitor Centre, Ballincollig, Cork (with Emma O'Neill; 1991-2); Terraced Garden, Cork (1994); House, Cualadh (1994); Sculpture Studio, Cork (1995); Íosfacht Building, Dublin (1995); Wallpaper House, Cork (1996-); Hardware Shop, Dublin (1996-); House, Killiney, Dublin (1996-); Foyer Building, Galway (1996-).

NOEL DOWLEY *b.* 1932

Studied at University College Dublin, graduating in 1961, and at the University of Pennsylvania under Louis I. Kahn (1963-4). Practised privately in Dublin (1965-9), in the partnership Curley and Dowley Associates (1969-78) and, since 1978, as Noel Dowley Architects. Currently Consulting Architect for the Master Plan (Landside) at Dublin Airport for Aer Rianta. He has taught at University College Dublin since 1965. Fellow of the RIAI in 1995.

Works include: Church, Cong, Galway; Workshop, New Dock, Galway (1977); Car Park Buildings, Airport, Dublin (1991); School, Ashbourne, Meath (1995).

JOSEPH VINCENT DOWNES *b.* 1891, *d.* 1967

Studied at University College Dublin and as an apprentice with Callaghan and Webb, graduating 1920. Worked in London with Herbert Baker, Robert Atkinson — acting as site architect for the Gresham Hotel, O'Connell Street, Dublin — and in Dublin as a partner in McDonnell and Dixon (1927-35). Practised privately in Dublin (1935-44) before establishing Downes Meehan with F. Bernard Meehan (1944) and Downes Meehan Robson with Harold S. Robson (1949). Served as Professor of Architecture at University College Dublin (1943-51), established a remarkable library of architectural slides and was a leading spokesman on behalf of the modern movement in Ireland.

Works include: Bank of Ireland, Belfast; Housing, Kincora Road, Dublin (1930); Insurance Offices, Dame Street, Dublin (1934-5); Hospital, Kilkenny (1935); Church, Our Lady of Lourdes Hospital, Drogheda (1935; demolished); 'Dunboys', Foxrock, Dublin (1939); Science Buildings, Belfield, Dublin (1964).

PETER AND MARY DOYLE ARCHITECTS

Mary Doyle

Studied at University College Dublin, graduating 1959. Worked in Boston, USA, before returning to Dublin to work in the office of Michael Scott. Established Peter and Mary Doyle Architects in 1972, whose work together has received numerous awards, including the Gold Medal of the RIAI.

Peter Doyle *d.* 1995

Studied at University College Dublin and the Illinois Institute of Technology, graduating with a Master's Degree in Architectural Science in 1965. Worked with Ludwig Mies van der Rohe before returning to Dublin to work in the office of Michael Scott. Established Peter and Mary Doyle Architects in 1972. He has taught at University College Dublin and the Dublin Institute of Technology.

Works include: Health Centre, Maynooth, Kildare; Health Centre, Athy, Kildare; Health Centre, Bride Street, Dublin; Sheltered Housing, Rathmines, Dublin; Electricity Depot, Ardee, Louth; Factory, Newtownmountkennedy, Wicklow; Factory, Rathdowney; Community School, Birr, Offaly; Community College, Firhouse, Dublin; Water Treatment Buildings, Clare; Water Treatment Buildings, Bray, Wicklow; Offices, Standard Life Assurance, Dublin (renovation); National College of Art and Design, Thomas Street, Dublin (landscaping); School, Cashel, Tipperary; Interpretative Centre, Valentia Island, Kerry.

DESMOND FITZGERALD *b.* 1910, *d.* 1987

Studied at University College Dublin, graduating in 1935, and in London. Worked on housing in London before returning to Ireland to take up the appointment of Architect for Airports with the Office of Public Works for the airports at Collingstown (Dublin) and Rynanna (Shannon). Received the Gold Medal of the RIAI for his work on Dublin Airport. He held the Chair of Architecture at University College Dublin (1954-73).

Works include: Airport Buildings, Dublin (1937-41); Airport Village, Shannon (1946); Housing, Naas, Kildare (1946); Housing, Athy, Kildare (1949); Housing, Boghall Road, Bray (1950); Moyne Institute, Trinity College Dublin (1950-3); Factory and Office, Hanover Street, Dublin (1954); Café, Bray Head, Wicklow (1956);

Housing, Dominick Street, Dublin (1959); Offices, O'Connell Bridge, Dublin (1960-1); Apartments, Seafield Road, Clontarf (1962); Offices, Pembroke Road, Dublin (1963); Apartments, Ailesbury Road, Dublin (1963).

ARTHUR GIBNEY *b.* 1932

Studied at the Dublin Institute of Technology and at the National College of Art. Worked as an assistant to Michael Scott before establishing the partnership Stephenson Gibney Associates with Sam Stephenson in 1960. In 1975 he established Arthur Gibney and Partners and in 1976 he received the Gold Medal of the RIAI for the Irish Management Institute building. He has served as President of the Society of Designers in Ireland (1975-7) and of the RIAI (1988-9) and is currently professor of architecture at the Royal Hibernian Academy.

Works include: Offices for Coras Tráctála, Dublin (1970); Irish Management Institute, Sandyford, Dublin (1973); School, Leixlip, Dublin (1979); Royal Hibernian Academy Gallagher Gallery, Ely Place, Dublin (final execution; 1987-9); Dublin City University Masterplan (1990); the restoration of Dr Steeven's Hospital, Dublin (1994).

FRANK GIBNEY *b.* 1905, *d.* 1978

Apprenticed to Frank Russell. Member of the Institute of Registered Architects and an Associate Member of the Town Planning Institute. With Patrick Abercrombie, Ernest Aston and Manning Robertson he was one of the major figures in town planning in Ireland after Independence, preparing Town Plans for Waterford, Tralee, Drogheda, Meath, Navan and Tullamore. From 1951 to 1958 he worked for sixteen separate Local Authorites and built almost 300 houses per year, particularly in the Midlands. His most noteworthy housing schemes are those for Bord na Mona and at Clarecastle and Ballinasloe.

Works include Housing at Bordna Mona, Kilcormack, Offaly, Rochfortbridge, Westmeath, Lanesborough, Westmeath, Cloontuskert, Roscommon, Derraghan, Westmeath, Timahoe, Offaly, Bracknagh, Offaly, Clarecastle, Clare and Ballinasloe, Galway; House, Carrickbrack Road, Sutton (1945-6); Housing, Coill Dubh, Kildare; House, Blackbanks, Raheny, Dublin.

GRAFTON ARCHITECTS

Yvonne Farrell

Studied at University College Dublin, graduating 1974. Established Grafton Architects in 1977, whose work together has received numerous awards and has been published extensively internationally and exhibited at Dublin, London, Paris, Madrid and Zurich. A member of Group '91 Architects, she teaches at University College Dublin.

Shelley McNamara

Studied at University College Dublin, graduating 1974. Established Grafton Architects with Yvonne Farrell in 1977. A member of Group '91 Architects, she has taught at University College Dublin since 1976 and has lectured in Britain and Jordan.

Works include: Offices, Ormond Quay, Dublin (1989); House, Doolin, Clare (1994); Motorway Bridge, Bray, Wicklow (1994); Temple Bar Square and Building, Dublin (1995); Department of Production Engineering, Trinity College Dublin (1996).

NEIL HEGARTY

Studied at the VEC School of Architecture, Cork, and at Oxford University, England. Established private practice in Cork before joining Cork County Council in 1974 and Cork Corporation as City Architect in 1985. Received the Gold Medal for Housing from the RIAI for the Housing at Dundannion Court.

Works include: Housing, Dundannion Court, Cork; Housing, Dunmanway, Cork; Housing, Ard Bhaile, Cork; Housing, Knocknaheeny, Cork; Housing, Mayfield, Cork.

WILLIAM HENMAN b. 1850, d. 1917

Apprenticed to his father, Charles Henman, before establishing independent private practice in 1871 at Stockton-on-Tees, England, moving to Birmingham in 1879. Elected Fellow of the RIBA in 1895. He specialised in hospital planning and construction. He wrote extensively and contributed many articles to the RIBA Journal before resigning his Fellowship in 1913.

Works in England include: New General Hospital, Birmingham; Guest Hospital, Dudley; Hospital Buildings, Stockton; Hospital Buildings, Thornaby; Hospital, Great Malvern; Hospital Buildings, Darlington. In Ireland: Royal Victoria Hospital, Grosvenor Road, Belfast (1900-3).

FREDERICK GEORGE HICKS b. 1870, d. 1965

Studied at the Architectural Association and the Finsbury Technical College for Building Construction in London and was apprenticed to J. W. Stevens there (1886-90). Moved to Dublin in 1890 and, after working for several offices, established his own practice in 1896. Founding member of the AAI and its President in 1896. President of the RIAI (1929-31), receiving the first Gold Medal in 1934 for the Church of St Thomas, Cathal Brugha Street, Dublin. He retired from practice in 1945.

Works in Dublin include: Housing, Rathmines (1900-2); Iveagh Markets, Francis Street (1906); Martello Tower House, Malahide (1910); Housing, Bettyglen, Raheny (1910); Corner Building, Abbey Street-O'Connell Street (1917); Housing, Marino (1922-5); St Thomas Church, Cathal Brugha Street (1930-2); Grain Silos, North Wall (1936).

ALAN HODGSON HOPE b. 1909 Liverpool, d. 1965 Dublin

Studied at Liverpool University (1927-32). Worked briefly in Germany before moving to Ireland. Worked with Frederick George Hicks on the hospital building programme. On Hicks's retirement in 1945, Hope took over the practice. Received the Gold Medal of the RIAI for the Aspro Factory in 1950. Served as a Council Member in the RIAI and in the RIBA. He was an accomplished watercolourist throughout his career.

Works include: Methodist Hall, Belfast (1934); Meander House, Foxrock, Dublin (1939); Aspro Factory, Dublin (1947; demolished); Factory, Sir John Rogerson's Quay, Dublin (1949); Fever Hospital, Cherry Orchard, Dublin (1950); Pediatric Clinic, Rotunda Hospital, Dublin (1950).

RICHARD HURLEY

Studied at the Dublin Institute of Technology, graduating 1955. Worked in the office of Tyndall and Hogan before being made a partner in 1968. Established Richard Hurley and Associates in 1988, which specialised in hospital and church buildings. President of the AAI (1967-8) and Chairperson of the Irish Hierarchy National Commission on Sacred Art and Architecture.

Works include: Apartments, Mespil Estate, Dublin (1967); Lansdowne House Offices, Ballsbridge, Dublin (1967); Canada House Offices, St Stephen's Green, Dublin (1973); Hospital, Tullamore, Offaly (renovation); St Michael's Hospital, Dun Laoghaire (renovation); Beaumont General Hospital, Artane, Dublin; St John the Baptist Cathedral, Eldoret, Kenya (1987); Mercy International Centre, Baggot Street, Dublin; Esposito Hall, Royal Irish Academy of Music, Dublin; St Stephen's Cathedral, Brisbane, Australia; Our Lady and St Philip Howard Cathedral, Arundel, England (renovation); Clinical Science Building, Beaumont Hospital, Dublin.

JOHN MacLANE JOHANSEN b. 1916 in USA

Studied at Harvard University, graduating 1942. Worked with Marcel Breuer and Skidmore, Owings and Merrill in New York before practising privately from 1948 in New Canaan, Connecticut. Transferred his practice to New York in 1968 and established a partnership in 1970 with Ashok Bhavnani.

Works include: Warner House, New Canaan, Connecticut (1957); United States of America Embassy, Ballsbridge, Dublin (1962-4); Clowes Hall, Indianapolis, Indiana (1964); Taylor House, Westport, Connecticut (1966); Morris Mechanic Theatre, Baltimore, New Jersey (1967); Goddard University Library, Worcester, Massachusetts (1968); L. Francis Smith School, Columbus, Indiana (1970); Mummer's Theater, Oklahoma City (1970); Johansen House II, Stanfordville, New York (1974); Housing, Roosevelt Island, New York (1976).

DELISSA JOSEPH b. 1859, d. 192?

Began practising privately in 1882. He was responsible for numerous building projects in London, including apartment buildings, town and country houses, office buildings, warehouses, factories, hotels and synagogues.

Works include: Chelsea Court, Chelsea Embankment, London; Hotel Rembrandt, South Kensington, London; Peninsular House, Monument Street, London; Adelaide Court, Queen's Gate, London; Railway Station, Moorgate Street, London; Iveagh Trust Housing, Bride Street, Dublin; Dye Works, Mina Road, London; Synagogue, Higher Broughton, Manchester; Synagogue, Hampstead, London.

DAVID KEANE

Studied at University College Dublin, graduating 1954. Established McCormack and Keane in 1954 and Keane Murphy Duff in 1977 with Ian Duff and Noel Murphy. Studied law (1974-7) and was called to the Bar in 1977. He has written several books on building and law. President of the RIAI in 1996.

Works in Dublin include: Augustinian Novitiate, Ballyboden (1956-7); Church, Finglas West; Texaco Offices, Pembroke Road; Church, Ballyboden; Shopping Centre, Phibsboro; Shopping Centre, Blackrock; Leo Laboratories; Offices, Kinnear Court; Offices, Palmerstown House.

SARAH KELLY b. 1961

Studied at University College Dublin, graduating 1984. Worked with the Housing Research Unit at University College Dublin, Simon J. Kelly and Partners, Galway, and Chapman Taylor Architects, London, before returning to Simon J. Kelly and Partners in 1989, of which she has been a director since 1992. Currently director of the Galway Civic Trust.

Works include: Racecourse Development, Galway; Granary Suites Apartments, Galway; Ardilaun House Hotel, Galway; Western Health Board Training Centres, Loughrea and Tuam, Galway.

STEPHEN KELLY b. 1891

Apprenticed to R. M. Butler and studied at the Dublin Institute of Technology. Worked with J. J. Robinson until establishing partnership of Jones and Kelly with Alfred Jones in 1919. In their first year together they won the competition for the new Town Hall at Ballymena, and four years later won the competition for the new City Hall at Cork. President of the RIAI in 1947, in which year he was elected a Fellow of the RIBA.

Works include: Town Hall, Ballymena, Antrim (1920); City Hall, Cork (1932-5); Church, Nutgrove Avenue, Dublin; Housing, Mount Merrion Estate, Dublin (1934-5); Franciscan Church, Athlone, Westmeath; Church, Kimmage Manor, Dublin; Church, Clontarf, Dublin; Franciscan Church, Limerick; Ireland Pavilion, Glasgow Exhibition, Scotland (1938); Church, Mount Melleray, Waterford (1941); St Francis Church, Liberty Street, Cork (1951); Green Cinema, St Stephen's Green, Dublin.

VINCENT KELLY b. 1896

Studied at University College Dublin, of which he was the first architectural graduate. He was one of the original members of the Irish Hospital Committee of Reference and was responsible for much of the hospital building programme of the 1930s. President of the AAI.

Works include: ESB Offices, Fleet Street, Dublin (1931); ESB Substation, Milltown, Dublin (1931); Hospital, Nenagh, Tipperary (1932-6); Hospital, Cashel, Tipperary; Hospital, Naas, Kildare

(1939); Hospital Buildings, Grangegorman, Dublin; Holy Rosary Convent, Killeshandra, Cavan; New Ireland Assurance Offices, Dawson Street, Dublin.

JAMES B. KENNEDY

Studied at the Harris Academy and the School of Architecture in Dundee (1951-9). Worked as an assistant architect with the Northern Ireland Housing Executive before joining the design team responsible for the Belfast Airport Buildings at Aldergrove as principal architect. In 1963 he joined Shanks and Leighton Architects, becoming an associate in 1964 and a partner in 1970. His work has received numerous British and Irish awards, including an RIBA award for the Belfast Airport Buildings and an RIAI Gold Medal in 1985.

Works include: Belfast Airport Buildings, Aldergrove, Antrim (1960-3); Portadown Technical College, Craigavon, Armagh (1972-6); Valley Leisure Complex, Belfast; Council Offices, Dungannon, Down (1979-83); St Colman's Church, Lambeg, Down (1989-91); Theatre, Omagh, Tyrone (1995); St Brigid's Church, Malone Road, Belfast (1994-6); Theatre, Armagh, Belfast (project; 1996).

PAUL KEOGH

Studied at University College Dublin and the Royal College of Art, London. Worked with Stirling Wilford and Associates, London, de Blacam and Meagher, Dublin, and the Office of Public Works before establishing Paul Keogh Architects with Rachel Chidlow in 1984. His work has received numerous awards and he is a member of Group '91 Architects. He has lectured in Europe and America and teaches at University College Dublin.

Works include: House, Cleaboy Stud, Westmeath (1985); Avonmore Creameries Pavilion, Zoo, Dublin (1986); Garden Room, Percy Place, Dublin (1988); Housing, Ballsbridge, Dublin (1988); Housing, Earls Street South, Dublin (1990); Housing, Portmarnock, Dublin (1990); Charlesland Golf and Country Club Hotel, Greystones, Wicklow (1991); House, Simmonscourt Road, Dublin (1992); Urban Building, Meeting House Square, Dublin (1993-6); Visitor Building, Avoca, Wicklow (1994); Apartments, Haddington Road, Dublin (1994); Apartments, Aungier Street, Dublin (1994); House, Carrickmines, Dublin (1994); House, Monkstown, Dublin (1994); Apartments, Hanbury Lane, Dublin (1995); New Urban Square, Finglas, Dublin (1996).

PAUL KORALEK b. 1933

Studied at the Architectural Association, London, graduating 1956. Worked with Powell and Moya, London (1956-7) and with various architects in France and Canada before working with Marcel Breuer in New York (1959-60). Established Ahrends Burton and Koralek in 1961 and won the international competition for the Berkeley Library at Trinity College Dublin in the same year. Elected to the Council of the Royal Academy of Arts, London, he has taught at University College Dublin, Leicester Polytechnic, the University of Manchester, Kingston University and the University of Wales.

Works include: Berkeley Library, Trinity College Dublin (1961-7); St. Andrew's College, Booterstown, Dublin (1968-72); Arts Faculty Building, Trinity College Dublin (1968-9), Maidenhead Library, Berkshire, England (1972); Polytechnic Library and Development Plan, Portsmouth, England (1975-90); House, Wicklow (1979-80); John Lewis Stores, Kingston Upon Thames, England (1979-84); Sainsbury's, Canterbury, England (1982-4); Heritage Centre, Dover, England (1988-91); Techniquest Science Centre, Cardiff, Wales (1991-5); Dental Hospital, Lincoln Place, Dublin (1995-).

SIMON ALOYSIUS LEONARD b. 1903, d. 1976

Studied agriculture at Trinity College Dublin and farmed in Meath before joining the office of William Henry Byrne in 1927. Studied architecture at Liverpool University (1931-5) and graduated from University College Dublin in 1937. In 1937 he became a partner in W.H. Byrne and Son and took over the practice on the death of the Principal in 1947. President of the AAI in 1940, he was elected Fellow of the RIBA in 1956.

Works include: Church, Belturbet, Mayo (1954); Purcell House, All Hallows College, Dublin (1955); School, Ballyfermot, Dublin (1956); Church, Dunboyne, Meath (1956); House, Kilkenny (1956); Church, Carrabane, Galway (1959).

EDWIN LANDSEER LUTYENS b. 1869, d. 1944

Studied temporarily at the Kensington School of Art, London, before becoming an apprentice in the office of Ernest George and Harold Peto (1887-9). He established his prolific and distinguished practice in 1889. Collaborated with Gertrude Jekyll in house and garden design (1896-1916). Knighted in 1918 and awarded the Gold Medal of the RIBA (1921) and the Medal of the American Institute of Architects (1924). He was President of the Royal Academy of Arts from 1938 until his death.

Works include: Jekyll House, Munstead Wood, England (1896-7); Lindisfarne Castle, Holy Island, England (1903-4); Country Life Offices, Tavistock Street, London (1904); Lambay Castle, Lambay Island, Ireland (1905-12); Municipal Art Gallery project bridging the River Liffey, Dublin (unbuilt; 1911-12); Viceroy's House Complex, New Delhi, India (1912-31); War Memorial, Etaples, France (1918-24); Somme Monument, Thiepval, France (1927-32); War Memorial and gardens, Inchicore, Dublin (1931-9); Campion Hall, Oxford, England (1935-42).

HENRY J. LYONS b. 1880, d. 1947

Apprenticed to Kaye, Parry and Ross before establishing a private practice in 1927. Elected Fellow of the RIBA in 1925. Specialised in commercial buildings, particularly cinemas and factories, before being joined by his son Samuel Lyons in 1939. His office continues to practise under his grandson, Anthony Lyons, who joined the office in 1967.

Works include: House, Seafield Road, Clontarf, Dublin (1926); House, Irishtown Road, Dublin (1926); Chocolate Factory, Inchicore, Dublin (1932); House, Mount Merrion Avenue, Dublin (1933); Grand Cinema, Fairview, Dublin (1929); Cinema, Dungarvan, Waterford; Odeon Cinema, Dundrum, Dublin (1942); Lemon's Factory, Drumcondra, Dublin (1951); Odeon Cinema, Phibsboro, Dublin (1953); Offices, Westmoreland Street, Dublin.

PATRICK McCABE b. 1960

Studied at University College Dublin, graduating 1984. Worked with Chandler Lavin, Dublin, Noel Heavey, Athlone and Chapman Taylor Architects, London (1986-8). Returned to Galway in 1989 and practised privately until being appointed director of Simon J. Kelly and Partners in 1992. He has served as Chairman of the Western Group of Architects (1994-6).

Works include: Mill Development, Ennis, Clare; Moorings Restaurant, Galway; Niland Warehouse, Galway (renovation); Fox's Bar/Hostel, Galway; Alley Nite Club, Galway; Houses, Mincloon, Galway (1986); Greene House, Brownville, Galway (1992).

LIAM McCORMICK b. 1916, d. 1996

Studied at Liverpool University, graduating 1943, before working as an architect and planner at the Ballymena Urban District Council. Established Corr and McCormick with Frank Corr (1948-68) after winning the competition for a new church at Ennistymon in 1947 and continued to specialise in church design and construction. Formed McCormick Tracey Mullarkey in 1968 and continued to be distinguished in church design until retiring in 1982. He received the RIAI Gold Medal in 1971.

Works include: Church, Ennistymon, Clare (1948-54); Church, Lahinch, Clare; Church, Milford, Donegal; Church, Murlog, Donegal; Church, Southampton, England; Church, Burt, Donegal (1964-5); Church, Creeslough, Donegal (1970-1); Church, Glenties, Donegal (1974-5); Church, Maghera, Londonderry (1975); Church, Fossa, Kerry (1977-9); Church, Balally, Dublin; Church, Steelstown, Derry; Church, Toome, Antrim; Church, Carrickfergus, Antrim; Church, Bettystown, Louth; Church, Julianstown, Meath; Church, Artane, Dublin; Church, Clogher, Tyrone; Church, Dartford, England; Church, Redhill, England.

McCULLOUGH MULVIN ARCHITECTS

Niall McCullough

Studied at University College Dublin, graduating 1981. Spent a year studying and working in Rome before returning to Dublin to work with Scott Tallon Walker. Established McCullough Mulvin Architects with Valerie Mulvin in 1986. He was a member of Group '91 Architects. He has published three books on Irish architecture, including The Lost Tradition (1987) with Valerie Mulvin and Dublin: An Urban History (1989). Received the AAI Downes Medal for the Black Church Print Studios in 1995.

Valerie Mulvin

Studied at University College Dublin, graduating 1981. Spent a year studying and working in Rome before returning to Dublin to work with An Taisce, Scott Tallon Walker, Arthur Gibney, de Blacam and Meagher, and Brian O'Halloran and Associates. Established McCullough Mulvin Architects with Niall McCullough in 1986. Mulvin was a member of Group '91 Architects. Undertook postgraduate studies at Trinity College Dublin (1990-1), which will result in the publication The Irish Town.

Works include: Institute of Engineers of Ireland Headquarters, Clyde Road, Dublin (1989); Free Church Community Centre, Great Charles Street, Dublin (1989-90); Housing, Debtors Prison, Green Street, Dublin (renovation; 1993-5); Abbey Theatre Extension, Marlborough Street, Dublin (1995); Temple Bar Gallery and Studios, Temple Bar, Dublin (1991-4); Blackchurch Print Studios, Temple Bar, Dublin (1991-4); National Music Centre, Curved Street, Dublin (1992-5); Cliffs of Moher Interpretative Centre, Clare (1993-); Dun Laoghaire-Rathdown County Hall, Dun Laoghaire, Dublin (with Robinson Keefe Devane Architects; 1994-6).

McGARRY Ní ÉANAIGH ARCHITECTS

Michael McGarry   b. 1955

Studied at University College Dublin and at the University of Virginia, USA, graduating in 1978. Worked with the Richard Rogers Partnership on the offices for Lloyds of London, with Professor J. P. Kleihues on the Wülfen Centre in the Ruhrgebiet, Germany (1975-9), and with the IBA Berlin (1984-7). Returned to Ireland in 1984. Established McGarry Ní Éanaigh Architects with Siobhán ní Éanaigh in 1985 and has worked as a member of the City Architecture Studio on projects for the City Quays, Dublin, and with Group '91 Architects. He has taught in Schools of Architecture in Ireland, Britain and the Netherlands, and is currently a visiting critic at University College Dublin, the Dublin Institute of Technology and Queen's University, Belfast.

Siobhán Ní Éanaigh   b. 1955

Studied at University College Dublin and at the University of Virginia, USA, graduating in 1978. Worked with de Blacam and Meagher on the Church, Firhouse, and on projects at Trinity College Dublin, with Professor J. P. Kleihues on the Museum of Pre- and Early History, Frankfurt am Main, Germany, and with the IBA Berlin (1984-7). Returned to Ireland in 1984. Established McGarry Ní Éanaigh Architects with Michael McGarry in 1985 and has worked as a member of Group '91 Architects. She teaches at University College Dublin.

Works include: Small Country House (1987); Táin Interpretative Centre (1988); House on a Drumlin (1989); Brick House (1990); Medical Consulting Rooms, Drogheda (1991); 'Making of a Modern Street' (unbuilt project) and the 'Temple Bar Framework Plan' (with Group '91 Architects; 1991); House on a River (1992); Traveller's Housing (1993); Poddle Bridge (unbuilt; 1992-5); Museum at Mellifont Abbey (1995); Software Company Headquarters (1996).

RAYMOND McGRATH   b. 1903, d. 1977

Studied at Sydney University, Australia, Westminster Art School and Brixton Building School, London, and Cambridge University. Worked as an artist, graphic designer, interior designer, exhibition designer and architect, and wrote extensively, producing two major publications: Twentieth Century Houses (1934) and Glass in Architecture and Decoration (1937). Involved as consultant in the design of many of the BBC Radio Buildings in England, including the Headquarters Building in Portland Place, London. In 1940 he emigrated to Ireland to work as a senior architect with the Office of Public Works, to which he was appointed principal architect in 1948. With the Office of Public Works he was responsible mainly for the renovation of many state buildings, including Aras an Uachtarain, Dublin Castle and many of the Irish Embassies abroad. Elected fellow of the Society of Industrial Artists in 1961. Nominated Professor of Architecture at the Royal Hibernian Academy (1967) and President in 1977.

Works in England include: Finella, Cambridge (renovation; 1928); BBC Studio, Manchester (1933); Frognal House, Hampstead, London (renovation; 1933-4); House, St Anne's Hill, Chertsey, (1936-7); House, Galby, Leicester (1938-41); Aspro Factory, Slough (unbuilt; 1938-9) In Ireland: Thomas Davis Memorial, St Stephen's Green, Dublin (unbuilt; 1945); Cenotaph, Leinster Lawn, Merrion Street, Dublin (1950); JFK Memorial Concert Hall, Dublin (unbuilt; 1964); Royal Hibernian Academy Gallagher Gallery, Ely Place, Dublin (unfinished; 1973-4); House, Southwood, Carrickmines, Dublin (1974).

DESMOND McMAHON

Studied Art and Arts and Crafts before entering the Dublin Institute of Technology, graduating 1969. Established Gilroy McMahon in 1971. Received first prize in the Department of Education architectural competition for generic solutions to the national community school brief (1973). Received the RIAI Triennial Gold Medal in 1993 for the Extension to the Dublin Institute of Technology, Bolton Street, Dublin. He has lecturered in Ireland, the United Kingdom and Finland, and has taught at the Dublin Institute of Technology.

Works include: Stadium, Croke Park, Dublin (1989-95); South County Dublin Civic Offices, Tallaght, Dublin (1992-3); National Museum of Ireland, Collins Barracks, Dublin (1994); Research Laboratory, College of Catering, Dublin (1995-6); Viking Interpretative Centre, Temple Bar, Dublin (1995-6); Housing, Temple Bar, Dublin (1996-).

FREDERICK MacMANUS   b. 1903 d. 1985

Apprenticed to Vincent Kelly (1920-4) and later studied at the Architectural Association, London (1925-6). Travelled throughout France, the Netherlands and America before working at the office of Sir John Burnet, Tait and Lorne. Although most of his work is in Britain, he received many commisssions for private work in Ireland before joining the Directorate of Post-War Building in Britain.

Works include: Houses, Bray, Wicklow (1928); Hosiery Factory, Blackrock, Dublin (1930-2); Factory, North Circular Road, London (1935); Hosiery Warehouse, Blackrock, Dublin (1936); House, Newpark Stillorgan, Dublin (1937); House, Avoca Avenue, Dublin (1937); Offices, Ringsend, Dublin (1938).

JAMES FINBARRE McMULLEN   b. 1859, d. 000

Studied privately and with the City Engineer and Architect in Cork Corporation. Appointed City High Sheriff for Cork (1907-8). He was made Knight Commander of the Order of St Gregory the Great and awarded a Papal Distinction for his work for the Roman Catholic Church.

Works include: Alexander Grant Warehouse, Patrick Street, Cork; Honan Hostel Chapel, University College Cork (1915-16); Munster and Leinster Bank, Mill Street, Cork; Munster and Leinster Bank, Newcastle West, Limerick.

HUGH MURRAY b. 1949

Studied at Rice University, Texas, graduating 1975 with a Master's degree in Urban Design. Worked with Liam McCormick in Derry before practising privately in Limerick (1975-9). Established Murray O'Laoire Associates with Seán O'Laoire in 1979. He has taught at the Dublin Institute of Technology and the Regional Technical College, Limerick.

Works include: Regional Hospital, Limerick; Library and Information Building, University of Limerick; Steamboat Quay, Limerick; Regional Technical College, Limerick; Mill House and the Red Church Office Development, Limerick; Cutlass Hall, Limerick; Holiday Housing, Mountshannon, Clare.

For work with Seán O'Laoire, see p. 000.

PADRAIG MURRAY

Studied at the Dublin Institute of Technology, graduating 1954. Worked with architects in Belfast and Edinburgh before establishing a partnership with Doherty and Grant, Derry, in 1957. Practised privately in Dublin (1959-63) before establishing Murray and Beaumont (1963-71). Established Costello Murray Beaumont in 1971, since when he has specialised in restoration, commercial and educational projects. He has served as Council Member in the RIBA and the International Union of Architects, and has been President of the RIAI. He is an Honorary Fellow of the American Institute of Architects and of the College of Architects of Chile. He has taught at the Dublin Institute of Technology and University College Dublin, where he also lectures in Professional Practice Management.

Works include: Cistercian Monastery, Portglenone, Antrim (1962); Shopping Centre, Stillorgan, Dublin; Offices, South Leinster Street, Dublin (1973); Shopping Centre, Dun Laoghaire, Dublin; restoration of the Royal Hospital Kilmainham (1979-84); Offices, Royal Hibernian Way, Dublin; Community School, Balally, Dublin; Town Centre, Tallaght, Dublin; Restoration of the Four Courts, Inns Quay, Dublin; Clarence Hotel, Wellington Quay, Dublin (renovation; 1995-6).

JOHN McBRIDE NEILL b. 1905, d. 1974

Studied at the Royal Belfast Academical Institution and as an apprentice with Robert Lynn in Belfast (1922-6) while attending architectural and building construction lectures at the Belfast School of Art. On the death of Robert Lynn in 1928 he established a private practice specialising in the design of cinemas. Although many of his best drawings were destroyed in an air raid on Belfast in 1941, he remained a great admirer of German architecture and design. He retired from active practice in 1965.

Works include: Apollo Cinema, Belfast (1933; now remodelled); Mountpottinger Cinema, Belfast (1934; now demolished); Tonic Cinema, Bangor (1934; now demolished); Strand Cinema, Belfast (1935; now remodelled); Curzon Cinema, Belfast (1935-6; now remodelled); Majestic Cinema, Belfast (1935-6; now closed and altered); Troxy Cinema, Belfast (1935-6; now demolished); Regal Cinema, Larne (1935-7; now remodelled); Forum Cinema, Belfast (1937; now demolished); Cinema, Omagh (now demolished); Ritz Cinema, Ballybofey, Donegal (1946; now remodelled); Lido Cinema, Belfast (1954-5); Tivoli Cinema, Finaghy, Belfast (1955); Iveagh Cinema, Banbridge, Down (1956); Alpha Cinema, Rathcoole, Belfast (1957).

BRENDAN O'CONNOR b. 1911, d. 1986

Studied at University College Dublin. Practised privately not long after graduating, specialising in simple modern forms that drew admiration from, among others, George Bernard Shaw. His Clinic for Handicapped Children in Sandymount was the first of its type in Ireland.

Works include: House, Carrickmines, Dublin (1949); Warehouse, Wolfe Tone Street, Dublin (1950); Substations in Dublin at Donore Avenue (1950), Russell Place (1951) and Binns Bridge (1952); Church, Rossguil, Donegal (1954); Sheltered Housing, Dun Laoghaire, Dublin; Technical School, Garristown, Meath; Technical School, Kilternan, Dublin; Clinic, Sandymount, Dublin (1957); Factory, Harmonstown, Dublin (1962); Housing, Shannon, Clare.

O'DONNELL TUOMEY ARCHITECTS

Sheila O'Donnell b. 1953

Studied at University College Dublin, graduating 1976. Worked with Spence and Webster and Colquhoun and Miller in London (1978-80) before completing a postgraduate degree at the Royal College of Art in 1980. Worked with Stirling Wilford and Associates (1980-1) before returning to Dublin. Established O'Donnell and Tuomey Architects in 1988 with John Tuomey, whose work together has received a number of awards. She has worked as a member of Group '91 Architects and was elected Fellow of the RIAI in 1994. She has been involved with architectural education at University College Dublin since 1981, and was a visiting critic at Princeton University, New Jersey (1987), and a member of the Architecture and Culture Conference, Venezuela (1993).

John Tuomey b. 1954

Studied at University College Dublin, graduating in 1976. Worked with Stirling Wilford Associates, London (1976-80) before returning to Dublin to work with the Office of Public Works (1981-7). Established O'Donnell and Tuomey Architects in 1988 with Sheila O'Donnell has worked as a member of Group '91 Architects. Fellow of the RIAI (1994) and President of the AAI (1992-5). He has taught at University College Dublin since 1980. He has been a visiting critic at Princeton University, New Jersey (1987-93), at Harvard University, Cambridge, Mass. (1988-9), and has served as external examiner to the Architectural Association in London (1988-94), Cambridge (1993-5) and Oxford (1993). While at the Office of Public Works he designed the State Laboratories, Abbotstown, Dublin (1981-5), and the Courthouse, Smithfield, Dublin (1983-7).

Works include: National Youth Federation Offices, Dublin (1989); Irish Pavilion, Frieslandhal, Leeuwarden (1990-1); Bridge Centre, Dundalk, Louth (1991-4); Irish Film Centre, Eustace Street, Dublin (1987-92); House at Garristown, Dublin (1992-3); Blackwood Golf Club, Clandeboye, Down (1992-4); National Photography Centre, Temple Bar, Dublin (1992-6); Furniture and Design School, Letterfrack, Galway (1994-); School, Ranelagh, Dublin (1995-7); Campus Development Plan and Buildings, Good Shepherd Centre, Cork (1995-).

SEÁN O'LAOIRE b. 1946

Studied architecture at University College Dublin, graduating in 1970, and for a Master's degree in Urban Design at the University of California in Los Angeles. Worked in Italy, Britain and America before returning to Ireland. Lectured at the Dublin Institute of Technology (1976-9). Established Murray O'Laoire Associates with Hugh Murray in Limerick in 1979, in Dublin in 1982 and, as Murray O'Laoire International, in Moscow in 1992. Elected Fellow of the RIAI in 1993 and Vice-President in 1995. Among his urban design projects are the Framework Plan for the Custom House Docks Area and the Bord Gáis Grand Canal Docks Area, Dublin, and Mount Shannon Holiday Housing, Clare. He has lectured and published extensively, broadcast on television and, in 1966, was curator of the L'Imaginaire Irlandais' exhibition in Paris.

Works include: Food Centre, Raheen, Limerick (1986); Housing, Adare, Limerick (1987); Milk Market Building, Limerick (1991); Civic Park and Tourist Office, Limerick (1991); King John's Castle Visitor Centre, Limerick (1992); Leo Laboratories, Dublin (1992); Dublinia Centre, Dublin (1992); Green Building, Crowe Street, Dublin (1992); Stolichny Bank, Moscow (1994); Student Housing, Trinity College Dublin (1996).

CATHAL O'NEILL

Studied at University College Dublin and for a Master's degree under Ludwig Mies van der Rohe at the Illinois Institute of Technology, graduating 1959. Worked with Mies van der Rohe until returning to Ireland to establish Cathal O'Neill Associates, Architects in 1961. Apart from his building projects, he has been primarily involved in architectural education since 1961: he held the Chair of Architecture at University College Dublin for twenty-three years (1973-96) and has lectured and served as visiting critic and external examiner throughout the world.

Works include: House, Mart Lane, Dublin; Meehan House, Monaghan; Shannon House, Westmeath; Apartments, Sandymount, Dublin (1970); Egan's Warehouse, Phibsboro, Dublin (1971); School of Architecture, University College Dublin (renovation; 1981); Chaplaincy Building, University College Dublin (1989); Student Housing, University College Dublin (1989); Shop, Aungier Street, Dublin (1990); Offices, University College Dublin (1991); House, Temple Road, Dublin (1991); Traveller's Housing, Castletray, Limerick (1992); Traveller's Housing, Mountmellick, Laois (1992); Housing, Wicklow (1993); Arts Centre, Blanchardstown, Dublin (1994); Laboratory Offices, Monaghan (1994); Housing, Abbey Street, Dublin (1995).

EMMA O'NEILL

Studied architecture at University College Dublin, graduating 1990, and landscape architecture at University of Virginia, USA (1994-6), where she received the Certificate of Honour of the American Society of Landscape Architects. Working with Tomás de Paor, she won the national competition for a Visitor Centre at the Royal Gunpowder Mills in Ballincollig in 1991. She has worked with O'Donnell and Tuomey Architects, Derek Tynan Architects, and Cathal O'Neill Architects in Dublin, and is currently working in New York.

Works include: Visitor Centre, Ballincollig, Cork (1992); Interiors, Hard Rock Café Hotel, Las Vegas (1994).

SHANE O'TOOLE b. 1955

Studied at University College Dublin, graduating 1979. Worked with Lynch O'Toole Walsh Architects (1979-86) and then as Project Manager at the Energy Research Group, University College Dublin (1986-91). Director of Group '91 Architects since 1990, he has practised privately since 1991 and has been architect with Tegral Building Products since 1994. President of the AAI (1982-3) and Vice-President of the RIAI (1988). Founder of the Irish DoCoMoMo Working Party in 1991, he has received awards for his architectural work, including the Grand Prix at the Kraków Biennale (1989) and the AAI Downes Medal (1996). He has written widely on architectural subjects and curated the exhibitions 'Collaboration: The Pillar Project' (1988) and 'Tales From Two Cities: Emerging Architects in Dublin and Edinburgh' (1994). He has taught at University College Dublin and at the University of Edinburgh.

Works include: Temporary Papal Church, Drogheda (with James O'Toole, Turlough McKevitt and Michael deCourcy; 1979); the 'Temple Bar Framework Plan' (with Group '91; 1991-2); The Ark Children's Cultural Centre, Eustace Street, Dublin (with Michael Kelly and Susan Cogan; 1992-5); Pedestrian Archway, Meetinghouse Square, Dublin (with Michael Kelly and Susan Cogan; 1992-6).

JOHN J. ROBINSON b. 1887, d. 1965

Initially studied for the Ministry before turning to architecture and being apprenticed to George O'Connor (1907-11). Worked in London with Leonard Stokes until returning to Dublin in 1913. Entered into partnership with R. C. Keefe, forming the practice Donnelly, Moore, Keefe and Robinson, which became Robinson & Keefe in 1922. Initially specialising in church architecture, in 1932 he was appointed architect for the Eucharistic Congress and received an Honorary Master's Degree for his services. President of the RIAI (1939) and elected Fellow of both the RIAI and the RIBA.

Works include: Housing, Dun Laoghaire, Dublin (1922); Church, Lusk, Dublin (1922-5); Church, Killester, Dublin (1925); Housing, Temple Park, Blackrock, Dublin (1925); Sweet Factory, Rathmines, Dublin (1926); Gas Company Offices, D'Olier Street, Dublin (1928); Technical College Extension, Bolton Street, Dublin (1929); Housing, Dollymount, Dublin (1932); Empire Theatre, Galway (1933); Technical Institute, Marino, Dublin (1934); Carlton Cinema, O'Connell Street, Dublin (1934); Church, Foxrock, Dublin (1935);

College, Cathal Brugha Street, Dublin (1936); House, Knocksinna, Dublin (1937); Hospital Sweeps Offices, Ballsbridge, Dublin (1938); Corpus Christi Church, Griffith Avenue, Dublin (1938-41); Garden of Remembrance, Parnell Square, Dublin (1946); Adelphi Cinema, Dundalk, Louth (1947).

MICHAEL SCOTT b. 1905, d. 1989

Studied at the Metropolitan School of Art, Dublin, and was apprenticed to Jones and Kelly Architects. Worked with the Office of Public Works before practising privately from 1929 to 1975. Intensively involved in all aspects of architectural life, he was foremost in promoting modernism in the arts and architecture in Ireland. His work has been published and exhibited internationally. He received the Royal Gold Medal for Architecture from the RIBA in 1975.

Works include: County Hospital, Portlaoise, Offaly (1933-6); County Hospital, Tullamore, Offaly (1934-7); 'Geragh', Sandycove, Dublin (1937-8); Ritz Cinema, Carlow (1938); Irish Pavilion, World's Fair, New York (1939); Ritz Cinema, Athlone, Westmeath (1939); Ritz Cinema, Clonmel, Tipperary (1940); Housing, Charlemont Street, Dublin (1944); Busáras, Store Street, Dublin (1944-53); Bus Garage, Donnybrook, Dublin (1946-51); Chassis Factory, Inchicore, Dublin (1946-8); County Offices, Roscommon (1954); Housing, Bridgefoot Street, Dublin (1955); Abbey Theatre, Marlborough Street, Dublin (with Ronald Tallon; 1958-66); Radio Telefís
Eireann Studios, Donnybrook, Dublin (with Ronald Tallon; 1959-61).

HENRY SEAVER b. 1860, d. 1941

Studied at Queen's University, Belfast, and graduated in engineering in 1880. Worked as an apprentice with Young and McKenzie in Belfast before practising privately from 1886. Early commissions included offices for the Belfast Telegraph Newspaper, St John's Church, Malone, and St Barnabas's Church, Duncairn Gardens. Served as President of the Ulster Society of Architects (1912-13). He taught at Queen's University, Belfast, and at the Ulster Academy of Arts.

Works include: Scottish Mutual Offices, Donegall Square, Belfast (1904); House, Cultra, Down (1907); House, Jordanstown, Antrim (1924); Heyn Memorial Hall, Holywood Road, Belfast (1928-9); St Christopher's Church, Mersey Street, Belfast (1931); St Patrick's Memorial Church, Saul, Down (1932-3); St Martin's Church, Kenilworth Street, Belfast (1933); Seaver Hall, Osborne Park, Malone (1938).

HERBERT GEORGE SIMMS b. 1898, d. 1948

Studied as an apprentice in London before moving to Dublin to work in the office of A. V. O'Rourke (1923-5). He worked with the Housing Department of Dublin Corporation (1925-9), receiving a Diploma in Town Planning in 1928, before moving to India to work as a town planner in the Punjab. Returning to Dublin in 1930, he was appointed City Housing Architect in 1932 and also succeeded Horace O'Rourke as City Architect. He was responsible for the design and construction of 18,000 new dwellings before his tragic death at his own hand in 1948.

Works include: Housing, Hanover Street, Dublin (1934-6); Housing, Townsend Street, Dublin (1934-6); Housing, Chancery Place, Dublin (1935); Housing, Watling Street, Dublin (1937-8); Housing, Poplar Row, Dublin (1938).

SAM STEPHENSON

Studied at Dublin Institute of Technology. Further studies in France, Italy and Switzerland followed, and in 1972 he was awarded an Honorary Diploma in Architecture by Dublin Institute of Technology in recognition of his contribution to architecture in Ireland. Elected Fellow of the RIAI in 1975, he received its Gold Medal in 1985. He has lectured in Ireland, Europe and America.

Works include: Public Bar, Grafton Street, Dublin (renovation; 1957); Mews House, Dublin (1970); Hotel, Killarney, Kerry (1970); Hotel, Galway (1970); Irish Pavilion, Expo 70, Osaka

(1970); Northside Shopping Centre, Coolock, Dublin (1970); Institute of Advanced Studies, Burlington Road, Dublin (1971); Hotel, Airport, Dublin (1972); Offices, Bride Street, Dublin (1974); Fitzwilliam Lawn Tennis Club, Appian Way, Dublin (1974); Electricity Supply Board Offices, Fitzwilliam Street, Dublin (1975); Offices for Central Bank, Dame Street, Dublin (1975); Offices for Educational Building Society, Westmoreland Street, Dublin (1975); Civic Offices, Wood Quay, Dublin (1976); Offices for Bord na Mona, Baggot Street, Dublin, (1979).

RONALD TALLON b. 1927

Studied at University College Dublin, graduating 1950. Worked with the Office of Public Works in Dublin under Raymond McGrath (1950-6) before joining the office of Michael Scott in 1956. In 1958 he was made a senior partner and has served as chairman since Scott's retirement in 1975. His work has received awards both nationally and internationally, including two Gold Medals for Building and one for Housing from the RIAI.

Works include: Abbey Theatre, Marlborough Street, Dublin (1958-66); Kire Factory, Kinsale, Cork (1960); Buildings, RTE, Dublin (1961-7); Church, Knocknanure, Kerry (1964); Industrial Estate, Dun Laoghaire, Dublin (1966); Buildings, Galway University, Galway (1970-8); Carroll's Factory, Dundalk, Louth (1967-9); Bank of Ireland Offices, Baggot Street, Dublin (1968-78); House, Foxrock, Dublin (1971); Goulding House, Enniskerry, Wicklow (1975); Master Plan for Trinity College Dublin (1976); Master Plan for University College Dublin (1976); Artist's Studio, Gorey, Wexford (1980); Guinness Hop Store Gallery, Dublin (1984); Civic Offices, Wood Quay, Dublin (1992-5).

DEREK TYNAN

Studied at University College Dublin, graduating 1977, and at Cornell University, from which he received a Master's degree in Urban Design. Established Derek Tynan Architects in 1985 and practises both as an architectural design and an urban design consultant. Appointed Director of the Urban Design unit at the National Building Agency (1986), he was involved in the design and implementation of the developments at North End, Wexford, and Spanish Arch, Galway (1986-9). He has received a number of awards for his work, including the Downes Medal (1995) and a nomination for the Mies Van der Rohe Award for European Architecture (1994). A founding member of the City Architecture Studio and a contributor to the Liffey Quays Project (1984), he is also a member of Group '91 Architects and project director for the eastern section of the Temple Bar Framework Plan. He has taught at Cornell University, the University of Virginia, Queen's University, Belfast, and University College Dublin.

Works include: The Park and the City, Kingsbridge and Parkgate urban design, Dublin (1982); Dublin City Quays (with the City Architecture Studio; 1984); Apartments, Carlow (1985); House, Athy, Kildare (1986); North End urban development, Wexford (1986); Spanish Arch urban development, Galway (1988); Double House, Monkstown, Dublin (1990); The Printworks, Temple Bar, Dublin (1994); John Rocha Studio, Temple Bar, Dublin (1994); Library, Roebuck, Dublin (1995); Offices, Francis Street, Dublin (1995); Mews House, Dublin (1995); Hughes House, Dublin (1995); Housing, Earl Street South, Dublin (1996).

CHARLES FRANCIS ANNESLEY VOYSEY b. 1857, d. 1941

Apprenticed to J. P. Seddon (1874-80) and worked with George Devey (1880-1). Practised privately from 1881. He was one of the most prominent figures in the Arts and Crafts movement in Britain. Foremost among his works were houses and their furnishings. As a designer, architect and writer, he approached a synthesis of practice and theory. Received the Gold Medal of the RIBA in 1940.

Works in England include: Lakin House, Bishop's Itchington (1889); Forster House, Bedford Park, London (1891); Grove Townhouses, Kensington, London (1892); Horniman House, Frensham (1894); Sturgis Stable, Guildford (1896); Briggs House, Lake Windermere (1898); Voysey House, Chorley Wood (1899); Wells House, Sandgate (1899); Wallpaper Factory, Chiswick (1902); Cotterell House, Combe Down (1909); Simpson House,

Kendal (1909); Atkinson and Company Store, London (1911). In America: Tytus House, Tyringham, Massachusetts (1904). In Ireland: 'Dallas', Malone Road, Belfast (1911).

ROBIN WALKER b. 1924, d. 1992

Studied at University College Dublin (1942-7), the Ecole des Beaux-Arts, Paris (1947-8), and, under Ludwig Mies van der Rohe, at the Illinois Institute of Technology, Chicago (1956-8), from which he received a Master's degree in City and Regional Planning. Worked with Le Corbusier while in Paris and then joined the office of Michael Scott in 1948, occasionally working in Zimbabwe and Chicago before being made a senior partner in 1958. He has been twice awarded the Gold Medal of the RIAI for his work (1967, 1970) and was President in 1968-9. He taught at University College Dublin after his retirement from Scott Tallon Walker in 1982.

Works include: Bord Failte Building, Baggot Street Bridge, Dublin (1962-6); O'Flaherty House, Kinsale, Cork (1967); Master Plan and Buildings, Wesley College, Ballinteer, Dublin (1964-9); Restaurant Building, University College Dublin (1967-70); Master Plan and Buildings, St Columba's College, Dublin (1968-71); Master Plan and Buildings, St Patrick's College, Maynooth (1968-77); Master Plan and Buildings, St Gerard's College, Dublin (1976-8); Anco Training Centre, Ballyfermot, Dublin (1978-81).

REGINALD SHERMAN WILSHERE b. 1888, d. 1961

Studied at Leicester College of Art and apprenticed to G. Lawton Browne of Leicester (1904-9). Further studies at the Architectural Association, London, and at the Royal Academy of Arts under Reginald Bloomfield, Sir Edwin Lutyens, Aston Webb and Ernest Newton. Worked in several offices in London before a distinguished service in the First World War. On his return to England he was appointed Deputy County Architect of Essex, before moving to Northern Ireland to take up the post of Education Architect to the Belfast Education Authority. Before his retirement in 1954 he had designed and constructed over thirty schools and several housing schemes in the Belfast area. Twice President of the Royal Society of Ulster Architects (1935-6, 1954-5).

Works include: School, Fane Street, Belfast (1927); School Mount-collyer, Belfast (1927-30); School, Glenwood, Belfast (1928); School, Strandtown, Belfast (1928-30); School, Linfield, Belfast (1929); School, Elmgrove, Belfast (1930-3); School, Seaview, Belfast (1932); School, Avoniel, Belfast (1933-5); School, Nettlesfield, Belfast (1934-6); McQuiston Memorial School (now Belfast School of Music; 1935-6); School, Cliftonville, Belfast (1936-8); Botanic Senior Public Elementary (now Botanic Primary) School, Belfast (1936-9); Grove School, Belfast (1937); School, Carr's Glen, Belfast (1938-40); School, Wheatfield, Belfast (1949-54); Domestic Science College, Garnerville, Belfast (1954).

ANDREJ WJECHERT b. 1937

Studied at the Faculty of Architecture, Warsaw Polytechnic, and worked with the Design Office of City Buildings in Warsaw (1959-64). In 1964 he won the international competition for the Master Plan for the new Campus and Arts, Administration and Aula Maxima buildings at University College Dublin and established an architectural practice in Dublin. In 1984 he established A & D Wjechert, Architects with Danuta Kornaus Wjechert. He is a member of the RIBA, the Association of Polish Architects and a Fellow and former Vice-President of the RIAI.

Works include: Central School, Plock, Poland (1962-6); Campus Development Plan and Administration, Arts, Bank, Computer, Industrial MicroBiology, Sports and Water Tower buildings, University College Dublin (1964-81); Community School, Ballincollig, Cork (1976); Holy Trinity Church, Donaghmede, Dublin (1978); Ailwee Caves Visitor Building, Clare (1979); Church, Blessington, Wicklow (1982); Anco Training Centre, Loughlinstown, Dublin (1983); House, Loughrask, Clare (1983); School, Brookfield, Dublin (1985); Offices, Beresford Place, Dublin (1991); Offices, Lower Mount Street, Dublin (1991); Student Centre, University College, Cork (1996); Housing, Smithfield, Dublin (1996); Shopping Centre, Blanchardstown, Dublin (1984-96).

Photo Credits